PUBLICATIONS
OF THE
ARMY RECORDS SOCIETY
VOL. 23

MILITARY MISCELLANY II

Wynendael, woven by De Vos after L. de Hondt, showing a sergeant holding a pike. (Blenheim Palace, Duke of Marlborough)

MILITARY MISCELLANY II

Manuscripts from Marlborough's Wars, the American War of Independence and the Boer War

Edited by
DAVID G. CHANDLER in collaboration with
CHRISTOPHER L. SCOTT,
MARIANNE M. GILCHRIST and ROBIN JENKINS

Published by
SUTTON PUBLISHING LIMITED
for the
ARMY RECORDS SOCIETY
2005

First published in the United Kingdom in 2005 by
Sutton Publishing Limited · Phoenix Mill · Thrupp · Stroud
Gloucestershire · GL5 2BU

British Library Cataloguing in Publication Data
A catalogue record for this book is available from the British Library.

ISBN 0-7509-4088-3

Typeset in Ehrhardt.
Typesetting and origination by
Sutton Publishing Limited.
Printed in Great Britain by
J.H. Haynes & Co. Ltd, Sparkford.

This volume is dedicated to
Dr David Chandler,
a former councillor of the
Army Records Society.

Contents

Part I The Journal of John Wilson, an 'Old
Flanderkin Serjeant', who served 1694–1727 1

Acknowledgements 3
Introduction 5

The Journal of John Wilson 13

Appendix I Biographical Notes 97
Appendix II Place Names 105
Appendix III Names of Regiments 107
Notes 111
Bibliography 127

Part II Captain Hon. William Leslie (1751–77):
His Life, Letters and Commemoration 133

Acknowledgements 135
Introduction 137

The Letters of William Leslie
1 Home and Ireland 139
2 America 149
3 Death and Burial 165
4 Commemoration 173

Notes 181
Bibliography 195

CONTENTS

Part III   **The Diary of Private Robert Edward
             Cross, 1st Battalion, The Leicestershire
             Regiment, September 1899–April 1901**   197

             Introduction   199

             The Diary of Private Robert Edward Cross
1   Talana Hill and the Defence of Ladysmith   201
2   After Ladysmith   223

             Notes   249

             Index to John Wilson's Journal   261
             Index to William Leslie's Letters   265
             Index to Private Cross's Diary   269

Part I

The Journal of John Wilson, an 'Old Flanderkin Serjeant' of the 15th Regiment and Later of the 2nd Troop of Life Guards, who served 1694–1727

Edited by
DAVID G. CHANDLER in collaboration with
CHRISTOPHER L. SCOTT

Acknowledgements

I would first like to thank His Grace, the Duke of Northumberland, for his kindness in permitting me to work as the editor for John Wilson's Journal, our 'Flanderkin Serjeant'. I also thank Mr Colin Shrimpton, Librarian at Alnwick Castle, for his advice and assistance over the last ten years. I am especially grateful to General Sir Anthony Farrar-Hockley, GBE, KCB, DSO, MC, B.Litt., The President of the Army Records Society, and the Chairman, Professor Ian Beckett, BA, PhD, FRHist.S., together with my friends, councillors of the Society, for giving me the opportunity to prepare this volume. I am also grateful for the help and encouragement of the late Field Marshal the Lord Carver, GCB, CBE, DSO, MC, D.Litt. I especially wish to thank Bishop Michael Mann for his constructive criticism of my early drafts and my friend the late Dr John Pimlott for his support and efforts to guide the work through its revision stages. I would like to thank my sometime researcher, Jenny Toyne Sewell, who has been most helpful to me since 1991 from Government House at RMA Sandhurst and more recently from London. She has been deeply involved with this particular volume, with personal interest in the task, and she has been kind and supportive of me during this difficult time. I especially wish to thank my good friend Christopher L. Scott, BA, Cert.Ed., CMS, who kindly offered to write the introduction and to assist me in his general collaboration during my illness. Naturally any errors or mistakes remain my own. Chris Scott would like to thank Richard Ellis for his advice, Pam Golding for her reader advocacy, and Guy Loveday and Katharine Oram, students at New College, Swindon, for their technical assistance.

David G. Chandler
Yateley, January 2004

Introduction

Historical documents always pose editors problems whether it is scrutinising minute secretary script or following tortuous routes around the sides of pages. Sometimes the fundamental physical act of reading is a trial. At other times we are faced with deciphering personal shorthand codes, deducing from initials names omitted for politically correct reasons or applying crossword skills to Latinate phraseology. There are no such problems with Serjeant Wilson. He writes in a neat, bold hand with a certain flourish and he appears to be meticulous about the sharpness of his nib and the clarity of his text. However, he is no professional writer, often repeating himself and, indeed, employing the same phrases and expressions over and over again. He can be tedious, with seemingly endless laudatory passages, and he can be infuriating with his penchant for recounting strategic manoeuvres in generalised, sweeping terms and noting marches and campaign moves from hearsay. His style too is weakened by a tendency to use passages from other published works, particularly Thomas Lediard, whose three-volume *Life of John, Duke of Marlborough* (1736) was for many years the standard account.[1] At times Wilson copies exactly, while on other occasions he works upon the piece, adding a grandiose tone and his own replete stock of superlatives. Added to this, although we may excuse his phonetic approach to spelling, Wilson is an appalling speller, even for his period; and he is no advocate of consistency. Apart from these 'faults', Wilson is a fascinating man who undoubtedly saw action in Marlborough's wars and at times he gives us new glimpses into them and the special place they held in the memories of 'Corporal John's' soldiers.

Studying Wilson we also suffer from the special problems involved in reading the work of one writing about the late 1600s and early 1700s. Although there were some good maps in existence, they were in their infancy; they were frequently inaccurate and place names were written as they were spoken by the person recording their location. Flanders is notorious even today for dual naming in Flemish and French, and British tourists confuse matters even further by using the First World War Tommy's pronunciation for places such as 'Wipers', 'Proper-inky' and

'Eat apples' in France. Add to that the way names change with the passage of time, the reliance upon phonetic interpretation and the deliberate renaming of towns and regions, and one can appreciate the difficulties. By tracing marches upon old maps and transposing them to more modern versions we can usually determine where Wilson meant even if the place he wrote of no longer exists.

It could be argued that Wilson is unworthy of publication, being tedious and secondhand, but despite his shortcomings he is a contemporary source and he was present at many of the events he describes. He is also exciting in his amount of detail for some actions and we can glean from him camp life minutiae previously unknown to us. C.T. Atkinson of Exeter College, Oxford, stated that the scarcity of original works by early eighteenth-century soldiers alone made his publication of the memoirs *A Royal Dragoon in the Spanish Succession War* worthwhile and that they were worth studying if only for their rarity value. We know of only one other journal of a non-commissioned officer of this period, and currently understand there is only one copy of Sergeant John Millner's *A Compendious Journal . . . begun A.D. 1701 and ended in 1712* (London 1733) at the Ministry of Defence Library. Millner, however interesting, especially for his errors, is no rival to Wilson as his journal is basically a series of dates and times. Wilson too could be accused of adding very little new information to the body of knowledge known about these campaigns, but it is the looking beyond the statement of facts that tells us so much more. Wilson helps us see these campaigns from the point of view of one who underwent them. Period thought is a difficult concept but Wilson gives us yet another window into the mind-set of the professional soldier of Marlborough's wars. We see what was looked upon as normal practice, what was regarded as unusual, what was deemed of value, and even what was so commonplace that it goes unremarked. We are given a better ability to understand the decisions and the actions of 'the good and the great' by coming to understand the men they led.

Until recently historians working with contemporary sources had the writings of officers, such as General Orkney, Brigadier General Kane, Colonels Blackadder, Cranstoun, St Pierre and Sterne, Captain Parker, Field Marshal Mérode-Westerloo and Chaplain Dr Hare. A small enough selection, but the published writings of the 'lower ranks' were even more limited to the anonymous Royal Dragoon and Private Deane whose *Journal of Marlborough's Campaigns* was first thought to be by Captain Hunter, but is clearly by Private Deane (see Society for Army Historical

Research Special Publication no. 12 (1984), p. 984). Now there is
Serjeant John Wilson. These gems are so few and far between that to
withhold them because we do not like their spelling, their style or their
interpretation, or because they relay so few new facts, seems a little
pedantic. It is vital we give them publication, even in part, so as to open
them up to the scholarly minds of others, especially to those who draw
from them so much more than lists of actions, men and dates.

To our minds, Wilson wrote his Journal both to record his life's
history and to ingratiate himself with his patron, and commanding
officer, Algernon Seymour, then Earl of Hertford, by providing him with
a reference book for his campaigns. Wilson seeks assurance in his preface
that he has not presumed too much and offers his 'strong memory and
honest heart' although he must have entertained hopes of gifts of cash or
other favours. We must not be too condemnatory about 'ingratiating
texts' as they were the style and practice of an age which revolved around
patronage. Laudatory dedications and even verses extolling important
men's virtues were the rule for those who wished to make their way in
the world. It was the way society operated. For Wilson to believe Lord
Hertford would finance the publication of his journal he must have
served his commander well, and been useful to him in the past –
promotion to the Guards was not won easily. Wilson's valiant attempt to
gain further patronage was certainly a good gamble and the Earl and
Marquis of Hertford was a powerful and influential force in
contemporary eighteenth-century society.

He had been Wilson's commander from 1709 in what became the 15th
of Foot, and, when he was honoured with the lucrative and highly
desirable post of Captain of the Second Troop of Horse Guards in 1715,
Wilson followed, although we do not know the date this was effected.
Lord Hertford was then a general and a line colonel but the command of
troops in the Guards was a royal appointment and very important to both
military and political careers. Similarly a move from the Line to the
Guards was a great honour for an ordinary soldier. Wilson, then a
veteran Sergeant of Foot, transferred to the Horse Guards as a trooper;
however, this was only a titular reduction, as troopers ranked as
equivalent to non-commissioned officers in the Line received equal pay
and had far better service conditions. It was not uncommon for newly
appointed officers to bring several of their experienced NCOs with them
into Guards units as private sentinels or troopers, but the move from
Foot to Horse is, as far as we can deduce, unusual. The background to his
transfer is unknown although we are told the new Colonel of the infantry

regiment, Harrison, did not want to lose him. When and why he transferred is not clear but Lord Hertford must have recommended him. Whether Lord Hertford knew of the journal being written and the role and praises Wilson was ascribing to him is also unknown; all we have is the dedication penned in 1736. It is not beyond belief that being immortalised in print did not have its attraction.

However, despite the laudatory dedication, which contradicts itself about flattery, Lord Hertford was apparently unmoved and failed to become the patron of Wilson's literary work. As an eighteenth-century author of lowly origin, Wilson had to seek a noble patron if he was to gain the means to publish, but Lord Hertford's seeming literary uninterest meant Wilson went unpublished, the manuscript being kept by the Dukes of Northumberland until now, but Lord Hertford clearly remained useful to our Serjeant's military career.

It was a career which spanned William III's campaigns in the Netherlands from 1694, through Anne's wars against French expansion and into George I's attempts to secure a European peace. Wilson fought under several notable commanders, including the great Duke of Marlborough and the more politically oriented Duke of Ormonde, and his views on them and other princes and general officers percolate through the text. The original journal is a long document, and well over half has been omitted. In editing his journal we have tried to present the reader with the more personally relevant sections. Where we have made cuts is where Wilson relies very heavily upon the works of others and we do so safe in the knowledge that readers may easily read those pages in their original form. (The Bibliography, pp. 127–31, lists a number of contemporary memoirs, both British and continental.)

Despite remaining unpublished for so many years John Wilson comes over to us a 'testy old sweat', and it is tempting to see him as the role model for such mainstays of popular fiction as Sharpe's Sergeant Harper in Bernard Cornwell's novels. This 'Flanderkin Serjeant' is an honest man who uses honest words. He casts the occasional askance remark but never denigrates individuals, indeed he is slow to point out failings and he is particularly and strangely quiet about the removal of Marlborough which must have been a very fierce campfire debate.

Wilson has an extraordinarily vivid long-term memory about his enlistment and we are left to wonder why this Colonel took such pains about a local lad. And he tells us what the ordinary soldiers did on campaign, sleeping in their clothes, their early rousing, long marches and camping routines. We learn of the duties of camp colour men and from maps can plot the series of moves and distances covered per day by armies during the War of the Spanish Succession. We hear first hand of their deeds in war and how, even in victory, they had to remain alert, sleeping in ranks lest a French counter-attack should be delivered. As well as what they did, Wilson also informs us about the beliefs and values of the common soldiers and how they reacted to things. Through his comments about the French deception at Arleux, we share his soldierly disgust at their cowardly acts and we can understand his revulsion at the murders they carried out in the name of war. Wilson's is an ordered war. His emphasis upon parades and reviews for visiting military dignitaries reflects a man with certain over-riding concerns – turnout and drill being high on the list of priorities for a non-commissioned officer, even in the early 1700s.

Wilson lets us look into the conduct of warfare in the age of elegance and discover that formality was not only an officer convention. He pays great attention to the rules and form of campaigning, and he is most meticulous in his timings for marches and rests. The playwright Peter Shaffer spoke once about the author's art in writing in different voices, using phraseology, vocabulary, and imagery to express thoughts particular to each character throughout a scene. He added that the more distinctive the voice the better the audience understands them and 'what made them tick'. We are privileged through Wilson's journal to hear the voice of an old soldier and, through it, come to a better understanding of how the English Army of that age functioned and influenced the lives and way of thinking of its members: the wry humour involved in perpetuating the term 'Forlorn Hope' for the advance party, the familiarity with the complicated terminology of fortress design, the regard for the enemy until he does something 'out of order', and the permeating respect for status, rank and privilege.

Unfortunately we do not know when Wilson began his work, certainly after the Act of Union in 1707 as he refers to the 'King of Great Britain' when recording the events of 1697, and we only have the dedication date as a guide to his cessation of work. Wilson never really completed his enormous task, and it is obvious he chose to leave out certain years completely, such as 1720 and 1721, although why, we do not know. The later chapters are brief in the extreme but he was still writing in the 1730s.

We know he first tried an underage enlistment and was taken into the 15th in 1695 (probably aged around fourteen or fifteen) and from then on he was continually serving, rising from what later was to become a boy-soldier, to a senior non-commissioned officer and still serving in the Lifeguards when he stopped writing his journal in 1736, possibly in his late fifties. Wilson's life did not end with the completion of his journal, but we know little of the man's private or retired life, nor do we know when he died. However, we can be sure John Wilson went to his grave still styling himself 'an old Flanderkin Serjeant'.

To the Right Hon: the Earl and Marquis of Hartford Baron Piercy,[1] Governour of Tinmouth Castle and Captain of His Majesties Second Troop of Horse Guards

My Lord.

I had the good fortune to commence – soldier in the same Regiment[2] that Yor Lo^PP[3] commanded; I shared in the common felicity that every private soldier and every officer enjoyed under that command. I was witness to Yor Lo^PP's gallantry in the trenches and also in the Marshal fields.[4] Your contempt of death and love of yor country I (and every officer and private man that was ever under yor command) can give testimony of yor humanity, generosity, affability and sweetness of temper. The nobleman, the soldier and the fine gentleman was so conspicuous that even people of my rank could distinguish them. Yor blood made us reverence you as your humanity made us enter upon the greatest dangers with alacrity. Wee saw in you the sweetness of the Dutchess; nor could we forbear running back to the greatness of yor royal ancestors.

This, my Lord, to strangers may look like flattery; but an old Flanderkin Serjeant scorns to flatter for if I could abroad, or since I have had the hon'r of riding in yor Lo^PP's troop, find a fault in yor Lo^PP, I would scorn the attempt of a Dedication and let this Journal rot with my bones.

But the world doth endeavour to do yor Lo^PP justice and attempt to do it to yor bountifull family (who bless and blessed by you). My Lady Hertford (next to the Queen) is the ornament of the Court and shares the praises (both in publick and private) of all that approach her.

Lady Betty shines in beauty, goodness and right understanding as Lord Beachamp both in every promising quality that can adorn a nobleman of his birth and age.

I should say something, my Lord, to excuse the want of style and method in this journal and also for my presumption in this Dedication but that I know yor Lo^pp's noble heart will suggest more things in favour than I can say for myself; for I have nothing to offer in justification of this undertaking but a strong memory and honest heart and a violent desire to tell yor Lords'pp that you are beloved in yor troop as much as you were in yor Regiment, and that out of downright affection you may command the last drop of blood that can flow from the veins of

May it please yor: Lordsp

Yor: Lordsp's

Most dutiful,

most obedient and

most faithful Servant

JOHN WILSON

Anno. 1736

A Journal of the Most Memorable Transaction's

from the commencement of the campaigns of Anno 1694. Which was carried on in the Netherlands, under the command of his late Ma[jes]tie King William the 3ʳᵈ. and after his death during the reign of her late Ma[jes]tie Queen Anne in Germany and in the Netherlands under the command of his Grace John Duke of Marlborough and James the late Duke of Ormond.[5]

And after the death of Her Ma[jes]tie during the Reign of King George the First, which ended in 1727, being the space of 33 years[6]

Written By
JOHN WILSON
now in the 2d. Troop of Life Guards and during the greatest part of the said time was Serjeant in that Regiment now commanded by Brig. Henry Harrison.[7]

Anno 1736

Before I enter upon the particulars of the ensueing journall I think it not amiss to give my reader an acco't of my first entering into the Army and Regiment aforesaid, then comand'd by Sr. James Lessley.[8] I entered as soldier with Ensigne William Haliday to serve in the Regiment afores'd upon the 25th day of March 1694, and came to the Regiment, then quartered at Cannongate, Edenburgh the day following, and the next day was shown to Sr. James with severall other recruits. Upon Sr. James takeing a view of me, he was pleased to say to Ensigne Haliday, 'What, my friend Haliday. Do you bring me children for soldiers? I did not expect this from you, for you know I do want men.'

Ensigne Haliday answered in an humble manner, that he must confess I was too young,[9] but that it was intirely my own desire and that my parents could not diswade me from it. Therefore they were disireous I should be under His Honour's care. Whereupon Sr. James askt whose childe I was and if he had any knowledge of my parents. The Ens. told Sr. James my father's name, whom Sr. James knew, and said he knew my grandfather also, whereupon Sr. James turned to me with a frown and said, 'You young rogue, how came you to run away from yo' parents?' I answered him, 'I did not run away but came with their consent to be a soldier.' 'A soldier,' says Sr. James with a smileing countenance. 'Go home you young rogue and go to school.' To which Ens. Haliday made answer and said, 'Sr. If you turn him back he will certainly go with some other recruiting officer and that would very much vex his parents.' Then Sr. James said I should go home upon furloe, 'and lett him have three months pay advance and his furloe for a full year,' both w'ch I had next morning and comitted to the charge of Ens. Haliday's brother to see me safe home w'ch the gentleman performed. And I went again to school and continued until such time as I broke up for Christmass at w'ch Ens. Haliday came from

Flanders to Scottland in order to raise recruits. I, being informed of his arrival at his brother's in the evening, went the next morning like a dutiful soldier to wait upon my officer; desired one of his brother's serv'ts to acquaint him I was come to wait his comands. And he ordered the serv'ts to bidd me come up to him and I imediatly went up to his chamber. He asked me very kindly how I did, and whether I continued my resolution of going abroad. I answered, 'Yes Sr., indeed I do and will continue it.' Then said the Ensigne, 'It's Sr. James's orders that I shall give you the remainder of yo'r pay what you are behinde.'

And he paid me accordingly and ordered me to go home and keep close to school untill such time as he wanted me, w'ch was not till the 27th of April following.

At w'ch time he sent a Serj't for me to meet him the next day at Kircaldie, w'ch I accordingly did. And then he asked me again in the presence of the Provost of the town, Sr. Rob't Douglass and his brother, if I continued stedfast in my resolution to go abroad. I answered them I did, and was come there for that purpose. Whereupon he gave me my pay to the 30th day of April inclusive.

And the day following, being the 29th, we went on board a transport and on May Day weighed anchor and sett sail. The Fleet was designed for Ostend, the vessell wee were in made Campheer and from thence went in Billindors[10] to Sluice [Sluys][11] in Flanders and from thence to Bridgos [Bruges] by land.

And the next day, being the 27th of May 1695, wee arrived at the Regiment's headquarters about two in the afternoon, at Lafine in the Camborland of Ambought, where Sr. James reviewed the recruits. And when he came to me he asked Ens. Haliday if I was the furloe boy. The Ens. answered I was. 'Very well,' says Sr. James, 'Haliday, take care and have an eye over him.' The Ensigne answered Sr. James, 'Obliged so to do.' And then wee were dismissed and sent to our quarters. The regim't continued in their q'rs about a fortnight afterwards before the campaign opened.

Wilson then describes the marches and manoeuvres of the English contingent in the previous year.

1695

*Wilson continues to relate the story of the campaign during 1695
with an account of the siege of Namur, the efforts to relieve it and
a stirring tale of the escalade and subsequent capitulation. This is
worth reading, both for its vivid description and for an account of
the deeds and military decisions of William III, but most of it is
second hand.*

The town, [Namur] having been invested upon the 23^d of June and
all things necessary prepared for the opening of the trenches, the
same was opened ag't the town the 30th, at night, in two attacks;
the 1st. along the Maese [Maas] and the second on the adjacent
riseing ground. W'ch, the enemy perceiving, made a salley next
morning but were repulsed w'th considerable loss and the
trenches next night were caried on with little or no loss; and so
continued advancing our approachm'ts untill the 5th and
commenced the raising our batteries upon the 6th, w'ch were
compleated and our cannon mounted by the 9th, in w'ch time the
trenches on this side of the Meuse were advanced from one side to
the other. And the day following they were advanced 900 paces
farther at what time the beseiged fired with much fury, made a
sally, and after some resistance retired.

But upon the 10th they made another sally, about 3 in the
afternoon, with 1200 foot and 4 Squadrons of Dragoons and
crossed the Meuse. And fell upon the trenches on the right hand
of the bridge, took a redoubt that was unfinished and fell w'th
great fury both in front and flank upon the beseigers, who were in
some measure obliged to give way. But resumeing fresh courage
they rallied again [and] beat them back with the loss of 300 men.
This combate proved also very bloody to the besigers. But His
Maj'tie, perceiveing that the trenches were advanced within
muskett shott of the counterscarp and a considerable breach made
in the wall, ordered the same to be stormed upon the 11th in the
evening, an hour before sun sett. W'ch was performed by a
Brigade of Foot Guards comand'd by Gen'l Ramsey[12] seconded by
nine Battalions of English and Scottch with a reserve of eight

Battallions of Forreignors comanded by Major Gen'l Salish.[13] This attack was performed w'th extraordnary bravery and with such success that the French, after a dispute of two hours, were beat'n out of their works.

The King, according to his usual manner, remained upon the place during the whole action where there was sev'l persons killed abo't him. The loss of the Conferates was not very great considering the resistance the enemy made, but it was too great in the main; the killed and wounded amounting to upwards of 800 men. But this did not at all daunt the courage of the Army who resolved to surmount the greatest difficulties, so that they advanced the trenches upon the 12th, at night, as farr as the village brigg [bridge] towards St. Nicholas Gate, as also those next the Meuse as well above and below, with a design to draw two parralell trenches along the River on that side next Jamb, opposite to the Castle Bridge. Whereupon the beseiged sett fire to the suburbs; by w'ch the approaches w'ch Gen'll Colhorn[14] had begun were retarded.

On the 13th the Batterie was finished on that side next St. Nicholas Gate, and the trenches advanced 100 paces towards the river that runs in the bottom w'ch the French had swilled w'th water. Next day they began to play upon a bastion before St. Nicholas Gate w'th a battery of 18 peices of cannon. And the Brandenburgh's Battery began to play at the same time on the water stock[15] in order to lett the water out of the moat but with little or no success because it was lyned w'th a large free stone. But notwithstanding all those difficulties, wee continued advancing our approachm'ts as also battering the walls w'th all diligence and bombarding the town in a most terrible and furious manner. So that upon the 15th, at night, we took an out-bastion where there was a kinde of a counterscarp,[16] oblidgeing the enemy to surrender the same at discretion. And by the 17th in the morning wee made an alodgem't at the foot of the redoubt of ballast and imediatly made ourselves masters of it. And this is not all, for after much resistance wee lodg'd ourselves on the foremost covered way of St Nicholas Gate that evening; but in regard that the Meuse lay low and the great number of our Batteries, wee had made breaches in

St. Nicholas bastion, the Domy Bastion of St Ruth, and the point of the counterscarp of the town. After w'ch wee adventured to creep along the river side and bravely to storm all those forts from whence wee were three times valiantly repulsed. But at last wee did prevail after a combate of four hours; wee lodged ourselves on the covered way[17] as also upon the point of the counterscarp next [to] the river. At the same time it fell out that some woolsacks took fire w'ch made us for sometime open to the fireing of the enemy, but wee again repaired the lodgem't as soon as possible.

During this time the Elector of Bavare[18] between the Sambre and the Meuse, forced the enemy's intrenchm'ts at the Abby of Salsine next the Sambre, [and] made himselfe master of a fort at the head of those intrenchm'ts [and] repulsed four Squadrons of Horse that came out of the castle, the w'ch had enough adoe to make their retreat back being almost surrounded. But this was not all, for after the French had disputed the water stock almost all night, the beseigors at length made themselves masters of it, then bridge'd the Sambre in midst of the enemy's firing. W'ch wee, having so farr advanced w'th soe much difficulty, there was no looking back. So the 19th wee entrencht ourselves in the post of the Ballart and the Abbey of Salsine.

And the same day there was a comand of all the Grenadeers and sixty men of each Regiment to make an attack near the front gate. And the same was defended by the enemy with a great deal of courage, at last obliged to retire. And the same evening the lines of comunication near the suburbs of Sambe was attackt and carried, w'ch disabled the enemy from making any more salys on that side. Next day was employ'd in attacking the lines before the castle, between the same and the Maes; both w'ch wee carried one after another with great bravery. On the 20th, in the morning early, wee attackt the great intrenchm'ts of the old wall between the Sambre and the Meuse. From w'ch, after the beseigers had made a long resistance by the favour of comunication and one redoubt and two running trenches, wee being attacked both in front and flank and that, too, w'th extraordinary bravery, yett the enemy was driven as farr as the Cowhorn Port and wee pursued them to the Devills House, where they had a Battery of sev'll peices of cannon loaded with cartriges,[19] as also an ambuscade of 900 men lying on their bellys. And wee being now come within reach of them, they lett fly upon us in a most dismall and horrible manner. But notwithstanding wee stood the brunt with incredible bravery and after forced them to quitt the counterscarp of the fort and made ourselves masters of it. Yett not being able to keep our ground, retired in as good order as wee could.

In the meantime the army found themselves under a necessity of quitting a redoubt, some advance batterys and their intrenchm'ts from the Sambre to the Meuse. The same day there was a mine sprung near St. Nicholas Gate w'ch turned [a] great part of the water back into the moat, and our cannon plaid all that day in order to widen the breach. Upon the 22nd wee entred the works and the breach that had been made at Nicholas Gate, from whence wee threw a great many bombs that did great execution, and at evening stormed the half-moon,[20] covered way and Demy Bastion.[21] And after the enemy had repulsed us no less than three times, wee at last lodged our selves on the counterscarp, all things being in a readiness for a gen'll storm.

Count Guiscard, the Governour, came and satt upon the Demi Bastion where he ordr'd Chamade to be beat and a white flagg to be displaid in order to capitulate. Whereupon all the Batteries were thereupon ordered imediatly to be silent and Col'ol Macartney who waited upon Major Gen'll Ramsay in the trenches, was sent to the breach to know what the Count desired; who required to speak w'th the Major General himself. And thereupon the Gen'll went to him and the Count, after mutual civilities, told him that the necessitated circumstances of their affairs was not so much to oblige them to capitulate, yett for the preservation of the town they were willing to give it up upon hon'ble terms.

Of w'ch Ramsay acquainted the Duke of Hulstonploen, whose Qrs was fast by, and promised to send the Count an answer in an hour's time. He also went himself to his Maj'tie to acquaint him therewith, who sent him back w'th power to exchange hostages. An Express of the same was sent to the Duke of Bavaria and a person was appointed to treat about the surrendery.

The Treaty lasted not long but after some contestation, the capitulation was signed the next day, being the 25th of July, on honourable terms. And upon the 3rd day following, a body of the troops in the town of Namur marched into the cittadell and joined the troops under the comand of Marshall Buffleurs and the remainder part in the Cohorn under the comand of Count Guiscard.

There then follows another description of various strategic moves involving forces under Prince Vaudemont and Marshal Villeroi. They relate to the French attempt to take Brussels and then their moves to bring reinforcements to the relief of Namur citadel. However, the story of Namur continues.

The Confederates likewise received a strong detachm't from the Rhine, under the comand of that brave and most exc'll't Prince, the Landgrave of Hesse Cassel. The w'ch enabled His Maj'tie both to carry on the seige of the Castle and Cohorn and at the same time defend the enemy in the feild; the camp being strongly fortified and His Maj'tie being very vigilant and indefatigable and present both in the beseiging army and grand camp, as there was occasion for his Royal Presence and direction.

And all things being gott ready after the surrender of the town, the trenches were opened ag't the Cohorn the 5th of August, at night, with a considerble body of workmen and a sufficient number of men under arms to cover them. The w'ch the beseiged perceiving, began fireing both great and small shott with a considerable number of mortars throwing bombs. Upon w'ch a bomb fell upon the magazine near the Devil's House where there was upwards of 1000 loaden grenades which took fire, were blown up and a considerable number of arms damaged and a great many men killed and wounded. And at the same time, by report from deserters, wee were informed that the Marshall Boufflers had putt his Cavalry all in a readiness in order to break through camp. Whereupon there was orders to secure all the passes upon the Sambre, and also on the Meuse, in order to prevent the s'd enterprise.

The trenches were carried on the following day with great success, though the beseiged fired furiously in the night time upon the workmen, and the day following. It proved to be very hott and desperate work on both sides; the beseig'd having 190 peices of cannon and mortars to play upon their fort and castle upon which sev'll of their cannon were dismounted, whereby their fireing very much abated. However upon the 10th they made a salley w'th 200 Dragoons more and 400 Grenad'rs. Whereof 150 made their attack on the right hand but were stoutly repulsed. And upon the left My Lord Cutts,[22] haveing just posted the cover of the workmen, 100 Dragoons fell upon a Lt's comand of 30 Fuzileers, lett them advance till they came very near them, gave them a round volley and then retreated to the main body. W'ch they pursued untill such time as the Spanish and Bavarian Horse fell upon them, sword in hand, drave them back to the castle gate killing and wounding a great many and makeing sev'll prisonrs.

During the time of the proceedings afores'd the Marshall Villeroy, with his great and potent army, advanced as farr as Herus in order to releive this great and seemingly impregnable castle and citty of Namur and gave the beseiged a signall by the discharge of 90 peices of cannon, w'ch they answered from the topp of the castle by a great many lights. W'ch approach of the Marshall Villeroy oblidg'd His Maj'tie to leave the charge of the Seige to Duke of Bavaria and the Duke of Holstenploen and repair to the Army to oppose Marshall Villeroy's attempts. Who's advance did no ways discompose His Maj'tie, he having been reinforced the night before by the troops under Prince Vaudemont's comand, as before cited and also those under the comand of the Earl of Athlone and likewise a considerable detachm't from the Rhine under the Landgrave of Hesse Cassell. By addition of w'ch troops and the situation of the camp, His Maj'tie thought himself in a condition to defend all the assaults of Villeroy, and also sustain his seige.

The next day following the Marshall Villeroy formed his line of battle, and advanced towards the Confederats' advance guard. Upon w'ch His Maj'tie ordered the Army to form the line of battle imediatly, in w'ch station both Armys continued from 4 in the morning till 8 at night, during all w'ch time His Maj'tie continued in the field at the head of the Army. At w'ch time the enemy attacked our advance guards, but being repulsed w'th a deal of courage and the Marshall finding he could not carry his point, he retired silently off in the night, and encamped next morning along the Meighon, w'th his Right extending to Perwys and his Left to Boness.

Upon w'ch His Maj'tie advanced with his Army towards Ostin in order to observe the march of the Marshalls. His Maj'tie, being now sensible he was secure from the assaults of his enemys from witho't but finding scarcity in his camp, resolved (w'th the consent of the Elector of Bavaria, Prince Vaudemont and all the Gen'll Officers) to make a gen'll assault which was putt in execution the 14th August in the following manner, viz to:

My Lord Cutts, with 3000 English, was to attack the Counterscarp and the breach of the Terra Nova and part of the line of comunication between the Cohorn and Terra Nova, w'ch was next to it. The Count Rivara, with 3000 Bavarians and other troops, was to attack the breach of the Cohorn[23] and another part of the forementioned lines of comunication next to the Cohorn. On the right of the Count Rivara, Major Gen'll Cave w'th 2000 Brandeburghers was to attack the upper point of the Cohorn and part of it, with part of the comunication to the Castle. Major Gen'll Swerin was to attack the Casotte with 2000 Dutch, and at the same time a Collol w'th 600 men was to attack the Lower Town, and a signall was to be made upon the Old Battery near Brussells gate, by blowing up a considerable quantity of gunpowder.

And the Elector of Bavaria gave the word of battle ('God with us') as alsoc gave orders to the afores'd sev'll Generalls comanding the s'd attacks in cheife, that they should appoint a certain number of men on the forlorn hope of each attack to be sustained by another number of men, and the remainder to be for a reserve. Anything else was left to the sev'l Generals' own conduct as occasion should require, but it was ordered that Count Rivara's attack, and those on his right, should begin some minutes before the English, w'ch was judged would be the hardest and more difficult than any of the other attacks.

My Lord Cutts, the night before the attack, received a detachm't of 1000 chosen men from His Maj'tie to be part of his 3000; His Maj'tie being at the Head of the Army to observe Villeroy and left Cutts to comand the English troops at the seige. But the Elector of Bavaria had order'd the sev'll troops to march into the trenches before day, such as were for the attacks to remain undiscovered till the signall was given. And my Lord Cutts, in obedience to the orders, marcht into the trenches some hours before day. But there not being room enough to cover his men, he was obliged to post 3 Battalions at Salsine Abbey, being the nearest to the trenches where the men could have cover.

My Lord Cutts made his disposition of the English in this manner: He comanded four Serg'ts, with fifteen men each, to go on the Forlorn Hope[24] promising, in the King's name, preferment to the Serg'ts and large rewards to the men according to their bravery. Those were to be followed by the Grenadeers of the Guards under the comand of Col'ol Evans and the rest of the Grenadeers designed for the attack of the Breach, to the number of 700 men under the comand of a Col'ol, and 300 Grenadeers to attack the line of comunication. Col'ol Corthorp and Col'ol Makay's Regiments were ordered to sustain those that attackd the breach. Col'ol Hamilton's and Col'ol Buchan's Regiments were ordered in reserve and, for the better performance, the Regiments of Col'ol Hamilton, Buchan, and Mackay,[25] w'ch were posted at Salsine Abbey were, upon the signall given, imediatly to march to the place of action and draw up in the rear of Corthop's Regim't and wait for orders.

The attack began about noon, and though the English had a hundred paces to march under the enemy's fire from the trenches to the breach, yett they drew up exposed to their great and small shott and marched forward to the breach with unparalel'd bravery and courage. And were, presently, followed by the Grenadr's with drums beating and colours flying, w'ch made the beginning of the attack. W'ch was carried on with such resolution and firmness seem very prosperous. But by some failure in the signall the Regiments at the Salsine Abbey not comeing up to the English troops then engaged, they were very much overpowered by the numbers of the enemy. And the fire of the great and small shott fell upon them, w'ch would have been otherwise employ'd if everything had succeeded as intended. In this grand attack Count Rivera, who comanded the Brandeburghers as afores'd, Count Marsilli w'th his Lt. Col'ol, Col'ol Courthope and his Lt. Coll'ol were shott dead upon the spott; My Lord Cutts dangerously wounded by a shott in his head and Sr. Matthew Bridges also desperatly wounded, with a great many brave officers of the Grenadeers and other officers and soldiers of all the severall corps of the Confederate Army.

After a short time the three Regiments from Salsen arrived and, as affairs stood, then were oblidged to comence a new attack in w'ch they had their share of suffering. Count Nugent and Mons'r L'Abdi, being come down by comand of Marshall Bouffleurs with 1200 foot and Dragoons of the French King's Household, with w'ch fresh supply they charged the English both flank and rear who were now in the middle of six fires.[26] And my Lord Cutts, having had his wound drest and finding affairs but in an indifferent posture, promised (in His Maj'tie's name) singular rewards to such as deserved them by their actions.

And as soon as my Lord came to the place of action, he repaired to the head of Makay's Regim't at w'ch place he found the Colo'l himselfe. Whom, in a most familiar manner, he caught by the hand saying, 'My Dear Hugh.[27] Our designs have proved this day not so successfull as I could have wisht they should have don, but I hope to retrieve our losses. And in relation thereunto, sure I am, Sr, you will exert yo'rselfe in the highest degree.' Whereupon he answered His Lords'p that nothing should be wanting in him, and he hoped in none under his comand.

Upon w'ch a Lieut. was ordered, with a comand of the choicest men in the Regim't, to attack the sailant angle next the breach with sword in hand and to maintain the same if possible and make a lodgm't therein. And at the same time he comanded the whole Battallion to advance and place their Colours upon the pallisades. W'ch the Battalion, under Col'ol Makay's comand did with so much courage and bravery, that to the admiration of their friends they struck a terror to their enemys. And all this had so good effect that the Regim't maintained their post, and the fore-mentioned Lieut., entred the Pallisades, beat the enemy from the covered way and lodged themselves in their Battery, where they turned their cannon upon them. For w'ch His Maj'tie rewarded the private men in a very handsome manner, and advanced the Officer both w'th preferrment and hon'r.

The Bavarians, perceiving that Makay's Regim't pitched their colours upon the pallisades and maintained their ground with undaunted vigour, renewed their attack w'th the like vigour, notwithstanding most of their officers were killed and wounded, by which this post was made good by them. During w'ch time the Elector of Bavaria exposed himselfe in a great degree and was very liberall both to his own and the English soldiers, and particularly to that comand of Makay's Regim't w'ch attackt the sailant angle next the Battery with sword in hand.

Wee having thus gained the covered way before the breach of the Cohorn and the Inferior Angle Sailant,[28] wee held ourselves contented to make a lodgm't thereon without makeing any farther attempt upon the breach. The w'ch enabled Maj'r Gen'll Caves to make his lodgm't on the covered way before the Ravellin and part of the Cohorn without sustaining any considerable loss. Major Gen'll Swarin, who comanded the right attack of all before the Casotte and so towards the Meuse, beat the enemy from their covered way and retrenchm'ts and made a lodgm't along the same of above 300 paces. Which lodgment he afterwards advanced to the left 140 paces more, and so joined the lodgm't of Major Gen'll Cave w'ch watched the Ravellin of the Cohorn so that the Confederates became masters of one of the greatest lodgments that ever had been made, at one assault, being near an English mile in length. Notwithstanding wee were frustrated in the enterprise of our great design, to have stormed and taken the castle w'th sword in hand and all the prodigious outworks thereto belonging.

This grand assault lasted untill night in the which there was many a brave man lost on this occasion of all nations that composed the Confederacie, being no less by computation than 1800 or 2000 men, and about two thirds of that number to the beseiged, and all this without any certainty.

But His Maj'tie, being resolved to overcome all those difficulties, ordered the Comanding Officer of each Regim't to infuse courage into their men, promising upon the word of a King preferrm't as well to the Non-Comissioned as Comissioned Officers that singuraliz'd themselves, as also suitable rewards to the private men. And pursuant thereunto, wee battered and bombarded the Castle and Cohorne the succeeding two days in a most furious manner with 120 peices of cannon and 60 mortars, and our miners continued with all diligence to forward their mines under the breach of the Cohorne till in and about the third day at noon. At w'ch time the enemy beat a Parley in order to bury their dead w'ch had been slain in the last assaults.

There follows a substantial account of the negotiations and final surrender including various personal vendettas and recriminations intermingled with the fate of the captured city and its garrison.[29]

And the Articles were accordingly signed and the ratifications exchanged next morning, being the 23[d] of August. And thus the supposed impregnable fortress of Namur, and the Castle therein, had capitulated to surrender after a seige of eight weeks and six days comencing on 23[d] of June and ending the 23[d] of August; haveing a numerous garrison therein headed by a Marshall of France, and an army of 10,000 men who came up to the releife of it, but could do nothing but remain spectators of our bravery. W'ch the enemy conceived was extraordnary and could not but be amased at it, they having made such additionall fortifications thereunto w'ch they presumed could never be forced. And therefore they vainly sett up this inscription over the gate: 'Reddi non vinci potest'.[30] But none could pretend to so much glory in this present important conquest as His Britanick Maj'tie and his veterans and experienced E'lish troops under his comand; under whose conduct and direction they behaved with such courage and resolution that even our enemys, as well as our friends, yeilded to us the glory of the seige.

On the same evening that the Castle capitulated orders were given in His Maj'tie's camp for all the Officers to lye in their clothes and the soldiers to do the same with their arms ready, and sixty men out of each Battalion were comanded to reinforce the camp at Massy. All this being carefully don to prevent any surprise from the enemy who, upon the news of the capitulation, might have presumed upon the Confederates' negligence and to have fall'n upon them; or they might perhaps have been prompted to an action from their own desperate and unfortunate state. But they were so farr from the thought of such an attempt that Mareshall Villeroy, when he was informed of the capitulation, was so extremely concerned at it that he would admitt no one to him for some hours, and at length marched away for the plains of Flans with so much haste and precipitation that he left many of his foragers and out guards behinde him.

1697

Wilson's own involvement in the wars began in 1697 and seems to have consisted of the time-honoured tradition of marching.

. . . both Armies took the field by the 1st of May. The English troops assembled at Brussells, from whence wee marched to Waterlow [Waterloo] where we were joined by all the Confederates and continued on that ground till the arrival of His Maj'tie, and then passed a Gen'll Review before him. After w'ch a body of the enemy, under the command of Count Catenagh[31] invested Aith [Ath]. Upon w'ch our Army marched for Notredam Hall and afterwards advanced to St. Quentin Lenock with a resolution to raise the siege. But being informed that the Army was so advantageously intrenched, His Maj'tie did not judge it proper to come to an engagement. Whereupon wee marched back to Notredam Hall and the next day to Seneff, where the Army encamped six weeks. But being informed that the French had marched and pitched again with their right to Notredam Hall and their left to'ds Gramont, our Army marched for Brussels and pitched our camp on the same ground the Prince decampt from the latter end of the last Campaign for Garrison.

At w'ch time, the peace being farr advanced, His Maj'tie left the field about the middle of August leaving comand of the Army to Prince Vaudemont.[32] After which Prince Vaudemont detached Gen'll Stewart, with five Battalions of Infantry w'ch was Brewer's, Stewart's, How's, Tiffeney's, and Collingwood's to march into land farr west, we being suspitious that the enemy would pass some partys over the Scheld in order to raise contribution. But as soon as wee were informed that the peace was concluded wee marched back again and encamped by Vilvord, where we were joined by 25 Battallions of Infantry and 30 Squadrons of Cavalry under the comand of the Earl of Athlone,[33] and marched the day following for Jouvong [Joudoigne]. Where that body of the Army under the comand of the Earl of Athlone encamped the remaining part of that Campaign.

The peace being proclaimed at the Head of the Army about the 20th of Sept., the which putt an end to a bloody and cruell war and comenced a glorious peace to the great honour of His Maj'tie and the good of Europe.

Wilson describes the arrival of peace and then begins a long narrative concerning the War of Devolution in general from 1672 to 1678 and the early events of the Nine Years War. Very little seems to have occupied him from 1698 to 1700 for he devotes only a brief paragraph to each, mainly to do with Ireland and disbanding of several units . Of 1701 he tells of troop transports and the death of William III. Much of his writings appear to come from second-hand sources. It is with 1702 that his tale begins to shed a more personal light upon the conduct of war – after a detailed eulogy upon the coronation of Queen Anne.

1702

. . . at Kizarswart and Cranenburghs where I finde the English troops, after Her Maj'tie's Declaration of Warr, in a condition to act offensively and defensively. And, in order thereunto, were joined as fast as possible by the troops from the Rhine, under the comand of the Duke of Wirtembergh[34] and a considerable number of troops belonging to the States under the comand of Count Tilly; the whole body still remaining under the comand of the Earle of Athlone. As also my Lord Cutts arrived in the camp with the Brigadeers[35] Withers, Stanley and Sr. Frederick Hamilton. The enemy at the same time strengthening the camp under Marischall Boufflers[36] with a large detachm't under Marish'all Villars,[37] the which enabled them to throw fresh supply of men, arms and amunition into Kizerwart, by w'ch means and the wettness of the season the siege was drawn out in great length. And at about the same time the Enemy had a minde to surprise either Nimeguen [Nijmegen] or the Grave,[38] and in order, if possible to cutt off our comunication with those Garrisons.

Of the which proceedings of the Enemy the Earle of Athlone being advertiz'd, about three a clock in the afternoon, called a Council of Warr wherein it was agreed to decamp and march to intercept and oppose the Enemy's designe. It was also ordered that Mar'r Gen'll Rhoo[39] with twelve squadrons of Horse and Dragoons, to march in order to possess himselfe of the eminence above Mook. And at the same time the train and heavy baggage was ordered to march with all expedition by the lower way for Nimeguen. But the train and baggage horses being scattered a-grazeing[40] in the meadows of the Rhine, the march was protracted till late at night before we could begin the same.

Whereupon His Lordship detached the Duke of Wirtemburg with twelve squadrons more, in order to second Major Gen'll Rhoo. And His Lordship followed with the remaining part of the Horse and ordered the Foot to take the road by Grossbeck to Newmegon. And His Lordship being advanced about halfe a league out of the defiles, the Duke of Wirtemburg sent him that he was posted upon the eminence above Mook, and that he had mist of Major Gen'll Rhoo but was informed that he had continued his march to the Grave and informed His Lordship further that he had perceived sev'll of the Enemy's squadrons in sight. Whereupon His Lordship ordered him to discover them as well as he could and to retire back to His Lordship if he found the Enemy too numerous to engage.

At the same time His Lordship posted forward with six squadrons of Dragoons and left the remaining part with Count Tilly with orders to advance as fast as possible. And by the time His Lordship had advanced as far as His Grace, he observed him wheeling his squadrons to the right abo't, whereupon His Lordship made a halt and dispatcht an Aid de Camp to Count Tilly to advance as fast as the Horse could ride. By w'ch orders His Grace and Count Tilly joined their squadrons w'th my Lord Athlone's much at one time. His Grace informed His Lordship that he had made as good a discovery as possibly he could of the Enemy and they were about thirty odd squadrons of Cavalry and, he thought, much about the same number of Battallions of Infantry advancing. Whereupon His Lordship ordered to put the Horse in Battallia[41] as soon as possible and, at the same time, ordered County Tilly with 4 Battallions of Infantry to march towards the Grave.

And then His Lordship made a feint to advance which putt the Enemy to some small stand. Upon w'ch His Lordship ordered his Squadrons to the right about and comenced his retreat towards his Infantry, the w'ch performed in very good order. Nothwithstanding the Enemy's Squadrons advanced and there was sev'll skirmishes on both sides with little or no loss, so that the Cavalry retreated in good order till they recovered the body of their Infantry and then formed the line of battall. Att w'ch time was perceived the Enemy's troops all to join and form the Line of Battle, and also blow up a barrell of gunpowder w'ch wee believed to be the signall for engageing.[42] Whereupon His Lordship, by the advice of the Gen'lls about him and perceiving the Enemy to be farr superior to his troops in number, thought it proper to retreat to Newmegen. W'ch they perceiving, advanced as quick as possible and, being come up with us about the rising ground of St Anns, began to press us very hard and putt some squadrons and Battlions in disorder. But some other of our Battallions and Squadrons faceing to the right about, gave them a great repulse and they were putt to a stand.

At w'ch time sev'll Brigades of the Enemy advanced with their cannon[43] in front of their Brigades. Wich the Earl of Athlone perceiving, ordered the retreat to be continued with all expedition till they were within the works of the towne and dispatcht an Express to the train and baggage to march with all expedition under the works of the town by the Upper Water Gate. But they not marching with such expedition as the extremity of the case required, eight small field peices and some part of the baggage were cutt off from the Line and fell into the Enemy's hands.

The Army being advanced to the works of the town, His Lordhip ordered the Foot to jump over the pallisades[44] and to putt themselves in order to defend[45] the Enemy in case they advanced any further. But they begun their cannonading upon our Cavallry by w'ch a considerable number of our horses was kilt before wee could march through the gates into the town, w'ch was performed w'th all expedition. As also the cannon of the town mounted on the batterys, w'ch cannonaded the Enemy w'th considerable success. Upon w'ch the Enemy drew up their Line without reach of our cannon, and our Cavallry marched over the river wall [Waal][46] upon a bridge of boats and encamped on the other side of the towne. In w'ch station both Armies continued the remaind'ng part of that day till the next morning. At w'ch time wee perceived the enemy making sev'll movements, sometimes to the right and sometimes to the left. Whereby His Lordship concluded that they had a minde to encamp about Duikenburgh which gave him a suspicion they had a designe upon the Grave. But Count Tilly, having crost the Wall and come up the other side to Newmegen, aquaint'd His Lordship that the twelve Squadrons of Horse und'r the comand of Maj'r Gen'll Rhoo, w'ch marched from the Army at Cranenburgh and the four Battallions that he had marched off from the Army dureing the time of the retreat, were all safely arrived at the Grave. As also a reinforcem't of four Battallions under the comand of Gen'll Fagle,[47] w'ch with the Garrison there before made eleaven Battallions of Foot and twelve Squadrons of Horse. With which His Lordship [was] very well assured the Grave was sufficiently garrison'd.

And by this time [he] perceived that the Enemy were drawing off, making their march towards the right. And His Lords'p, by this march, judged they were resolved to encamp between

Cranenburgh and Cleeve upon the ground wee decamped from. Whereupon His Lordship comenced disimbarrassing[48] the works of the town and sending all the Foot of twenty Battallions over the River; which body of Foot he ordered to be joined with twelve Squadrons of Horse and to encamp by the river side half way between Nimeguen and Skininsconce, in order to observe the motion of the Enemy.

The which march and encampm't was of very great service (as appeared the Enemy's next days procedings) the Enemy having designed to bridge the wall about a league below Skinkinconce. Of w'ch Duke Witenburgh, who comanded that body of troops by the water side being informed, marched imediately for to oppose him and, upon their advancing, gave them so warm a reception that he obliged them to retire before they could lay a pontoon on the river.

Upon this design and procedings of the Enemy, His Grace dispatched an Express to the Earl of Athlone, on receipt of w'ch His Lordship dispatched an Express to the Grave with orders to Major Gen'll Fagle and Maj'r Gen'll Rhoo to march with all expedition to Newmegen with the twelve Squadrons of Horse and eight Battallions of Foot under their command, and ordered at the same time that the pontoon boats should be in readiness to march. These orders having arrived at the Grave, the Gen'lls afores'd marched their troops according to orders with expedition, and as soon as they arrived at Newmegen they crost the river on a bridge of boats where they were joined with the two Battallions of Bleu [Blue] Guards, the whole being under the comand of Count Tilly, who marched directly for the Rhine having the pontoons along with him. And they bridged the Rhine about halfe a league below Skinkinconce and then marched over and encamped on the other side of the river. By which disposition of the troops we had secured a comunication with the besiegeing army at Kizerswart. In w'ch station both Armys continued during the time of the siege.

Wilson then digresses with the story of the Dutch Engineer-General Coehorn's operations against Fort St Donat, but soon returns to the Siege of Kizerwart.

By this time the Governour of Kizwerwart, perceiving that (by any diversion they could use) the French were not able to raise the siege, the Governour resolved to come to a capitulation. And in order thereunto, beat a chamede[49] and, the Articles being agreed upon, surrendered the Garrison, being made prisoners of warr after a siege of two months in which the besiegers suffered so much by the numerous sallys from the Garrison, as also by the frequent storms by them made, that the greatest part of the Regt's of Infantry were obliged to be sent into quarters of refreshment.[50]

After the Seige of Kizerwart the Confederate Army from all quarters assembled at Newmegen w'th all possible expedition, by w'ch place the whole Army were arived by the 28th of June. And the States Gen'll, being pleased to compliment the Earl of Marlborough w'th the comand of their forces[51] who arrived at the camp the 30th and took a Gen'll Review of the Right Wing and the day next after, being the 3d of July, the Left Wing past a Gen'll Review before His Lordship.

And upon the 4th, at night, there was orders for the Army to be in a readiness to march the next morning; the Gener'll to beat at 4, the Assembly halfe an hour after and to comence their march by 5ive. To the right Gen'l Cadogan[52] having orders at the same time to march by 3 a clock with the Q'r Masters and Camp Colour Men[53] and to pitch their camp at Duckenburgh, w'ch was to be my Lord Marborough's quarters, with their right joining the Meus[54] a league above the Grave and the left of the line extending to Mook. The Enemy being then encamped and intrenched between Goch and Genapp, about two leagues right in our front. During our abode in this camp Prince Ernest Augustus, the Elector of Hanover's younger brother[55] came into the Army in order to make a campaigne with the Earl of Marlborough. Upon which His Lordship conferred the dignity of the comand of a Major Gen'll of the Line, w'ch the Prince was to accept of. And His Lordship did him the honour of takeing a view of the line.

Wee continued in this ground without any motion till the 14th, at w'ch time there was orders for the pontoons to march to the right in order to lay two bridges over the Maes, as also for the Train and wheel baggage to march that afternoon by way of the

Grave. And at night there was orders for the Q'r M'r Gen'll, the Vanguard and the Camp Collour Men to parade on the right of the front line by four a clock in the morning and the General to beat at 5; the Assembly halfe an hour after and the Army to march by six to the right. W'ch orders were all punctually obey'd and the Army decampt accordingly and that day past the Meuse and advanced about two leagues and a half and there encamped. Whereupon the Enemy decampt also and past the same river by Venlo and continued their march by Roremont and Stevensthwart and after turn'd their march towards Ash.

My Lord Marlborough continued the march of the Confederates right for Chateau Gravenbock at w'ch place, as wee were encamping, we were joined by my Lord John Hay's and Gen'll Ross's Dragoons, Rhoo and Ferguson's Regim'ts of Foot with an adition'l company to each Regiment, as also the English Train of Artillery.[56] Wee being then ecamped as before mentioned at Gravenbock, the English Train, according to the Antient custom of warr, fired the Tatoo Gun.

Upon w'ch all the drums of the Army according to order, beatt of the Tatoo and the French Garrison in Gravenbock beat their Tatoo at the same time, notwithstanding they were within the heart of our camp.[57] Of w'ch My Lord Marlborough being informed, replyed with a smile, 'If they beat a Tatoo t'night. I'll beat the Revellie in the morning.'[58]

Whereupon he ordered that each Regim't in the Army should make twenty faschines[59] imediately and carry them to the front of My Lord John Hay's Dragoons, and twenty four men of each Regim't under arms and twenty men of each d'to [ditto] without arms for work[60] to parade at the same places. As also six field peices and two mortars, with a sufficient quantity of amunition, as also sufficient waggons w'th tools, all to parade at 10 a clock that night. The whole to be comanded by Brigadier Withers,[61] the comand arms to be comanded by two Colon'ls, two Lt Colo'ls, two Majors and twenty Captains and proper subalterns and the comand without arms to be comand'd by Lt Colo'l Major and 6 Captains and proper subalterns. W'ch comands all paraded according to orders and marched imediately and opened the trench[62] and by break of day had a sufficient cover and the Batteries raised. W'ch the Enemy perceiving, fired some shott but with no great success, there being but one man killed belonging to Gen'll How's Regim't. For as soon as wee could see wee threw in sev'll bombs and cannon ball and the Govern'or offered to capitulate and promised to march out under arms. But the Brigadier sent them word they must be content to be prisoners at discretion[63] or he would enter the Fort sword in hand and then neither he nor any of them need expect q'rs. W'ch the Govern'r considered and submitted to be prisoners at discretion. Upon w'ch the comand under arms and also the workmen entred the Fort and pillaged and made booty of all they could find therin and afterwards demolished the same.

Wilson next tells of a difference of opinion between Marlborough and Athlone followed by Army Council changes in Allied strategy to respond to the French retiring to the Lines of Brabant: none of which he could have witnessed.

Marlborough's subsequent movements threatening Venlo brought a portion of the French Army once again into the field.

. . . it was the opinion of the Councill of Warr that the Army should march the next day in order to reverse their camp that they might face the Enemy in the manner following: w'ch was to march from left to right and that the Horse should be interlined with the Foot in order to forme a Line of Battell upon an imergent occasion. And Gen'll Updamh, Q'r M'r Gen'll to the States, had orders to march with the Vanguard and Camp Colour Men, through the defiles upon the right to Dunderslow Heath and, as soon as he had clear'd the defiles abo't half a league, to lay out ground for pitching the camp, bearing his left towards the Brabant Line in the same manner as was disposed by the Councill of Warr.

And Gen'll Cadogan had orders at the same [time] to march with the Camp Colour Men of those troops designed for the Seige of Venlo under the comand of my Lord Cutts, to pitch out the camp between the right of our present camp and the defiles. The w'ch orders was putt in execution the next morning by both the Q'r Master Gen'lls and the Army decampt about six next morning and comenced their march as before described from left, being interlined upon the same with a Brigade of Horse to a Brigade of Foot. And that body of the Army under Lord Cutt's comand to decline and fall in the rear of the Second Line, and after to incline gradually to the right and to cover the Right Wing of the Army. In which posture they were to continue till such time the Grand Body of the Army was incamped.

The w'ch disposition of the troops under my Lord Cutts proved to be (as will afterwards appear) of singular use and benefitt to the whole Army. For the Enemy, being advertized of these great dispositions and the reversion of our camp, were resolved, if possible, to attack us upon our march, if not as soon as wee were encamped. And in order thereunto, the Grand Body of their Army advanced towards us, their Right Wing being comanded by Marischall Tallard[64] and Duke of Berwick,[65] and their Left by Marischall Boufflers and Count d' la Motte; the latter having joined them the day before from Flanders with the greatest part of the body of these troops, which he had comanded in conjunction with the Marquis of Bedmar in opposition of Gen'll Gowhorne's [Coehorn] late designe upon the French Lines in Flanders. And the s'd designe of the Enemy had been of great advantage to them had not their Squadrons on their left wing advanced with too much expedition, by w'ch the Camp Colour Men under my Lord Cadogan's comand took the allarum. W'ch the Gen'll perceiving, ordered them to retire to the main body.

Wh'upon My Lord Cutts altered the march of the troops abo't a mile in the rear of his designed camp, by w'ch His Lordship had the advantage to take up the vacant ground between the right of the camp and the defiles. And at the same time [he] despatched an Express to My Lord Marlborough to inform of the Enemy's advancem't. Upon w'ch the Army was imediately ordered to take their arms but at that time under a great disadvantage, the Army having but just encampt and most part of the Horse being out aforrageing, the Train horses turned agrazeing, as also a great many of the Foot turn'd out for straw, by w'ch means there was not above one halfe of the Army in camp.

Notwithstanding, His Lordship and all the Gen'lls of the Army used their utmost diligence and endeavours to putt their men in Battallia and at the same time ordered three peices of cannon to be fired, being the proper signall to all absent from camp to return w'th great expedition. And the Army, then under arms, advanced abo't halfe a league in the front, there being a morrose.[66] It was resolved there to dispute the advance of the Enemy. And our people abroad, takeing the allarum from our firieng the afores'd 3 peices of cannon, the horsemen threw down their trusses, drew their forrage cords[67] and made all expedition imaginable to their respective Regim'ts. And the Foot likewise threw away their bundles of straw or anything else they had gott, and made an expeditious return also. And, likewise, the conductors of the train used all possible diligences to have the horses brought in. By w'ch expedition returne the Army appeared in a compleat line of battell in the space of two hours.

The w'ch fortunate expeditious conduct of our Gen'lls gave new vigour and courage to our Army. And the which non plus[68] and great disadvantage had the Enemy in that juncture had the courage to make use of and push on to their advantage, our Army, without all doubt, must have mett with such a defile, as might have laid in the way for the French King to prescribe laws and rules to most of all Europe.

Both Armies having thus advanced, having nothing but the small morros to intercept them, comenced cannonading each other with a great deal of vigour but without any great execution, both Armies being in some measure under cover of small sandhills. And at the same time, sev'll of our Gen'll Persons, particularly the Heriditary Prince of Hesse Casell[69] importun'd as much as possible with the Earle of Marlborough, the Earl of Athlone and the States Deputys to force the Enemy to an engagem't. But all the importunitys could not prevail upon the judgements of those experienced Gen'lls who, considering the morros on the front w'ch would hinder the Cavalry to support the Infantry and would be vastly to disadvantage.

Therefore in that situation their Lordships was resolved to content themselves and act defensively and the cannonading continued with great vigour till the darkness of the night oblidg'd them to cease.[70] And as soon as it was light next morning renewed the same with the like vigour, both Armies being very eager for an engagem't but the disadvantage of the ground between them hindered both Armies from acting offensively by close engagem't, for w'ch reasons as afores'd, both Armies continued still cannonadeing till darkness prevented. And when the Enemy perceived they could not come up to their design and wisht for success, retired in the night. W'ch we perceiving next morning ordered a considerable body of both Cavalry and Infantry to beat up their rear.

After this stand-off, Wilson describes the march on Venlo and, although quite detailed, much of his story of its fall is second-hand. He devotes other pages to the various manoeuvres of the 1702 campaign, most of which were aimed at securing and counter-threatening lines of communication and important fortresses.

Wilson's personal recollections of the 1703 campaigns are also glossed over as he focuses upon putting the year's events into the context of the whole war, and outlining grand strategy and movements of the armies in a series of attempted engagements, and further stand-offs. These are punctuated by the siege and fall of Bonn, the Battle of Eckeren, the loss and capture of several strategic locations including Tongres and Huy. Much of what he writes is recounted in more detail elsewhere for Wilson wishes to find room to explain the political manoeuvres of the Archduke Charles of Habsburg as Charles II of Spain. It is not until 1704 that he returns to events at which he was presumably present.

1704

The English troops assembled at Hartogenbosch upon the 25th and 26th of April and comenced their march upon the 27th for Roremont, under the comand of the Earle of Orkney,[71] where we arived upon the 28th and were joined the next day by the detachments of our troops comanded by Brigadeer Ferguson. Which detachments had marched about two months before in order to relieve those troops which had that winter garrison'd Venlo, Roremont and Stevenswart. In order for them to march towards the Rhine, Gen'll Churchill,[72] My Lord Cutts, Gen'll Lumley, Gen'll Ingoldsby, Gen'll Ross and Gen'll Withers, with sev'll other Comanding Officers all joined the Army the same day.

And on the day following the whole body of the English troops, under the comand of Generall Churchill, crost the Maes, marcht thro' Roremond and so continued our march gradually for Coblants [Koblenz], where we crossed the Moselle and the Rhine[73] and marched through the town where it was designed to have pursued our march the next day towards Hesserland [Hesse]. But there falling such a flood of rain by w'ch there came such a torrent of water from the mountains that the roads were rendered so bad that there was no possibility of moveing the train. And the camp, being on a levell ground, by the violence of the water was in danger of being washt away into the Rhine. Notwithstanding after the rain was over, the Gener'l designed to have pursued his march and, in order thereunto, order'd the Train and wheel baggage to march. But the roads were so bad and the ground so boggy w'th the excessive rain, that not one peice of cannon could be mov'd. Upon which there was orders for the country to bring in fresh straw for the men and another day's forrage for the Horses. And next day fifty men without arms were ordered to goe before a mile or two to prepare the way. And the s'd 50 men of each Regim't haveing repair'd the roads, the Train was ordered to march gradually after them. Which they did but with a great deal of difficulty, they being obliged to putt double horses, if not more, to each peice of cannon. W'ch rendered the march so tedious that it was three a clock in the afternoon before the train had made the riseing ground about two miles from the camp, where they were obliged to draw up and pitch again. At w'ch time there was orders for the Q'r Masters and Camp Colour Men to pitch the camp adjoyning to the Train. And the troops marched halfe an hour after and encamp there that night and pursued our march next day for Nasted, where we were obliged to halt the next day in order to refresh our train and baggage horses, w'ch were so much fatigued by the baddness of the roads.[74]

Wilson then devotes himself to retelling the story of Marlborough's rule-defying 250-mile march to the Danube, including the tales of favourable comments made during various reviews; especially the famous words ascribed to Prince Eugene of Savoy about the Allied cavalry. The Allied and Habsburg armies linked up near Launsheim, concentrating some 85,000 men and forty-eight guns.

And the next day after the Army join'd, being the 18th, the Gen'lls held a Grand Councel of Warr wherein it was unanimously resolved to force the Pass of Donewart [Donauwörth]. And in order to prepare for the same, there were orders sent to the Burgomasters of the sev'll adjacent villages to make a considerable number of faschines sufficient for the same, and to bring them in by waggon to a small village upon the left of Onderingen. And there to continue till further orders. And not so much as a man or horse was to leave the place upon any pretence whatever. The w'ch comand the country obey'd and had the waggons with faschines ready at the place appointed by the 21st in the morning. Upon the 19th, the Army continued their march in sight of the Elector of Bavaria, then encampt at Dillingham on this side of the Denbie, and encampt again with our right at Almerdingen and our left at Onderingen.

Whereupon the Elector of Bavar[ia] sent a detachm't of the best of his troops, under the comand of Gen'll Lee[75] to reinforce Count de Arco[76] who was posted at the Pass of Schelinberg on a riseing ground betwixt Danawort and a wood about a mile from it, who arrived there upon the 21st by-times in the morning. As also a sufficient number of pioneers, who fell to work imediatly to intrench their camp.[77] Notwithstanding, the Duke of Marlborough was resolved to drive the enemy from this important post, and accordingly all necessary orders were given and disposition made of the Army upon the 21st,[78] w'ch was as follows, viz.t: all the

Grenad'rs of the Army and twenty Battallions of Horse, thirty Squadrons of English and Dutch Cavallry, with three Battallions of Imperial Grenad'rs. The English troops of the Infantry were the Battalion of the 1st Regim't of Foot Guards, the 1st Battal'n Royall,[79] Ingoldsby's and Meredith's. All w'ch had orders to parade at 10 a clock at night, upon the left of the front line, as also a sufficient number of the Train of Artillery. And likewise, the country waggons w'th faschines were to follow in the rear of the train.

Wee continued upon the parade till 3 in the morning, at w'ch time wee comenced our march, the Duke of Marlborough being at our head, and continued on the same towards the River Werentz, the Grand Army having orders to follow with all expedition. But by reason of the length of the way and the badness of the road, wee did not come to the river till about two of the clock. And about four a clock wee had laid our boats and passed the river with our Artillery, and all within sight of the enemy. Upon which His Grace advanced in order to veiw the enemys endeavours, at which time the Earl of Orkney and Gen'll Gore[80] used all their endeavours to form the English and Dutch Grenadeers and the rest of the Battallions of Foot in Line of Battle.

And Brigadeer Blood used his uttmost diligence in posting the Artillery to the best advantage and comenced cannonading the enemy with all vigour imaginable; the which they answered as bravely from th'r Batteries w'ch gave us to understand the action would be what indeed it was, both bloody and hott. But there being no time of looking back, wee resolved to attack them.

And the first line, w'ch was made up by the Grenad'rs,[81] the Guards, the Roy'lls, and Ingoldsby's Battallions, had order to throw down all their luggage on the ground. The country waggons, at the same time, had come along the front of the line and thrown faschines down in parcells. And also the Cavallry were then formed in Battalia under the comand of Gen'll Lumley, Gen'll Ross and Gen'll Humpesch. And His Grace, haveing taken the most advantageous ground in order to disperse necessary orders from time to time, it being then about six a clock at night, the attack was ordered to begin in the maner following.

The front rank had orders every man to sling his firelock and take a faschine in his arms, in ord'r to break the enemy's shott in advanceing.[82] After which wee advanced with all courage and vigour in life. And the enemy received us w'th such warmth, both from their own shott and prodigious fire of cartridge shott from their Batteries that they obliged us to retire with considerable loss, and which had likely to have been of great damage further, by the retreat, to putt our second line into confusion and disorder. But the Gen'lls at their head, useing all diligence to keep their troops in order, as also Gen'll Gore and Gen'll Blenheim who comanded the front line, used all diligence to compleat that line and to rally again. But about that time it began to rain, w'ch by the slipperiness of the ground, rendered the procedure of the action very difficult.

Notwithstanding of all those difficulties, the Grenadeers made a second attack, with as great courage as the former, and was as vigourly rec'd, our right being intirely beat back again w'th as great loss, if not greater than before. But our three English Battallions, afores'd, w'ch made up the left of the front line, and the Companys of Grenad'rs of the 2nd Battallion Royall, How's, Rue's and Primrose's Regim't, w'ch join'd the said three Regim'ts, having in the attack (though not without great loss), obliged the Enemy to give way, by which they made themselves masters of the wood upon the Enemy's right and stood their ground.[83] W'ch His Grace perceiving, order'd the action to comence in gen'll. W'ch held for the space of three quarters of an hour with continued fire and great slaughter on both sides.

At w'ch time Gen'll Humpech and Gen'll Ross advanced with the English and Dutch Dragoons on the Enemey's right, as also the Prince of Hesse Cassell comenced his attack upon the Enemy's left and our right near the walls of Denevart,[84] by the three Regiments of Imperiall Grenadeers as before mentioned, being seconded with three other Battall'ns of the Imperial Infantry, under the comand of Major Gen'll Pallandt,[85] w'ch were imediatly sustaind by 10 Squadrons of Imperiall Cavallry and Hussars, under the comand of Count Horn. At w'ch time Prince Lewis of Baden,[86] advanced from the grand body of our Army and came in the best of the action. Who, like a wise and experienced Gen'll, dispersed his necessary orders and by this time the action was very hott, wee sometimes oblidgeing the Enemy to give way and they, in their turn, oblidgeing us to retire.

But at last our English troops oblidged the Enemy to quitt the trenches on the right. Upon which Humpass[87] and Ross charg'd their right wing of Horse, both w'th courage and good success. W'ch the center of their line perceiving, gave way and Gen'll Lumley and Gen'll Wood advanced w'th great courage and charged the Enemy so briskly that there ensued a violent slaughter: the Enemy retireing towards the river and our Horse pursueing them so hard that by the crowd of the Enemy, their bridge broke and great numbers were glad to escape, as well Generals as priv't soldiers, to save themselves by swimming the river.[88] The Imperial Troops, on their left, endeavoured to push the Enemy with a great deal of bravery at the same time, but being so much under cover of the walls of the Town w'ch gauld them sore on theuir flanks with cartridge and small shott, gave the Enemy an opportunity to fall back within their works.

The night comeing on putt an end to this terrible engagem't w'ch was fought with a great deal of courage and resolution, to the glory of all the Confederate troops under His Grace the Duke of Marlborough comand, and in an emenent manner to His Grace's own particular honour. Who, dureing the whole, behav'd himselfe like a wise and experienced Generall, and undauntedly exposed himselfe every where to disperse orders as he judged necessary. But as the engagem't was comenced w'th the English and Dutch troops, it was believed they were the greatest sufferers. Especially those three Battallions and four Companys of Grenad'rs before mentioned, who maintained their ground and stood the force of the Enemys fire on the right dureing the intervals of second and third attacks. The Imperialist, as before mentioned, comeing up just as wee began our third attack, and not come to any great action until the Conferates have drove the Enemy from their trenches, and even then but with small success.

Notw'thstanding it was computed that the Enemy, in this action had killed and drowned 6,000 men,[89] being at the comencem't of the engagem't abo't 14,000 strong; all choice troops comanded in chief by Count d'Arco and under him three Bavarian and two French Lieut Generals. By this it must be believed that our loss was also very considerable, and especially by the loss of Gen'll Gore and Gen'll Blenheim and sev'll other officers of note killed upon the spott. Prince Lewis,[90] the Prince of Hesse, Count Horn, Major Gen'll Wood, Major Gen'll Pallandt was all (w'th sev'll other officers of note) wounded. Wee took in this action sixteen peices of the Enemy's cannon, 13 colours and standards, as also all their tents and camp equipage.

After w'ch our troops continued all night in the feild of battell, the battell being thus ended. And about sunriseing next morning had orders to stand to our arms in order to march into our camp which was then pitching abo't a mile in our rear. And, accordingly, the drums beat to arms by which wee were roused up and looking abo't us beholding the fruits of our last nights labour, the feild of battell all strawed with the killed and wounded, w'ch was a very melancholly sight to behold, &c more in particular the groans of the wounded then the sight of the dead. Wee being thus roused, the Earl of Orkney came along the Line and order the Comanding Officers to march back into the Camp.

W'ch wee accordingly did, and as soon as wee had refreshed our selves a little after pitching our tents, there was orders for an hundred men of each Regim't without arms to go and search in and abo't the feild of battell and bring all the wounded men as well those of the Enemy as those of our own people, and carry them to the Chirurgeons of our respective Regiments in order to have them drest and taken care of. As also an Express to the comanding Majistrates of the sev'll adjoyning villages, to send men against next day at farthest to bury the dead.

And also, at the same time, ordered that 100 men of each Regim't that had not been on the attack the day before, with twelve Squadrons of Horse, to parade at the head of the Imperialists by nine of the clock, under the comand of My Lord Cutts, Gen'll Ingoldsby, Gen'll Wyndham, My Lord John Hay, in order to force the town of Donavert if the Enemy withstood it. But upon their advanceing the Bavarian Garrison quitted the same, broke down their bridges, but had not time to destroy their amunition and provision as they had orders to do. Notwithstanding they had sett fire to sev'll of their magazines but by our expeditious arrival wee extinguished the same. In w'ch wee found 2000 sack of meal and a great quantity of oats, salt and other provisions.

The effect of all these victorys were of very considerable service whereby the Confederates had opened a passage into the heart of Duke of Bavar[ia's] country, and he himselfe being oblidged to retire with his Army, under the canon of Ausburgh. All this glorious action being (by the blessing of God) completed on the 22^d and 23^d of June. Next day, early in the morning, wee laid four pontoon bridges over the river and also repaired the Town bridge w'ch the Enemy had broke down. And the body of our Army passed the river by twelve a clock and our train and heavy baggage marched through the Town. After which the Q'r M'r Gen'll was ordered to pitch the Camp on the plain by Marteningen, in the Elector of Bavaria's country.[91]

And the day following, being the 25th, was ordered for a day of Gen'll Thanksgiving throughout our Army, to Almighty God, for his great blessings on our arms, in giving us victory over our Enemys. And it was notified also that His Grace, in company with Prince Lewis, would see the Camp in the morning before divine service, at w'ch time His Grace came to the head of each Regim't to return hearty thanks to both Officers and men for their forwardness and great courage. And for their further encouragement gave the Army to understand that as farr as they should go into the Duke of Bavaria's country, they had liberty to make as free plunder.[92] The Day of Thanksgiving being observed religiously according to orders, the evening was also concluded with a flood of joy.[93] And His Grace, the Duke of Marlborough, being designed not to give the Enemy any time to recover out of their consternation, and considering that the Army was also considerably refreshed after their great fateique upon the 28th, ordered the Army to hold themselves in a readiness to march. And, in order thereunto, the Gen'll was ordered to beat in the morning by 4, the Assembly halfe an hour after and to march by five. Which they accordingly did and that day passed the River Lech upon which the Enemy abandoned Newburgh and retired to Ingolestat. W'ch His Grace being informed of sent a detachment to take possession of it [Newburgh]. And after, the Army encamped near the Rain, a small fortification[94] belonging to the Duke of Bavaria, which place the Duke ordered to be invested on the next day, being the 30th of June. And on the 3d day following, Count Voghlin,[95] Gen'll of the Palintine Horse came to the Confederate-Army from Prince Eugene with an Express to His Grace the Duke of Marlborough, that the Marischalls Tallard[96] and Villeroy[97] had passed the Rhine near Fort Keil[98] with 50,000 regular troops. Upon which, Prince Maximilian [of] Hanover was detached w'th 30 Squadrons of Imperial Horse to join Prince Eugene in order to enable him to observe . . . the Enemy.

The Garrison of the Rain came to a capitulation on the 5th and marcht out the next day being conducted by a party, to the Elector of Bavaria's Camp near Ausburgh. Upon which His Grace ordered Newburgh, the Rain and Donivart to be magazines for the Confederate Forces, and the Army marched the next day. And so continued till they encamped upon the 12th with our Right at Wolvertshausen and our Left at Ostmaring, Friedburgh being in the center of the Line, whereby the Elector of Bavaria's comunication with his own country was cutt off.

Nothwithstanding, His Grace and Prince Lewis were so civill to dispatch Count Wartislaw to His Electorall Highness with proposealls of an accomodation[99] which, at first, had the aspect of a good understanding. But His Electoral Highness, being informed that Count Tallard had passed the Black Forrest, he desired to aquaint Count Wartislaw that he was assured that His Most Christiain Maj'tie had made powerfull efforts to support him. He, therefore, thought himselfe oblidged in honour to remain firm to his allyance.[100]

This procedure was so much resented by the Duke of Malbrol that he sent out 30 Squadrons of Horse and sev'll partys of Hussars[101] to burn and plunder the Elector of Bavar[ia]'s country, even to the very gates of Munich, his capital citty. Upon which deputations was made to His Grace from sev'll parts of the country, offering to pay contribution and to accept of his protection. To which His Grace made answer, that the Queen of Great Brittain did not send her troops there w'th a veiw of levying mony off the country but to reduce their Prince to reason and obedience to his Lord and Soveraigne, the Emperor. And so the burning and plundering his country continued as farr as parties could reach.

After which His Grace and Prince Lewis resolved to beseige Ingoldstat and the Army marched in order thereunto and incampt between Newburgh and Ingoldstat. And the next day following, being the 27th of July, Prince Eugene arrived in the Camp in order to conferr with His Grace and Prince Lewis, who agreed that Prince Lewis should comence the Seige of Ingoldsat, and His Grace and Prince Eugene should observe the motion of the Enemy.[102] After which Prince Eugene returned to that body of the Army under his comand where he rec'd intelligence upon his arrival that the Elector of Bavaria and Count Tallard had join'd their Armys and past the Danube and, as was beleived, had a design to fall upon him seperatly. Of w'ch he dispatcht an Express to His Grace; Prince Lewis haveing marched off that morning for Ingoldstat and His Grace upon his march for Lech near the Rhine.[103]

As the troops were encamping wee had a full information of the Enemy's proceedings, His Grace order'd twenty Squadrons of Horse under Gen'll Humpech's and Gen'll Ross's comand and twenty Battallions of Foot under the comand of Gen'll Ingoldsby and Generall Withers. The whole under the comand of General Churchill to march in order to join Prince Eugene with all expedition. Which comand marched according to order, passed the Danube that night and encampt near Donivert, and the intire Body of the Army comenced their march by two in ye morn'g.

That detachm't under Gen'll Churchill, joined Prince Eugene between 10 & 11 of the clock. And by 7 in the morning the Express afores'd from Prince Eugene, came to His Graces hands. To which His Grace answered that he had information of the enemy proceedings as yesterday, and that he had detached twenty Squadrons of Horse and twenty Battallions of Foot under his brother's comand, w'ch he concluded had joined His Highness's comand by this time. His Grace said no more but presented his service by the messenger to Prince Eugene and bidd tell him that if possible he would join him that evening. Wee, accordingly, continued our march and passt the Danube by Donavert, and so on till wee joined the Prince's Army and then encamped, haveing Appershoven on our right and Munster on our left.

And the next day following, being the 1st of August, the Duke of Marlborough and Prince Eugene accompanied with all the Gen'll persons except those of the day, under the eschort of 4 Squadrons of Cavallry, went out in order to observe the motions of the Enemy; the which, by their propectives[104] they could observe were all in a motion. And after upon a more stricter observation, they could observe their camp pitched out between Blenheim and Lutzingen.

Whereupon the Gen'lls returned and ordered out a detachm't of men without arms in order to work, and a considerable strong guard under arms to open the ways, and lay bridges in the front cross some little rivuletts, that the Army might march upon occasion in a regular manner. And by twelve of the clock wee could plainly discern from the Tower of Thissingen, as also had certain information, that the Enemy was encamped in a very advantageous manner; their right being flanket by the Danube and the village of Blenheim and their left by a wood and the village of Lutsingen; as also a rivulett in their front,[105] whose banks were very high, and the meadows very morrossie. So that it was judged to be very hard to bring the Enemy to an engagement or to attack them in that convenient seituation.

Whereupon His Grace ordered a Grand Councel of Warr to assemble with all expedition, to whom His Grace and Prince Eugene remonstated [demonstrated] the seituation of the Enemy's camp, and how hard it would be to attack them.

Yett they did declare there was an indispendable necessity for doing it before they should intrench themselves in their camp; first because the country about our camp was so exhausted of forrage, so as wee should be straitened very much in a sho[r]t time; secondly that the Marischall Villeroy was upon the point of makeing an incursion into Wirtenburgh; and thirdly that after the Elector of Bavaria and Tallard were entrenched, they could spare such detachments from their camp to join Villeroy, as would enable him to establish a free comunication from the Rhine to the Danube, and force all to submitt to their crueltie as farr as the River Mein. And also that it would be in the power of the Elector of Bavaria to make such detachment from his camp as might ruin the Circle of Franconia, by which the Allies would finde no sustenance for winter quarters upon the Danube nor in Upper Germany.

Upon these considerations the Prince and the Duke, as also all the members of the Councell of Warr, came to a final resolution to engage the Enemy next morning, depending upon God for the victory. And in order thereunto sent away the wheel baggage to Ruttlingen, a village betwixt Munster and Donowart, as also made a disposition of the Army for the attacks.

Of which My Lord Cutts, being the first General upon comand, ma[r]ched off in the evening with 16 Battallions of Foot and twenty Squadrons of Horse comanded by Gen'll Humpech and Gen'll Wood. All w'ch marched silently in the dark, close by the river at where wee had laid our bridges, and there lay upon our armes till it was light.[106] At w'ch time wee perceived the Grand Body of our Army advanceing towards us, and abo't six a clock there came orders to My Lord Cutts that as soon as the Grand Body advanced within muskett shott of his rear he should advance over the rivulet and there draw up and wait for further orders. The w'ch was performed much abo't 7-a-clock, at which time the Enemy took the allarum. Who by their long silence did not (as was supposed) expect, so early a visitt, but before I proceed farther I leave our Army to pass over the rivulet, and the Enemy to forme their Line of Battell, and give you an acco't of the Army on both sides, their strength [at] this present juncture.

The Confederate Army, under the comand of the Duke of Marlborough and Prince Eugene, to consist of sixty four Battallions of Infantry and one hundred sixty and six Squadrons of Horse, a Train of fifty two peices of cannon and ten feild mortars.

And the Army of the Enemy, under the comand of the Elector of Bavaria and Count Tallard, consisted of eighty two Battalions of Infantry, and one hundred forty and seaven Squadrons of Cavallry, with a train of one hundred and four peices of cannon and thirty mortars. Which being a true state of both Armys, I proceed to the actions of the ensueing engagem't.

Where I finde the Confederate Army past over the first rivulett and still continuing advanceing till about eight a clock. At w'ch time the Enemy began cannonadeing us, as wee also did them, with great success on both sides but in this they had a great advantage over us by their great superiority in their number of their cannon. Notwithstanding, our troops continued advanceing till they had passed the second rivulett, after which His Grace took up the most proper ground to veiw the Lines, and dispersed his most necessary orders from time to time, as also Prince Eugene took up his ground upon the right; wee being then formed in two bodys, on the right comanded by Prince Eugene and that on the Left by the Duke of Marlborough. The Enemy, likewise, were formed in two bodys; that on the Right comanded by Count Tallard and that on the Left by the Elector of Bavaria and the Mischall Marshein. Thus all things were in a readiness for a close engagement but by reason of the great moross on the front of the Enemys Left, Prince Eugen was obliged to take a considerable compass of ground before he could come to engag'd them, by which ye engagem't was hindred for some time.[107]

And as soon as wee judged that Prince Eugene had gained his point, the action could [be] comenc'd on our Left by My Lord Cutts against the village of Blenheim w'ch wee fought with a great deal of courage and resolution; w'ch was seconded on the Right by Prince Eugene and the Imperialists with equall courage and resolution. And the Enemy received us with as great courage as wee could advance on them and obliged both our attacks to retire after such. My Lord Cutts ralied again with his troop, and haveing rec'd some fresh Regiments he, w'th My Lord Orkeney, made a second vigourous attack and were again repulsed, but they still rallied their men with all the resolution imaginable. By which time wee perceived Prince Eugene make his second attack from our Right and the Enemy's Left, w'ch were again, in some measure, repulsed. But the Prince continued to pour in fresh Battallions to support his attack.[108] At w'ch time our attacks began on the Right and also in the center of the lines, it being then about three a clock of the day. At w'ch time the action became generall, cruell and bloody; wee oblidgeing them in some places to retire and they, in their turn, oblidgeing us sometimes to give way. In w'ch close and furious manner both Armies continued till halfe an hour after six.

At w'ch time Prince Eugene advanced his troops on the Right, soe closely on the Enemys Left, that he broke the body of the Bavarian Guards w'ch made up the Left of their front line. By which the Imperial Dragoons gott the advantage of flanking them w'ch oblidged the Enemy to recoile back and incline very much to the morrose of Rochstet.[109] Upon w'ch the Prince poured in his imbattelled Squadrons in a most bold and daring manner and the Enemy rec'd them with as great courage, pouring in their retreating Platoons[110] in a terrible manner till they had recovered the Pass of the Morose of Hochstet. Which, His Highness perceiving, and considering how much his troops were gauled, did not think it proper to make any further pursuit. Upon w'ch he ordered to halt and compleat[111] the troops, and there so to remain till further orders.

In which station wee will leave them and take a veiw of the two bodys of the Armys under His Grace, the Duke of Marlborough and Count Tallard's comands, who all this time were attacking each other in a violent and bloody manner with little or no success on either side and especially at the village of Blenheim. The which place was so strongly situated by nature, as also fortified by art of the Enemy, that the place proved impregnable to us the whole day, haveing been attacked at least four sev'll times by the troops under My Lord Cutts, My Lord Orkney and Gen'll Churchill's comands. And as often repulsed, as also our Cavally being oblidged to charge the Enemy three or four sev'll times with little or no success.[112]

Whereupon the whole body of our English Infantry, and some of the auxiliary troops, attacked the village again with all the courage imaginable and were as bravely repulsed by the Enemy. Upon which Count Tallard, judging it then a convenient opportunity, advanced w'th the most part of his wing of Cavallry, in order to have cutt our Infantry in peices before they could have retired under the cover of our Cavallry. But our Horse, advanceing with a great deal of courage and resolution, they charged each other with a deal of vigour. But wee, crouding in our imbattell'd Squadrons, oblidge them to give way.[113] At w'ch time the Count Tallard and sev'll other Officers, were taken prison'rs[114] and our troops, haveing pusht the Enemy so hard, bore them down into the Danube; that it was computed twenty six Squadrons were pushed into the river where the greatest part, both men and Horse, perished in the stream.

Which the Infantry then in village of Blenheim perceiveing, as also being informed that the Elector of Bavaria had declined the feild of Battell and retired to the Morrose of Hochstet, were in a great consternation how to gett out of that laberynth of difficulty. And findeing no hopes of makeing any safe retreat, was resolved to make themselves Prisoners of Warr.[115]

Upon which they ordered a Brigadeer from the village to our Line with proposealls, who comeing to My Lord Orkney, aquainted His Lords'p that he was come with an intention to surrender these troops in the villages Prisoners of Warr. To w'ch My Lord Orkney replyed they must expect no better conditions then to be prisoners at discretion, and if they would not, they would finde themselves attacked on all sides and then they must expect no quarters.

Whereupon the Brigadeer replyed, that they were a good body of troops and thought His Lords'p's proposealls too hard, to which My Lord returned, 'What? Is not your left wing beat out of the feild, as also your right wing of Horse and your Gen'll taken prisoner? And wee have a considerable body of troops that have not yett engaged and are now upon their march to joyne the troops under Generall Churchill's and my comand. But I give you halfe an hour's time to go into the village and consult your Comanding officers, and if you don't return within that time, the event will be as I have already declared.'[116]

Whereupon the Brigadeer returned to the village and after a short consultation with the Comanding Officers, they agreed to submitt themselves Prisoners at Discretion;[117] the which resolution and agreement the Brigad'r returned to aquaint My Lord Orkney with and proposed to march out and lay down their arms upon the plain. But His Lordship, haveing that singular p[r]esence of minde, that the troops on that side being pretty much shattred, and also our Cavallry marched off w'ch had sustaind them, replyed, 'No S'r. You shall march out on the other side of the village and lay down your arms to My Lord Cutts.'

Upon w'ch the Brigadeer said they had made no conditions[118] with His Lords'p. 'No matter,' replyed Lord Orkney. 'Go you and gett your men ready, and I will send my Aid de Camp along with you through the village who shall aquaint My Lord Cutts of the conditions past between us.' Upon which he ordered S'r James Abercrombie to go along with the Brigadeer to My Lord Cutts, who accordingly went.

And just as My Lord Cutts was compleating his men, resolving to make his attack, he perceived S'r James Abercrombie comeing out of the village. Upon which he gave the word to the lines to halt and rid towards him, who aquainted him with the conditions agreed upon between My Lord Orkney and the Enemy. Whereupon he ordered the troops to the right about and ordered them to march about 300 yards to give the Enemy room to lay down their arms. After w'ch the Enemy marched out of the village to the number of twenty six intire Battalions, and laid down their arms in our front, marching through our intervales of the two lines.[119] As also twelve Squadrons of Dragoons, who submitted themselves at the same time and upon the same conditions to our English Horse.

And it being then much about sun setting and an end putt to this bloody and cruell battell, w'ch had been fought from the first begining for the space of twelve hours, with a great deal of courage and resolution on both sides, as could be no otherwise expected from two such great and potent Armys as was then in the feild; as also such wise and experienced Generalls at the head of both Armies, who contested so vehemently for the victory which (praised be God) was on our side.

The Earl of Orkney, being the first Gen'll person who knew himselfe at liberty, ordered the Comanding Officers of each Regiment under his comand to compleat their men, and then lett them lye down upon their arms.[120] And His Lords'p rode imediatly to the Duke of Marlborough to give him an acco't of what conditions he had made with the Enemy, and how the prisoners were disposed of. As also to congratulate His Grace upon the acco't that he and the arms under his comand had gotten so great a victory over the Enemy.

Whereupon His Grace returned his sword[121] with all the joy imaginable and said, 'Praised be God for this victory, and also for the stoppage putt to so great effusion of blood.' After which, in a most familiar and friendly manner, he took My Lord Orkney by the hand and said, 'George, thou art a happy man and a messenger of good tydeings. Praised, therefore, be Almighty God.'[122]

After which His Grace dispatched orders for the Army to draw up and range from Prince Eugene's left to the village of Blenheim; along this side of the Morose of Hochstet and so lye on their arms all night. In which station the Army continued dureing the dead of the night as silent as if they had been buried in oblivion of eternall rest.

And as soon as it was then light day, and wee being informed that the Duke of Bavaria and Marisch Marchien were marched off with the remainder of the troops under their comand,[123] there was orders for 100 men of each Regim't without arms, to go through the feild of battell and all the feilds and places adjoyning to search for wounded men, both of our own and the Enemy's troops, and give them to the care and charge of surgeons, with strict orders to dress them. As also a Capt. of Guides had orders to go w'th a party of Hussars, and press the country to come in imediatly to bury the killed men and dead horses. And if any village was disobedient to these orders, they were to fire the same.

His Grace also gave orders at the same time that all the prisoners of the Confederat Army under His Grace's comand should be brought to that body of prisoners under the charge of My Lord Cutts, being the place appointed for the gen'll rendezvous of the prison'rs. And also appointed Comissary and other proper officers to take an acco't of them according to their quality, posts and stations in the sev'll Regim'ts they belong'd to; from the Marischall Tallard to a private centinell. As also ordered that the tents and wheel baggage of the Army should be sent for; the performance of all which orders took up that forenoon.

After which our Q'r Masters and Camp Colour Men had orders to march and pitch out the Camp at Stenheim where wee remain'd encamped five or six days in order to look after and take care of the wounded, and dispose of the prisoners.

And the next day after was employed in impressing carriages to cary out wounded men to our Grand Hospitall at Narlin [Nordlingen]. And the next day following, being the 5th, His Grace ordered those whom he had appointed as Commissarys to take an acco't of the Prison'rs to bring in an exact return. And also the conductors of the train, to bring in an exact returne also of the cannon, mortars and ammunition waggons that were taken from the Enemy. And each Regim't also was ordered to bring into the Duke's Q'rs all the Standards, Colours, kettle drums &c., w'ch had been taken from the Enemy, where the Adjutant Generall was appointed to receive them, and make a return thereof to His Grace, as also a return of the number of coaches and laden mules, with a true acco't of the barrells and casks of ready silver taken in this engagement. And, likewise, a return of the killed and wounded of the Confederate troops under His Grace's comand in this action.

And he dispatched some of his most ingenious and brightest spies to the Duke of Bavaria's Camp, to discover as farr as possible the strength of his shattered troops, in order to [make] the computation of the loss w'ch they had sustain'd in the action. By which computation the Enemy lost in the feild of battell, and otherwise deserted from their Colours, to the number of 25,000 men, besides 13,000 that were made prisoners.[124] And also wee took 100 peices of cannon, twenty four mortars, 129 Colours, 171 Standards, 17 pair of kettle drums, 34 coaches, 300 laden mules, 24 barrels and 4 chests of silver, 270 amunition waggons, 3,600 tents with 100 and odd bread waggons and all their other wheel baggage intire.

The loss of the Confederates under His Grace's comand was 4,500 killed and 7,500 wounded.[125] Amongst the killed wee recon those that died of their wounds in a week's time after the engagem't; of which was the Prince of Holsteinbeck[126] and Brigadeer Row.[127] Feild Officers killed upon the spott; Colo'l White, Lt. Colo'l Dormer, Lt. Colo'l Dalzyel, Major Cornwallis, Major Campbell and Major Creed, Lord Forbes, and Major Chevnix. Amongst the wounded was Lord North and Gray, My Lord Mordant, Colo'l Hamilton, Lt. Colo'l Levingston, Lt. Collo' Peyton, Major Granvile, Major Morgan, Lt Colo'l Brittain, Major Armstrong, and Major Hatley.

Haveing now given an acco't of loss of the Enemy, and their killed and wounded, as also the loss of the Confederates under His Grace's comand, it may be supposed that the loss of the Imperialists under Prince Eugene, though they did not suffer so much as wee, yett all they might not be much inferior in the number of their killed and wounded, that by moderate computation of the whole wee had 8,000 killed upon the spott and about 1400 wounded.[128]

His Grace, haveing now had a very satisfactory acco't according to computation of the losses of both Armies in this terrible engagem't, judged it most proper and bound in duty, as he had begun with prayer to end with praise. And, accordingly, ordered the day ensueing to be a day of Gen'll Thanksgiving throughout the whole Army for the great blessings Almighty God had conferrd upon us, in giveing us victory over our Enemys. As also notified, at the same time, that His Grace designed to come along the Line next morning before Divine Service, w'ch he accordingly did. And at the head of each Regim't return'd thanks to both Officers and soldiers for their great courage and resolution, as also for their great fidelity to their country.

And likewise ordered that every Troop and Company of the English should, after Divine Service, receive four Pistoles each Troop and Company, upon his owne acco't,[129] in order to drink Her Maj'tie's health, the good of their country and the prosperity and success of the Army. This Day of Thanksgiveing, according to orders, was punctually observed and the evening concluded with a flood of joy.

As also during this time His Grace was not idle, but dispatched Expresses to the Court of Great Brittain,[130] and the States Gener'll of the United Provinces; the first with an acco't of the victory, the second with the confirmation of it. And a narrative (according to the best computation) of the particulars of the action. Prince Eugene also dispatched his Expresses to the Court of Vienna, and the sev'll Gen'lls to their respective Courts of this glorious success. At the arrival of w'ch Expresses the sev'll Courts expressed the greatest joy and satisfaction imaginable; and particularly the Emperor and the Court of Vienna, as plainly did appear by the honour and dignity conferred upon the Duke of Marlborough as soon as possible after, His Grace being made a Prince of the Holy Impire.[131] And also, a pillar of stone was erected on the place where the action was, with the Imperiall, Brittish and States Gener'll's arms engraven thereon, with an inscription to the perpetual memory of His Grace, the Brittish and Confederate arms, in Her Brittanich Maj'tie's auspicious reigne, for so signall and great a victory obtained by the blessing of God over the French and Bavarian Forces.[132]

Wilson then writes another poetic eulogy upon Queen Anne, Marlborough and the soldiery. His style is grand although at times sentimental and trite. He returns to his narrative with tales of general European rejoicing and the ferrying of the prisoners to Holland. He briefly mentions the sieges and capitulation of Ulm, Landau and Treves, Leopold I's grand tour of the Rhine and the reviews held in his honour, as well as the return of the armies to their Dutch winter quarters. He concludes the year by outlining the arrangements made to hold Tallard in Nottingham, the triumph staged in London and the proposal to pay the men a bounty.

1705

Wilson adds little to our understanding of the events of 1705 dealing, as he often does, with strategic manoeuvres; this time on the Moselle and those involved in the taking of the Lines of

Brabant. Yet he includes an interesting description of an attempt
by the Allies to forge a bridgehead over the Dyle.

And then it was determined in Councell, if possible, to pass the
Doile in two attacks near Welshwaver. And there was a disposition
made of the Army in order thereunto, who marched off by two in
the afternoon to the Left of the Line, where the Main Body for
that attempt was ordered to assemble. The English troops for the
same was Churchill's, How's, Godfry's, Ingoldsby's, Lord
Mordaunt's, Gen'll Ferguson's being comanded by Gen'll
Ferguson.[133] The Grenadeers of these 6 Regim'ts were drawn into
one body under the comand of Collon'l Godfrey who marched as
soon as it was dark in the front of the pontoons in order to cover
the lane of the bridges. Wee arrived at the river a little before
daylight without being discovered by the Enemy.

Notwithstanding they were just on the other side of the river,
yett we posted our selves under cover of a quick sett hedge without
so much as one shott being fired. Where wee continued the space
of a quarter of an hour untill such time as the pontoons on the
carriages came along a little causeway w'ch led to the river, in
order to lay the bridges. At the noise whereof the Enemy took the
allarum and so began their fireing very sharply on that place
where they judged the bridges would be laid. W'ch gauld our
workmen so prodigiously that they were not able to stand it. W'ch
Brigadeer Blood perceiveing, came to Colo'l Godfrey desireing
three Companies of the Grenadeers from the Right to advance to
the river side in order to fire upon the Enemy to divert them
dureing the laying of the pontoon bridges. And as the bridges were
finished the Grenadeers had orders to march over the same; w'ch
wee accordingly did and beat the Enemy from that ground. And
by this time our train was come up and our Batteries fixt and
comenced cannonadeing the French lines on their march with
great success for the space of an hour. Att which time His Grace
came up to the riseing ground in our rear and there took a Veiw of
the ground over w'ch the troops were to march to make their
attacks. And findeing the same to be so morasic that the Horse
could not march up to sustain the Foot, order'd those troops that

had passed the river to retire back with all expedition and the bridges to be taken up.

W'ch was don with great diligence and the Grenadeers lyned the same quick sett hedge from whence they marched when they passed the river, where wee were ordered to continue till the pontoons and all the other troops had marched clear off the morrose. After w'ch wee comenced our march.

Att w'ch time there was two Battallions of Irish in the French service advanced very briskly, close by the river side, beating the English march and flourishing St George's Cross.[134] And as soon as ever wee had marched clear of the cover of the hedge, they bore in their fire upon us in a terrible manner and did us a great deal of damage before wee could recover any advantageous ground to defend ourselves. But as soon as wee had recovered it, wee imediately wheel'd about, and threw in our fire upon them in so brisk and violent a manner, that wee tore them so to peices that wee judged most of them was killed or wounded before they recovered the hedges and ditches.[135]

The French, by this time haveing fixed their Batteries, comenced canonading our lines on their march but with no great success. The Battallions which were upon this expedition were ordered to fall into their lines upon the march; the Grenadeers excepted, who were to continue as a rear guard. W'ch as soon as join'd, Gen'll Ferguson order[ed] us to lye down and refresh our selves. And the Grand Body of the Army continued their march for Melder . . .

1706

Wilson's recollections of 1706 are dominated by the battle of Ramillies but there seems to be nothing new amongst them to interest the researcher save a reference to not many of the French soldiers being able to carry off their 'knapsacks' in the rout. He concludes the year with paragraphs on each of the cities and towns that subsequently fell into Allied hands in the course of which he recounts a unique verbatim story concerning the levelling of the French lines near Coutrai.

The confirmation of the surrender of Ostend being arrived in the French Army, they abandoned Courtray thereupon. Upon information of w'ch His Grace detached eight Battallions of Foot, under the comand of Prince Holstenbeck, to take possession thereof.

And the next day but one following, the Grand Army crost the Laies and encamped by Courtray, where they lay three days and encamped upon the fourth, with their Left to Holchen, so close to the old French line that the Qr Guard of the Front Line was pitcht thereon. W'ch lines wee levell'd effectually, during which time there happned one accident w'ch was worth remarkeing betwixt His Grace and the workmen.

W'ch was that His Grace, comeing along the line to see the workmen, said in a very jocose manner: 'Work, my lads. Work and levell the lines to perfection for I'll give you my promise, whilst the wars hold and I am yo'r Gen'll, they shall not be raised again.' Upon w'ch the workmen reply'd, 'My Lord. May it please Yo'r Grace. That is very well but that is not all. For if Your Grace thinks fitt wee will be glad of our mony for levelling the same.'

To which His Grace replied, 'What? Is nothing to be don without mony?' 'No,' replied the men, 'and that Your Grace well knows.' 'Very well,' replied he, 'Lett yo'r work be levell'd t'night and you shall be paid tomorrow.' The w'ch the men performed and His Grace was as good as his word.[136]

1707

Wilson contents himself with two pages outlining the strategic movements of the armies.

1708

In 1708 Wilson also brings into his panorama of events the actions of Bing, Baker and the Fleet during an attempted Jacobite rising, but he would have no first-hand knowledge of the events he relates. He may have picked up the information while aboard the transports, for he was shipped over to Flanders again in time for Oudenarde. His account of this battle is very incomplete, but perhaps it reflects what little he saw of it in his humble station as an NCO. Afterwards he unfortunately reverts to the grand manoeuvres, of marches and counter-marches and the progress of the Great Convoy and the Siege of Lille. However, during his general description of events around Lille he does recount two incidents worthy of mention.

And about 7 of the clock in the morning, His Grace had a full information that the Enemy was encamped again upon their old ground by Doway and that all their marches and countermarches hitherto was only to keep us in continual allarum and fateigue our troops. And also that they certainly designed to attack us but that they could not have all things in readiness in relation thereunto in less then three days time. Whereupon His Grace ordered the Army to encamp again and a General Councel of Warr was ordered to assemble by 9 a clock in order to consult and advise upon proper measures to hinder the Enemy from fateigueing the Army. The Councel of Warr mett according to order and unanimously agreed to intrench the camp and Prince Eugene declareing at the same time that there would be a sufficient breach in the counterscarp tomorrow by twelve a clock. And the Councel came also to a resolution to carry the same by storm.

And the next day following, being the 27th of August, there was a detachm't made of ten Grenad'rs of each company and 30 men of each Regim't of the Grand Army for ye same. W'ch was carried sword in hand that evening with a great effusion of blood on both sides. Wee having killed and wounded upon this attack, by computation, 2000 men and among the number (w'ch was very remarkable) there were abo't 17 or 18 Engineers.[137] The Army, according to the result of the Councel of Warr, comenced entrenching the camp the day before; had continued the same with all diligence which they had compleated by break of day by the 28th in the morning.

At w'ch time the Enemy, haveing all things in a readiness and being informed of our entrenching, thought it then high time to proceed in their design to raise the Seige. And in order thereunto, decampt that night and pitched the next morning abo't a league right in our front and took possession of a chateau about middway betwixt the two Armies. By w'ch they so much annoyed our forragers in the front that report thereof was made to the Gen'll of the day who reported the same to His Grace at Councel time.

Upon w'ch it was ordered that the piquetts of the Army should imediatly march to dislodge them but it was objected that would take up too long time and that there was Regiments entrenched by the Q'rs w'ch was more readier. And soe the order for the picquett was countermanded and How's Regim't and Sr. Rich'd Temple's were ordered to take their arms. Which they did accordingly and marched about 300 yards in the front of the Q'r Guard at w'ch place Gen'll Webb (being the Gener'l for the day) came in order to comand us. After w'ch wee imediatly advanced towards the chatteau.

How's Regim't attacked the gate w'ch was secured by a draw bridge and on the outside of the bridge there was two lodges and a pair of strong wooden gates where the Enemy had posted a Serj't and 20 men who, thro' the slitts and windows of the lodges as also the holes, broke in the gates. And likewise from the slitts and windows from the body of the chateau they fired upon us so violently and wee, being upon the plain without cover, they killed and wounded us at their pleasure without receiving any great damage from us in returne.

But notwithstanding all their great fire, wee broke open their outergates and took the Serj't and his comand prison'rs.[138] And if wee could have had proper time wee would have made ourselves masters of the chateau but, by the fireing, both Armies had taken the allarum. And the Gen'll perceiving that the French picquett of Horse was advancing very fast, ordered us to retire leaving all our killed upon the spott as also sev'll of our mortally wounded men to the mercy of the Enemy.

W'ch number of killed and wounded of Gen'll How's Regim't was incredible to think of. Wee having killed and left wounded upon the spott 107 and 161 wounded w'ch were carried off, whereof 47 died in 3 days and 114 was sent to Menin Hospit'll whereof 62 died of their wounds. And 52 came back to the Regim't

to Ghent whereof 27 were discharged for Chelsea, being unfitt for
service. So that there remained of the 161 that was wounded, only
25 for service. By which return it appeared that Gen'll How's
Reg't lost 243 men, Officers included, in the space of three q'rs
of an hour.[139] The loss of S'r Rich'd Temple's Regim't was
inconsiderable haveing only 7 killed and 13 wounded.

And the next day but one after Gen'll How's Regim't had
received this sad disaster, being upon the 29th of Aug't, the Enemy
advanced within cannon shott of our trenches with a vast Army
and a numerous train of artillery, being fully resolved if possible to
oblidge us to raise the Seige. Whereupon Prince Eugene drew off
all the troops that could be conveniently spared to joyne the
Grand Army. And His Grace, in conjunction with Prince Eugene
and my Lord Averquerque, ordered the camp to be struck and all
the wheel baggage, as also the tents, to march clear of the Army.

And then the front line marched into the intrenchm'ts
imediatly being sustained by the Second Line in the rear of us.
The Cavallry, being also drawn up in their proper order in the rear
of the Second Line, all things being thus prepared for an
ingagem't, being the 31th of August, betwixt two and three in the
afternoon.

Wee continued in this station without any motion till about 6 a
clock at night, at w'ch time the Comissarys of the bread waggons
sent to aquaint the Army that they were arrived with bread; a
report of which was imediatly made to the Gen'll persons for that
day who, considering the great necessity the Army had of bread
and also that seeing the Enemy had not as yett comenced their
cannonadeing and being now so late in the day, the Gen'lls
concluded they could come to no close action that night.

Whereupon it was judged proper that the men should go for
their bread, and accordingly the Q'r Mast'rs Serj't with a man of
each tent[140] should go to the bread waggons in order to receive the
same. Att which Cololl Durrell sent a Serj't to the Comissary of
the bread waggons to detach 31 waggons as soon as empty to the
rear of Gen'll How's Regim't. Whereof 27 was ordered for Gen'll
How's and 4 for S'r Richard Temple's Regim'ts. And also it was
ordered that the wounded men should be putt into the waggons

next morning,[141] as soon as it was light, in order that they might be clear off us before any action should comence.

W'ch orders was exactly performed and the waggons clear off the ground by sun riseing much abo't w'ch time the Enemy comenced their cannonading with a great deal of vigour, haveing no less then 130 peices of cannon by computation playing on our Lines, w'ch very much annoyed our Cavalry in the rear. Upon which there was sev'll Squadrons which stood most exposed, were order'd to remove to, a safer ground. Of w'ch the Enemy being sensible, turn'd their cannon to that advantage that evening that they flankt our intrenchm'ts. W'ch the Gen'lls perceiving, ordered the men to work to make blinds[142] at a proper distance one from another to prevent our receiving any damage from the Enemy's flanking ball. W'ch order was imediatly putt in execution and by day light next morning the blinds was raised so high and strong withall, that both the front and rear lines lay safe from any great shott that could come from the Enemy. It being then light day they renewed their cannonading with greater vigour, if possible, than what they had done the day before. And particularly upon the Brigade comanded by Brigadeer Evans, w'ch was advanced upon the Doway Causeway, about 300 yards in the front of the Line where there run a little rivulett in their front. Of w'ch they cutt the bridge and had entrenched themselves so strong both in their front and flanks, and had raised their Lines to that perfection that they did them little or no damage. Notwithstanding they continued cannonadeing the Brigade as well as the entrenchments with a great deal of vigour and resolution untill the darkness of the night putt it out of their power to pursue their designes any farther.

Whereupon wee lay all night very silently in the trenches, being the 3^d night. And the next morning our Generalls putt all things in a readiness, expecting that nothing could hinder a close engagem't from ensuing. And the Enemy comenced their cannonading but wee, perceiving imediatly that they did not fire such a numb'r of cannon as they had don the two days before, and there being a tall tree in the interval betwixt the first Battal'n Royall and How's, some of the men climbed the tree to observe the motion of the Enemy if possible.

At w'ch time the Earle of Orkney, in company with the Gen'lls
of the day and Feild Officers of the Picquett, were makeing their
tour in the trenches who, perceiving the men upon the tree, His
Lordship ordered to call to them to observe the motion of the
Enemy. To w'ch the men answered that they could observe a great
many of both Battalions and Squadrons under arms. Whereupon
His Lords'p desired them to observe if they could perceive them
moveing. Whereupon the men, takeing a higher observation,
replyed that they could not observe any motion of the troops but
one thing they could plainly perceive, that their train was moving
off their Batteries. Whereupon My Lord bid them take as strict an
observation of the troops as they could. W'ch the men did and
then told His Lords'p that the troops were marching off. 'Very
well,' replys My Lord, 'I do believe that the threatning fury of
Vendome, Burgundy and Berwick is, for this time, all over.'[143]

W'ch prov'd accordingly, for they drew back that night and
encampt with their Right to L'Abesse and their Left extending
towards Lans. Of which His Grace being fully satisfied, ordered
the tents and wheel baggage to return back to the Army and the
troops to pitch their tents as they lay in the Line of Battell in the
intrenchm'ts,[144] where wee continued for the space of six days. At
w'ch time we were very well assured that the Enemy had repast
the Scheld by Tournay.

Whereupon our Army marched to the left, bearing towards
Menin and so continued until our Right had cleared the left of our
intrenchm'ts abo't a league. And then pitched our camp haveing
the Enemy Right in our front; the troops under the comand of
Prince Eugene haveing marched back to the Seige. At that time
our troops pitched their tents in the intrenchm'ts and had by this
time so farr advanced their approachm'ts that it was judged proper
to carry the Outworks by storm.

And in order thereunto, there was a detachm't of the Grand
Army made the next day, being the 10th of September, w'ch
marched accordingly and made their attack about an hour before
sun sett.

W'ch they carried sword in hand and maintained the same but
not without a great slaughter on both sides; wee haveing had

upwards of 1000 men killed and wounded in the action. And Prince Eugene, at the same time, was wounded in the head[145] with a muskett ball by w'ch he was confined some time to his tent.

Lille finally capitulated but not before the Battle of Wynendael was fought. Although Wilson's description of Wynendael is second-hand, he has something useful to add about the siege which followed Lille, that of Ghent, despite much of the subsequent account apparently coming from Lediard.

The season of the year being now so farr advanced and His Grace being unwilling to slip any time, marched the same day with the troops under his comand from Gover and laid blockade to Ghent that night. In which station the Army continued for the space of four or five days untill such time as Prince Eugene arrived with his troops from the Seige of Lisle. And then His Grace made a disposition of the troops under his comand to beseige the town in form, which opened their intrenchments in three attacks,[146] the 1st attack opposite to St. Peter's Hill, the 2nd opposite to the castle and the third opposite to the Bastion, betwixt Brussell Port and the Scheld. For which attack, at the first, there was appointed but six regiments, the English Regiment of which were North and Gray's and How's.

The Army being thus disposed of for the Seige, comenced preparations for all things necessary for the breaking of grounds. Which, being finished, the three attacks opened their trenches all in one night. The attack at Brussells Gate being judged to be but of small consequence, there was but a small number of troops appointed therefor, by which wee were oblidg'd to make detachments of those Regim'ts which covered the trenches for carrying on the work. And on the first night the trenches were opened.

The Regim'ts for the cover of the attack were North and Gray's, How's and a Battallion of the Hanover Guards. And they each haveing a hundred men without arms at work w'ch much dimished the number of men under arms. And towards break of day, the trenches being in some measure perfected, to cover the men under arms, wee retired into the same and the workmen were order'd off into the camp.

In which station wee continued till about 10 a clock, we then apprehending that the Enemy had a designe to make a sally upon us. But the morning being very foggy and the Enemy, having the advantage of a barn which stood betwixt our trenches and their outworkes, advanced upon the right of our trenches with such surprise, courage and resolution that they drove Lord North and Gray's Regim't quite out of the trenches and Gen'll How's Regim't quite to the center.

At w'ch place they took Brigadeer Evans prisoner and carried him into the town without sustaining any loss from us, notwithstanding they had killed and wounded a great many of North's Regiment and also severall of How's both dead and wounded. The Battalion of Hanover Guards having formed themselves in very good order but could do no execution by reason Gen'll How's Regiment was in confusion betwixt them and the Enemy. Upon which Collo'l Gore called out in a violent manner for How's Regim't to run and give them liberty to fire upon the Enemy, but all in vain. For before How's Regiment could clear the front of the Hannover Guards, the Enemy began to retreat haveing, as aforementioned, the Brigadeer and severall other Officers of North and Gray's Regim't prisoners. Which proved a second dissapointment to the Hanover Guards which stood in ready order with their arms cock'd and recovered. But by reason the aforement'd Brigadeer and the Officers afore mentioned, they were incapacitated to fire upon the Enemy without prejudice of such pris'rs of note. On which they went off w'th the loss of one only man, wee being disapointed as afores'd and wee haveing received & sustain'd the damage aforementioned.

After which Collo' Groves, Collo'l Armstrong and Colloll Gore consulted to send an Express imediatly to the Gen'll who comanded that attack to aquaint him of which had happened [to] them in the trenches, who ordered those Regiments then encamped to take their arms imediatly and releive those that were in the trenches. And after dispatched an Express to Duke Marlbro' to the same effect. Upon receipt of w'ch His Grace order'd the Duke of Arguile's Regim't, with two Regim'ts of forreigners to reinforce us, as also to join with us equally in the attack. And upon Lord Orkny's takeing a veiw of the trenches next morn'g, judg'd that number of troops not yett to be sufficient for the attack. Whereupon three Regiments of forreigners was ordered for a second reinforcem't, by w'ch wee were sufficiently enabled to carry on the same. Which was don by us and the other two attacks in intire conjunction, w'th all diligence imaginable untill such time as our Batteries were raised and compleated, and our Artillery ready to fire.

The destruction of the town was then approaching so near that our balls were red hott in the furnaces and nothing wanting but day light to endeavour the destruction of this great and metropolitan Citty. Whereof the Majistrates being very well assured, assembled in the Town Hall between twelve and one a clock at night where they unanimously agreed, and were of opinion, that nothing could prevent the destruction of the Citty, w'ch then it was threatned with and would be putt in execution as soon as it was light if not timely prevented. And they being also very well assured that noe means to prevent the same was evident but by Count d'la Motte's order for a Chamede to beat and come to a resolution to surrender the Citty to the Allies.

A description of the capitulation of Ghent follows, coupled with that of Bruges and how the army then went into winter quarters. Thus ends what Wilson recalls as 'the longest and most fateigueing campaign that ever was known or can be read of . . .' But he cannot allow the termination of such an eventful year as 1708 to slip by without a couple of verses of doggerel to commemorate its achievements and its passing.

1709

The Grand Army assembled near Lysle where they continued for near the space of eight days during w'ch time they pass'd a Reveiw before His Grace. After w'ch wee comenced our march June the 16th at night,[147] in order to lay a blockade to Tournay, the which wee invested next day. In the w'ch station the Army continued for seaven days untill such time as there was a convoy of amunition, provision and forrage brought from Ghent by water. And there being also a disposition made of the Army in order to beseige the towne in form. The troops designed therefor marched in order to take up their ground for the same, being disposed of in three attacks; two against the Town and one ag't the Cittadel. And the Grand Army marched the next morning in order to form a proper camp, as also to encamp the Army in the most advantageous manner to defend the Seige, as there should be occasion and necessity did require.

The Armies being thus incamped as aforementioned the Grand Army, as also the beseiging Army, went to work in order to prepare all necessarys to break ground, during which there was orders dispatched for a great battering train to be transported to the camp with all proper utencills and necessarys to the same belonging in order for the seige. And as soon as the Armies had provided as was judged a sufficient quantity of necessarys for carrying on the seige, the beseiging Armie opened the trenches in three attacks as before mentioned, and continued working with all diligence imaginable in forwarding our approachm'ts untill such time as our battries were all finished.

And the battering train being arrived in the camp, the same was mounted upon the battries as soon as possible. All things being thus in a readyness, the fireing comenced next morning both ag't Town and Cittadel with all the vigour that the Art of Gunery could possibly devise; the cannons battering the walls in a violent manner, and the mortars continualy throwing bombs into the Towne and Cittadel in a most terible manner. As also the smaller hoiboites otherwise call'd Cohern's Grenadeers,[148] with several mortars w'ch threw stones perpetualy into the outworks and covered ways, by which the Beseiged who defended the works ag't our approachm'ts were soe annoyed that they found it impossible to withstand it.

And soe the fireing continued in this violent manner for the space of ten or eleven days, in which time wee had made a considerable breach in the main wall of the Town, as also a sufficient breach in the counterscarp which in some measure covered the same. And finding that the batterys from Count Lottam's attack, w'ch plaid over the Scheld, lyed so lowe that they could by no means be brought to bear upon the foundation of the main wall of the town untill such times as wee made our selves mast'rs of the aforsaid counterscarp and covered ways, betwixt the right of the approachm'ts ag't the Cittadel and the Scheld, the which wee were resolved to carry by storm as soon as possible. And in order thereunto, the attack ag't the Cittadel run a paralel trench from the right of their attack for abo't thirty yards in order to cover the advancem't of the storm, as also to support and sustain the same if necessity should req'r.

All things being thus in a readiness in ye morning, the storm was ordered to comence in the evening by a detachm't made of the Grenadeers of the whole Army.[149]

The w'ch attack comenced according to order, and carried both the counterscarp and covered way sword in hand.[150] Which wee maintained and made a lodgment thereon that night whereby wee were enabled to bring our batterie so close unto that advantage, that wee could raise the foundation of the main wall of the Town. Which the Beseiged's perceiving, and seeing that wee, in such a terrible manner, had stormed their counterscarp and covered ways and carried the same sword in hand, and also that the attack on the other side of the Town was so farr advanced that it was beleived there would be a storm in a very little time, w'ch, if the beseigers putt in execution they were assured wee should carry in the same manner as wee had done on the other attack. For they did beleive no power on earth, at least on their side, was able to withstand the force of our arms.

Whereupon Mons'r Sorville, who then comanded the troops of the Garrison in conjunction w'th Mos'r Agreenee, the then Governour, whom he knew to be a man of great wisdom as also a great ingeeneer and very well knew the fortifications of the Cittadell of Tournay and the mines thereto belonging, judged it proper to surrender the Towne in order to enable them to defend the Cittadell to the last extremity. Upon w'ch resolution Mons'r Sorville bought up all the stores of provision w'ch could be found in the Garrison and ordered the same imediatly to be sent into the Cittadell.

And farther, to enable him to make a most vigourous defence, Mos'r Sorville ordered all his own plate, as also that of all the officers of note in the Garrison, to be carried into the Cittadell, where he ordered the same to be cutt in peices and struck with a stamp and his own name at large w'th the number of pence of the value of the peice, w'ch he ordered to pass for currant mony of the Garrison.

Mos'r Sorville and Agreencc, having thus expeditiously putt themselves in an order of surrendring the town, ordered a Chamede to beat and a flagg to be displayed on the main breach to signifie their intentions. The w'ch being observ'd in the trenches, all acts of hostility imediately ceased. Upon w'ch the Gen'll then comanding the approachm'ts ordered his Aid de Camp to advance to the breach to know their intentions. Mons'r Surville being then advanced upon the breach in person, desired the Aid de Camp to return and aquaint the Gen'll that he was there and desired to speak with him in person. Upon whose returne and s'd answer, the Gen'll imediatly advanced to the breach where, after the usual ceremony and complem'ts passed, he made known unto the Gen'll his resolutions.

After w'ch the Gen'l returning, dispatched his Aid de Camp to Count Lottam to aquaint him thereof. Upon receipt of which he dispatched an Express to the Duke of Marlbro' and Prince Eugene to aquaint him thereof in order to know their pleasure thereupon. The which they agreed unto and sent an order back for Count Lottam to proceed therein. Upon receipt of which the Count ordered hostages to be exchanged on both sides and the host[a]ge which came from the Garrison brought Mons'r Sorville's proposealls in writing along with him into the trenches. W'th which he was safely conducted to the Duke of Marlbro's quarters, where all the persons principally concerned were assembled in order to know their resolution. The ten'r of which were in the words following.

'I, Mons'r Sorville, doe promise on my own part and also on behalfe of His Most Christian Maj'tie, my Gracious Soveraigne and Master, to deliver up to the Duke of Marlbro' the Garrison and fortifications of the Towne of Tournay in the condition they now are in, the Cittadel and the fortifications thereunto depending excepted, in the space of three days after the ratification of these Treaties, provided His Grace the Duke of Marlbro' grants me safe conduct and free passage without lett, hinderance or molestation according to the time stipulated in the Treaty, in order to remove the troops under my comand as also the stores of amunition and provison, from the town to the Cittadel.

'And I also promise that during the time of the Seige of the Cittadel there shall be no acts of hostility on my part acted on that side of the Cittadel opposite to the Town, provided His Grace promises, and also sees it be performed, that the beseiging army breaks no ground, nor comences any approachment upon the splanade betwixt the Towne and Cittadel, nor on any part of the fortifications of the Garrison whatever. W'ch Treaty I promise on my part upon my honour to perform, provided that the Gen'll who comands the Seige observe that no infringment be made contrary to the articles of this Treaty, w'ch if it be done it shall be taken for a breach of the hole.'[51]

Upon which His Grace the Duke of Marlbrough and the principall persons and powers concerned then with him, assembled after a short consultation, with little or no alteration, condescended to Mos'r Sorville's proposealls and order'd a counterpart of the said Treaty to be drawn out imediatly. W'ch being don and signed by Count Lottam as a ratification thereof and delivered to the hostage with safe conduct and free passage to return back to the Garrison.

Upon receipt of which the French Hostage begg'd that he might have the honour to speak one word with His Grace, which was that since this day was farr spent, he hoped His Grace would be so good as not to insist upon it for one of the three days stipulated in the Treaty. To which His Grace made answer, 'Give my service to Mon'r Sorvell and aquaint him that I do not insist thereupon.' Whereupon the French hostage, in a very becomeing manner, took his leave of His Grace and returned back to the Garrison, upon whose arriv'l our hostages had safe conduct back to the camp.

And upon the third day following, being the 18th of July, Mons'r Sorvell abandoned the town intirely and marched into the Cittadel w'th all the troops under his comand.[152] And the next day the acts of hostility were again renewed. The two attacks of the town being now releived by the surrendring thereof, His Grace thought it proper to releive that of the Cittadel also. Upon which twenty five Regiments were ordered to march from the Grand Camp to releive them, of which the Brittish Regim'ts were Gen'll Webb's, L'd North and Gray's, Gen'l How's, Colo'l Godfrey's and General Ingoldsby's, the which marched next morning after comenceing the second acts of hostility ag't the Cittadell and releive those upon that attack according to order.

And so wee continued forwards the Seige of the Citadell with all expedition, there being a sufficient number of Pioneers prest out of the country[153] in order to throw up the lines of circumvallation and counterscarp for the safety of the beseigers, both in front and rear, the which lines were compleated in the space of six days. By w'ch the troops on the attack of the Cittadell were safely encamped for any assault or attempt of the enemy by any surprise whatsoever.

After which the Grand body of the Army advanced towards the scarp in order to have forced the passage of the river, but the French, having possessed themselves so advantageously on the other side thereof and the ground on both sides of the river being very morrosy, it was judged not practicable to make any such attempt. Upon which the passing of our Army over the scarp was referr'd to a more favourable opportunity. And the Army continued in a settled camp at Orcheis during the time of the Seige of the Cittadel of Tournay and the enemy encamped at the same time between Doway and Valenchin.[154]

Wilson then relates the sapping, mining and countermining attempts that were made around the citadel at Tournai and the accidents attendant upon such works. Although it is a detailed and useful account of such proceedings, he reports upon events, designs and speeches he could not have witnessed. He does, however, give the soldier's view of the business.

The Seige being now so farr advanced and the Ingineers perceiving that the troops were very disconsolate and shockt, spar'd noe pains to perswade and also to infuse into the troops full confidence and beleife that wee were out of any damage from the Enemy from below ground. W'ch, indeed, was no more than their duty so to doe, for in my oppinion, of all the horrid schems of warr, this of bringing of mines and sapping to finde out the same was the most dreadfull, for it was with great reluctancie that even the boldest men in the Army then on this service have turned their backs and given way. Nay, even those who had seen death in all its shapes above ground was struck w'th horror to stand (as he supposed) on the topp of a mine in danger of being blown up every minute. And those who went under ground into the sapps had a co-equall reluctancie, if not more, they being in danger every minute either of being suffocated or buried in the rubbish in the like nature.

The story continues with the lengthy business of capitulation after the French commander realised the effectiveness of the mining operations which, when combined with another bombardment and the understanding of the Allies' determination to succeed, meant his destruction. Wilson next reports on Marlborough's and Eugene's manoeuvres to besiege Mons and the French moves to thwart them which led to Malplaquet.

. . . they pass'd the Scheld at Honneau and encamped again at Quiveron with their left towards the Hays and their right towards Bellginnes. Upon w'ch our Army made a motion at four that afternoon and passed the Heasne and Troville and then formed the Line of Battle. After which wee lay on our arms all night between two small rivulletts which runs into the Troville.

And the next morning wee advanced towards the Enemy, during which time the Hussars belonging to Prince Eugen's Army charged some of the Enemy's Squadrons and putt them to flight takeing a cololl, Lt Co'l, with four or five Officers and 100 men prisoners. But nothing farther being attempted that night on either side, wee encamped that night in the Line of Battell with the Right of Prince Eugene's Army towards Jennape not farr from St Gullian, and the Left of the Duke of Marlbro's Army near Bagnoise. The two bodies being so close join'd that they were seperate only by a small intervall by which encamp't the Right of the Confederates, properly under the comand of His Grace, was considerably on the right of the center of the Line of Battell.

Wee being thus encamped, the next day following the Enemy appear'd on the edge of the wood of Sart and made some motions as if they had a minde to attack our left wing, upon which His Grace advanced towards them.[155] Whereupon Prince Eugene ordered the troops under his comand to advance also. By w'ch motion the left wing of my Lord Duke's Army, w'ch was the States' troops[156] were very near to the Enemy. Upon which they began to cannonade each other with a great deal of courage and resolution as also with success on both sides. And so continued untill dark night, the which oblidged both Armies to decline for that time. After w'ch they both continued to lye on their arms in the Line of Battell for that night and all the next day.

At w'ch time the Prince of Hesse joyned the Army with fifty five Squadrons of the Horse under his comand, leaving the comand of the 3,732 Foot with five Squadrons of Horse, under the comand of Gen'll Dedin at Chippley, who received orders at the same time the Prince marched off to attack that place at night. W'ch orders Gen'l Dedin accordingly putt in execution and took it sword in hand with very inconsiderable loss, making the comand of the Enemy prisoners.

And that evening His Grace and the Prince, knowing that the 21 Battallions from the Seige of the Cittadell of Tournay were arrived within a league of the Army, ordered a Councel of Warr to assemble. In which (after sev'll weighty arguments being started) that notwithstanding our Generals were very well informed that the Enemy was casting up trenches in the wood of Sart, as also at the great Belagues and sev'll other places, yett they unanimously resolved to attack them next morning, lett the event be as God pleased.

Upon w'ch resolution, the next morning being the 31st of August, by break of day our Infantry marched according to the disposition made of the Army the night before; the Infantry in three lines and the Cavalry in two collums. The 21 Battallions which had been at the Cittadel of Tournay's Seige, by reason of their fateigue and their expeditious march were ordered for the Reserve. And in this man'r, as aforementioned, wee continued advanceing towards the Enemy in order to comence a Battell.[157] The w'ch prov'd so obstinate and bloody that none fought since the beginning of this Warr is to be compared with it for the great effusion of blood that was spilt on both sides.

The Enemy being encamped and strongly entrenched, as before mentioned, and being superior to us in number especialy in their Infantry, they judged that they had a great deal the advantage of us, they having that night thrown up several entrenchments w'ch wee were not aware of, and posted their Right to that advantage w'ch they had covered with a very thick wood whereof they had entrenched all the avenues and passes as also posted a considerable body of Infantry. And upon the Plain had cast up three entrench-ments, haveing a morrosy ground before them w'ch rendred our access to their entrenchments very difficult. Their Center, or rather towards the Left of their Line, was upon a little plain upon which they had cast up several entrenchments, one behinde the o[t]her. The Left Wing being also covered by a thick wood[158] w'ch they had precautiously secured, haveing planted a very good body of Infantry therein. Their whole body being defended in the most advantageous places w'th good Artillery, w'ch very much annoyed us in our advanceing, they had also cutt down the hedges and levell'd the ditches in the rear of their lines for the more speedy marching of their Cavallry from right to left, in order to support their infantry as occasion should require.

The Enemy being thus advantageously posted did no ways daunt our Army but wee continued advanceing towards them. Wee comenced cannonading each other by halfe an hour after 8 a clock with great courage and resolution on both sides and continued the same vigourously untill all our forces had march'd so close to the Enemy that wee were ready to begin the attack. Upon which the right wing of Prince Eugene's Army attacked the Enemy in the wood afores'd with a great deal of courage and resolution but were received by the Enemy with as great bravery. Wee beat them from that post and they beat us back again with as great courage and resolution as wee had them. Whereupon ensued an obstinate engagem't for the space of two hours in which there was a great effusion of blood on both sides; the Armys fireing at each other bayonett to bayonett. And after came to stabb each other with their bayonetts and several came so close that they knocked one another's brains out w'th the butt end of their firelocks.[159]

But notwithstanding all the courage of our Enemy, wee at last made ourselves masters of the wood and maintained the same, w'ch was a great advantage to our Left Wing in their advanceing. The which they did without any loss of time towards the Enemy and comenced a second attack which was more obstinate and furious then the first, if possible, for the Enemy's lines were covered on the plains by three strong intrenchm'ts w'ch wee were oblidged to attack one after another and their right being secured by a thick wood.[160] This action proved both desperate and bloody which continued for the space of five hours with incredible fury and resolution on both sides.[161] And all this while doubtfull of success because the Enemy rallied several times and regained, with extraor'dnary valour, the entrenchments from which wee had beat'n them.

During which time they endeavoured to drive us from the Wood which wee had gained from them. But wee maintained our ground there and the Confederate Troops, under His Grace's comand, much abo't the same time beat their Right quite out of their intrenchm'ts. Whereupon their Cavallry, w'ch was drawn up in the rear of their Infantry, advanced in very good order to charge our Cavallry in order to regain their entrenchments if possible, in which wee had taken post.

And this new engagem't proved very obstinate and bloody. The action being by this time become generall, both Armies contending violently for a victory, they forcing us somtimes in divers places to give ground and wee again forcing them in their turn to give way. And some Squadrons of the Right Wing of His

Grace's Army being repulsed by the greater number of the Enemy's Squadrons which, His Grace perceiving, advanced with the Danish Cavallry and some Squadrons of the Imperialists in order to support them. The which gave them time imediatly to rally again. After which they charged the Enemy a second time with such courage and resolution that they putt their Squadrons in great disorder and, at the same time, pressed them so hard that they could not rally again.

They endeavoured to do it behinde the hedges, which the Duke of Wirtemberg perceiving, ordered sev'll Squadrons of Dragoons to dismount imediatly and attack the Enemy on foot. Which the Dragoons imediatly performed with all the courage and resolution imaginable. But the Enemy being strongly supported by severall Battallions of foot, defended the hedges and the wood on the right w'th a great deale of courage. And this part of the action also proved very obstinate and bloody, in w'ch the troops of the States were great sufferers, notwithstanding the Enemy's bravery in defending their severall posts.[162]

Wee obliged them to retire in confusion after which they did not form again in any order till they came behinde a little hill some distance from us. Having a morrose in their front they formed again in order and their Infantry, by favour of the hedges and woods, made their retreat in very good order and formed again near the same ground w'th their Cavalry. The body of our Cavallry advancing in order to have made the pursuit good, but those hedges, ditches and morosses w'ch were in our front betwixt us and the Enemy, would not admitt us to perform the same further in any considerable body. Upon w'ch two Regiments of Hussars, with some Squadrons of Horse and Dragoons, were ordered to beat up their rear and annoy them as much as possible. W'ch comand advanced as farr as Bevey, at which place they made 300 Officers that were wounded prisoners. By which this great and terrible Battell of Mallplaquet was ended abo't 4 in the afternoon, wherein wee took several standards and Colours as also twenty nine peices of cannon with a considerable number of prisoners, among whom wee had a Prince of the House of Lorrain, son to the Count de Armagnac. This battell prov'd to have been fought with so much courage and resolution on both sides as any battell that has been fought this whole war, as appears by the great number of the slain on both sides as lay dead in the feild of battell which, by the moderatest computation that has been made, was upwards of 24,000 men.[163] The Confederate Army, under the comand of His Grace the Duke of Marlbro' and Prince Eugene, having maintained the feild of battel and also being informed that the Enemy had retired backwards betwixt Landrasee and Maubouge, ordered the tents to be sent for to the Army imediatly and the Camp to be pitch'd out imediatly in the rear of the ground that wee fought upon, in order to rest and refresh the men w'ch was very much wanting.[164] And much abo't the same time the Marschall Villars,[165] who comanded the French Army in Cheif, dispatcht an Express to His Grace and Prince Eugene, desireing to have a suspension of arms the day ensueing, that both Armies might bury their dead and search for persons of distinction that was kilt. And also desired that, seeing most part of the prisoners taken on either side were wounded, desired that His Grace and the Prince would be pleas'd to appoint proper Officers to treat with those whom he would appoint, in relation to the exchanging man for man, according to their several stations. And those that were superior in number, they should give their Parole of Honour to be answerable for the equivalent. To the which request of Marishall Villars, His Grace and Prince Eugene condescended to very willingly. And the next morning a suspension of arms was declared and all Acts of Hostility forbid for the space of twenty four hours.

And comands from both Armies came into the feild of battell with proper Officers to bury their dead and search for persons of distinction, and also wounded men that might be lying in the hedges and ditches and places adjoyning to the feild of battell, w'ch work took up most part of that day. And the next morning the Army fell back in order to lay a blockade to Mons.[166]

The campaign year ends with the story of the siege and surrender of Mons. Reporting the death of Lieutenant-General Howe, Serjeant Wilson includes his Patron, the Earl of Hertford, appointed to command the 15th Regiment of Foot on 23 October

*1709 in succession of Howe who had held the regiment from
1 November 1695. The campaign of 1709 had been the shortest
but also the bloodiest of the war.*

1710

*Yet again Serjeant Wilson focuses upon the marches and counter-
marches of the campaign and presumably this was his most
frequent experience of the wars. He rather blandly recounts the
sieges of Douai, Bethune, St Venant and Aire and the attempts
made by Villars to relieve them before their surrenders and then
relates the Allies' return to their winter quarters.*

1711

*This year opens with tales of more of the 'cat and mouse' strategic
moves played by Marlborough and Villars around the Lines of
Non Plus Ultra which Marlborough finally penetrated in August.
Most of the account of the campaign is devoid of detail or comment
but the surprise of the camp near Arleux outrages Wilson because
of the 'underhand' methods employed by the French in reaching
their goal and their subsequent behaviour.*

After w'ch His Grace, having the council of his Gen'll Officers in
these weighty affairs, gave orders to the Quarter Master Gen'll
to pitch out a regular camp, being resolv'd to continue on that
ground untill they could deliberate upon some expedition that
might prove more favourable than some already in this year had
done. The Marishch'l Villars being informed of our resolution in
pitching a settled camp resolv'd, if possible, to surprise and take
the Pass of Arlux. Proposeing to himself (if this was accomplish'd)
to prevent the Confederat's from making any attempt on that side
of the country for that Campaigne. Which indeed might have
prov'd so if they had been as carefull and diligent in maintaining
and keeping the same afterwards as they were secret and
expeditious in surprising thereof. Which was performed in the
manner following.

By detaching a sufficient body of troops from the Garrison at Arras w'ch marched w'th all the secrecie and expedition imaginable and came to the same break of day in the morning. The which they found but slenderly guarded they forced sword in hand, the same oblidgeing all that escaped to surrender prisoners at discretion.

An Express arriving that evening to His Grace of the surprise of Arleux as afores'd, it was judg'd proper that a detachm't of the Army should march imediately, consisting of 16 Squadrons of Cavallry and 10 Battallions of Infantry and incamp between Lewar and Doway in order to hinder the Enemy from making of any further inroades or approachm'ts near Doway. The which comand marched and there pitched according to order and the day following had orders that each Regim't of Foot should make 1500 faschines and each squadron of Horse 300. Which they accordingly sett to work about in order to have them compleated next morning, with which they design'd to have fortified right and left of their camp to prevent any surprise from the Enemy. But this design prov'd too late, not being in their power to effect their design of that number of faschines in that time.

For Marisch'll Villars, being timeously advertiz'd of their marching and encamping as afores'd, was resolv'd to surprise them if possible. And in order thereunto, most secretly and expeditiously detach'd a sufficient body of troops from his camp, w'ch marched by way of Arras for Arleux. At w'ch place they passed the morrose and came in upon the riseing ground between Arleux and Leward where they halted untill it was dark and put green bows in their hats,[167] w'ch is the Conferate sign of batle. And then comenced their march towards the left of our detchment untill such time as they came to the Grand Guard.

Of which the s'd Guard being advised, mounted imediately on horseback and detacch'd a Corporal and six men to reconnoite them. Which they perceiving det[a]ched the like number who advanced towards the Coporall who challenged in a customary manner who they were. Upon which they answered, 'Friends!' The Corpor'l demanded, 'What friends?' They answered, 'Good friends.' and a comand from the Grand Army who had been reconiteing the Scheld betweixt Marchiens and Vallenciens in ord'r to see how the country stood replenished with forrage,[168] a report of which the Corporal sent to the Capt. of the Guards, who ordered that they might be acquainted to march forward and his owne Corporal to return to his comand.

W'ch they accordingly did untill such time as they came to the Grand Guard on the Right which challenged them after the same manner as other guards had done and they had answer'd them as other guards before. And so the Enemy pursued their march, as to us appear'd right, towards our Grand Camp. Which march they continued untill such time as they'r rear had marched clear of the Grand Guard; about halfe an English mile. All this being done without suspition of an Enemy.

W'ch, to our great loss, wee afterwards found to be. For they imdeiately wheeled to the right and march'd directly to the right of our detachm't and there fell in a most violent manner, sword in hand, killing and making havock of our men, they being unadvertised and unprepared for any defence. By the which surprise they drove the whole right wing of our Horse quite out of the Camp, making a prise of a great number of our horses and barbarously us'd a great many, both men and women, cutting several of the latters tongues out and some their breasts of. Which cruel and unheard of barbarity they had a designe to persue throughout the whole of the comand and probably would, in great measure, have performed had not Gen'l Webb's Regim't, by the providence of God, been short of the number of faschines making the day before and being then turning out a comand in order to compleat the same, which was then parading by the Colours. Who observed the Right of the Line to be in a vast confusion all of a sudden, as also observing it to come nearer to them. Likewise hearing some dropping shot, took their arms imediately the most of them, except the comand and Piquett, being then in their shirts not having time to put on their cloathes, they forming imediately along a deep hollow on the right of their Grenad'r Company, making their front towards the right of the line. To which place the Enemy advanced, barbarously stabbing and murthering all that came in their way and as much as in their power lay all that offered to make any resistance.[169]

At which place Gen'll Webb's Reg't gave the Enemy such a warm reception that they put them to a full stand by which the whole line was in allarum. Which they perceiving, retired with all precipitation imaginable. Whereupon the Pickquets, both of Horse and Foot, made what haste they could to pursue them. But before they were in perfect readiness to pursue them, being in that confusion, the Enemy was quite retreated out of their reach so that it was judged not proper to pursue them without the Camp.

The subsequent pursuit was fruitless and the enemy troopers got away to Arras. Serjeant Wilson, unlike other contemporary British officers, such as Colonel Kane, Captain Parker and Corporal Bishop, makes little comment about Marlborough's fall from favour and replacement by Ormonde, preferring here to report upon other military matters. He describes the destruction of part of the New Channel to make floodwater defences and the bombardment strike against Arras before the armies retired from the field.[170]

1712

Wilson's narrative for this year tells of the assembly of the Allied army under Ormonde whose command, consisting of 295 squadrons and 143 battalions, advanced upon Cambrai. However, he gets involved in the politics of the Alliance, and the French efforts to 'buy' Britain out of the war. He devotes some of the chapter to the loss of the fortresses sustained by the Allied cause while the British, bound by their politicians, retired into Dunkirk and left the Dutch and Imperial forces to continue the war alone.

However, he does relate an interesting story of the Dutch capture of Fort Knocke.

. . . the surprise of Knoque which was don by a Partisan of the Hollanders in the following manner, to the great reputation of the Partisan[171] and all his party and to the great scandall and disgrace of the Governour and all the Garrison under his comand.

The afores'd Partisan, having obtain'd leave of the Governour of Mennin of a Partizan Party which consisted of six Serj'ts, six Corporalls and seaventy four choice men all pick'd out of the Garrison, with which the Partisan march'd that afternoon for Roofbucke, near the wood of Clarken where he halted to refresh his men. During which time he comunicated to the Sergeants his resolution, who approv'd thereof and declared they would stand by him in performance of that enterprise.

Upon which he desired to pick him out two of the boldest men of the party, with whom he went to a particular friend's house in the village where he exchang'd their arms for a spade to each of them, a satchell of bread and cheese and a wooden cagg of beer. As also their Regimental cloathes for a course Boor's habit. After which he desired they might go a back way out of the village and there wait at the skirt of the wood till the party came.

After which he return'd back to the party and desired them to stand to their arms and then devided them into six Platoons, each consisting of a Serj't, Corpor'll and twelve Priv't men. After w'ch they comenced their march, under the cover of the skirts of the wood, towards Mereken where they arrived betwixt ten and eleaven of the clock at night.

At which time the Partizan judg'd it proper to halt for an hour and there to refresh and cherish his men for which he ordered each man to have a quatern of brandy, a pynt of beer and a white manchett.[172] After which they still continued their march, under cover of the wood, the byway for Knoque where they arrived about an hour before day.

The Partizan, being now at the proper place where he design'd to fix his ambuscade and he knowing very well the seituation of the ground round the Fort, fixt upon a rank feild of hemp about a musket shot from the Port into which they went, taking the remotest places thereof on purpose that they should not be discovered by their tracks. And then laid themselves down in the silentest manner that could be and so continued till it was daylight all abroad.

At w'ch time the Port was opened as usual and the Serj't of the Guard marched out w'th a file of musketteers in order to reconiter all about the Port in case any party of the Enemy should lye in any ambuscade. All which the Partizan very well seeing and also observing the Serj't returning back. And that the Corpor'll who waited for the Serj't's return at the barrier sett the same open and posted a Centry thereat and after return'd back to the Guard. Where the Serj't then made a Report to the Officer of the Guard that all was well without and the Corporal went with ye Return of the Keys.

After which they all laid them down to sleep; the Guard's arms being lodged ag't the wall without the Guard. And the Centry which was over them, finding all things very quiet and still, sat himselfe down upon a bench and, being drowsie, fell fast asleep. In w'ch negligent and scandalous manner wee leave them taking repose and return to the Partizan and his party in the feild of hemp. Who now, by the computation of time, judged the Guard must be in the condition w'ch indeed they were as before described. So that the partizan now thought it high time to comence his enterprise and, having consulted all things suitable to put the same in execution, one of the two men in the Boor's habit crept privately out of the hemp into a hollow, from whence he went to the High Road and so on towards the Port when coming to the Barrier,[173] gave the Centry the time of the day. Who return'd him the same and asked him from whence he came and where he was going.

The pretended Boor answered the Centry that he came from Morekemp and was going to work at the by Cannal betwixt Furne and Osdunkirk, which was then a-cleaning.

'Very well,' replys the Centry. Upon w'ch the other sett down his spade, sachell and cagg against the Pallisadoe's and then pull'd a pipe out of his pockett and asked the Centry if he could help him to a little fire.[174] The Centry answered no, but he might go to the Guardroom; there he might have fire. Which the other very readily did, where he found a fire turf lying in the Guard window at which he lighted his pipe. And at the same time made a full observation of the state and condition the Guard was in and then return'd back again, very quietly, to the Centry, to whom he return'd a great deal of thanks for that favour and also said he had a partner who had promised soon to follow after and he did admire how he came to stay so long.

Upon which the Centry, looking along the highway to his great loss and destruction, perceived the second pretended Boor coming out of the hollow upon the riseing ground. And then asked the other supposed Boor, 'Is not that he a-comeing?' Who, pretending to take a sharp veiw of him, replyed, 'Yes.' Who, coming up to the barier, was very complisant in giving the Centry the time of day, setting his working tools down besides his comrades, asked to help him to a little fire which, the other pretending to doe, but instead thereof seiz'd the Centry, wrested his arms out of his hands, wrung his neck in two and threw him sidewise over the bridge. Which the Partizan, perfectly perceiving, advanced very quietly towards the Barrier and so along the drawbridge to the Guard, which they found all asleep as before described.

Upon w'ch the Partizan marched on with four Platoons towards the Case of Arms, leaving the two other Platoons to secure the Guard and the Port. W'ch they did in a most private manner, by securing of their arms, shutting to the Barrier and Gate and also drawing up the bridges. And the Partizan being, by this time, arrived at the Case of Arms, where he found the whole comand fast asleep, forced themselves into the rooms with firelocks cock'd and bayonetts fixed, roused the men in great surprise out of their sleep, gave them to understand that the place was surprised and they were Prisoners, charging them not to make the least resistance or noise. Who ever did that, he was a dead man. And at the same time, in order to clear them from their arms, drave them out of their rooms naked, scarce giving them so much time as to take their britches in their hands. Afterwards hurried them in to a waste house w'ch was empty and there secured them by shutting to the doors, only the wickate. After which the Partizan, with one Platoon, dispatched to the Comanding Officer's Pavilion. Where, the door being open and, as supposed, the serv'ts cleaning and setting the house in order. And the Centry, as it is to be beleived, thinking all things to be then very quiet and still, had left his post and gone into the Pavillion on purpose to toy and play with the maids.[175] By w'ch the Partizan entred the house, went upstairs, burst in the door of the Comanding Officer's bedchamber without being any wise discovered. The noise of the door having awak'ned the Governour in great surprise and seeing the Partizan with a cock'd pistol in his hand with men in arms by him, was struck in such a consternation that he had not power to speak. W'ch the Partizan perceiveing, said, 'Sir. The Fort is taken by surprize and wee are now masters of it. Therefore, If you would save your life, you must submitt and be my Prison'r.' Upon which he, after some consideration, perceiving himself to be in the hands of his enemy, reply'd, 'Sir. I hope you will use me as a Gentleman.' To which the Partizan made answer, 'Sir. That you may depend on, for there is nothing else in my nature. Wherefore I desire you to come down to your parlour.' Which the Govern'r imediatly condescended to, put on his night gown and other necessary apparell and went along with him. After which the Partizan desired the Governour to call for his serv'ts and sent them to the several pavillions where the Comission'd Officers were lodged to aquaint them with the present state of the Fort. And also to repair to the Comanding Officer's pavillion forthwith in order to submit themselves prison'rs. And that if any person was disobedient to these orders and did not perform the same in the space of a q'r of an hour, they must not expect, neither need they look for, any q'rs.

Upon receipt of which the most of them repaired to the appointed place with all expedition. After which the Partizan order'd to go w'th them to the place where the Body of the Garrison was confin'd. W'ch being done, he confin'd them in an adjoyning room thereunto, after which ordered a Serj't with a platoon of men to go to the Gate and rouse the Guard, and bring them along with them prisoners. All which being performed according to order, a Serj't, Corporal and twelve men went upon the ramparts in order to seize the Centrys on their posts. Whom they found in as supine and careless a posture as the Guard at the Port had been in. The which being done and they returned back to the comand.

The Partizan and his Serj'ts, finding then all things safe under their comand, thought it prop'r the poor men, then prisoners, should have their cloathes and provisions returned to them. Upon w'ch the Corp'lls, with two men each without arms, went into their several rooms and brought all things appertaining to them in, arms and amunition excepted. All w'ch being accordingly deliv'd unto them, the Partizan and Serj'ts then began to consider of their own estate and what necessity there was for a present reinforcem't.

Upon w'ch it was resolved to write to the Governour of Menin with an acco't of the proceedings and success of their enterprise, praying him for his aid and assistance in maintaining the same. The which Express was sent off with all expedition with one of the most cleverest of their party whom, for his better security, they dressed in one of the habits of the Boors. It being then much about 10 a clock when the man with the Express left the Fort, it is to be beleived he lett no grass grow under his feet, he delivering the same at Menin by two in the afternoon.

Upon receipt of which the Governour ordered that a comand of 244 of the best Light Horse and Dragoons, with proper Officers to comand them, the private men to carry neither carbines nor cloakes nor other luggage, to parade upon the Splanade without Ipre Port by 4 in the afternoon. As also a comand of six Serj'ts, 220 men, 6 Gunners and 12 Montrosses, to parade at the same time and place. And they to carry no more then one shirt apeice to shift them withal.

All which comands paraded according to order where the Governour in person acquainted the Comanding Officer of what had happ'ned in relation to the surprise of Knocke, as also full directions for his marching in order to reinforce the party there present and to bring those of the Enemy, w'ch were then prisoners, back along w'th the Comand of Horse. All necessary orders being thus given, each horsman took up a footman behinde him and so comenced their march right for Knoque, where they arrived much abo't 2 in the morning; a Serj't and 12 men of the Partizan party lying at the same time at the Outer Barier expecting their coming.

And finding they were arrived and also being fully convinced they were their own people, sent to aquaint the Partisan of their arrival. Who imediately went in person and, finding all things well and according to expectation, received those designed for the reinforcem't into the Garrison. And, as soon as possible that he could gett the prisoners in a readiness, march them out at the gate and deliver'd them to the Comand of Horse, who imediately marched off with all expedition back to Menin.[176]

The rest of the year's narrative is taken up with the negotiations of various conditions and treaty articles for the peace. Wilson does not mention the fact that, after all they had gone through, the joint victories won and the magnificent achievements of 'Castor and Pollux', Britain deserted the Allies for political gain.

1713

Wilson describes the signing of the Treaty of Utrecht and notes the fact that the Imperial representatives were still missing. He tells of the standing down of some garrisons, the manning of others and the moving of the British army to the transports, with a brief synopsis of how the Imperial army was brought to the table by the offensive of Villars and the wars concluded with the Treaty of Rastadt in 1714. He then produces an illuminating chart and computation of the cost of the war in casualties.

Those Articles, and all other in relation of this peace betwixt France and the Empire being agreed upon, signed and exchanged, there was an end put to the most obstinate and bloodiest war as ever had been in Europe, which had reigned and predominated for the space of thirteen yeares. In which there had been the greatest consumption of treasure, as also of effusion of blood that ever was known or can be read of in History to have been amongst the European Princes. As plainly will appear by the yearly returns of that branch of the War under the comand of His Grace, the Duke of Marlborough, Prince Lewis of Baden, Prince Eugene of Savoy when they comanded in conjunction with His Grace in Germany and the Netherlands. The which return, for the Reader's more satisfaction, I think it not amiss to insert a plan or schem thereof. And to add thereunto, by the nearest computation, the losses sustain'd in the other Branches through the whole course of the War. Computeing also the loss of the Enemy:–

The plan of the yearly return of the losses in the Confederate Army as afores'd

Date of Years	Kill' in Action	Died of the'r Wounds	Return'd Invalids	Deserted	Natural Deaths	Lost by Imprison m't	Totals
1702	6,910	1,442	1,254	375	773	242	10,996
1703	3,412	732	615	294	682	274	6,009
1704	15,768	3,856	3,593	271	897	145	24,530
1705	1,092	264	304	221	764	213	2,858
1706	5,742	1,325	1,249	197	684	192	9,389
1707	162	29	227	121	652	194	1,385
1708	14,232	3,724	4,724	92	966	157	23,895
1709	17,130	3,995	3,596	159	899	164	25,943
1710	6,589	2,007	1,927	146	929	157	11,755
1711	674	227	444	159	729	167	2,400
1712	12	5	624	16	1,229	—	1,886
Total	71,723	17,606	18,557	2,051	9,204	1,905	121,046

Wilson's conclusions about Allied casualties are not all that farfetched. For example: the worst casualties he gives are those for 1709 (which includes the Battle of Malplaquet) at 25,943 whereas modern calculations for that year are near the 25,000 mark.

Losses in the Confederate Army as afores'd	121,046
Losses sustain'd by the Confederates from the time of their comenceing the Seige of Quensnoy unto the surrendring Bouchine to Marisch'l Villars	20,971
This branch of the War being judged by computation to be one part in three thereof, by w'ch it may be computed that the loss of the other two in proportion accordingly must be	284,054
The Enemy's loss during the course of the Warr being computed at 6 to 5 of the Confederates it makes	511,298
Total	937, 379

Wilson's total of both Allied and French casualties brings us to almost one million casualties altogether. This demonstrates the terrible conditions in which the War of the Spanish Succession was fought. These huge losses (which do not include French or German civilians) explain the total exhaustion on all sides by 1714. Of course France – despite their considerable successes between 1711 and 1714 – did not recover economically for many years. Wilson next goes into detail about the reductions in the army.

Having now given my Reader a full account of the conclusion of the Peace as well that of the Emperor and Empire, as all the rest of Her Maj'tie's Allies as also a plan of the loss of the men killed and maimed and otherwise lost in the War, I shall return back to our native country and pursue the affairs thereof without any degression.

Where I finde Her Maj'tie, haveing taken into deliberate consideration the great hardship that her good and faithfull subjects had laboured under during the whole course of the War and in order to ease them of some part of heavy taxes, by advice and consent of her most Hon'ble Privy Councel resolved upon a regular and speedy reduction of the forces both by sea and land.

The which reduction comenced with those troops then in Flanders on the 1st of June in the manner following: which was ten men and a Corporal of each troop of the Light Horse; a Serj't, a Corpor'll and ten men of each troop of Dragoons; with a Serj't and Corporal and fifteen men of each Company and a Company intire of each Regiment of Foot. Of those in Garrison in Ghent, Bridges and Newport. And of those Regiments in Dunkirk, a Serj't, Corporal and ten men and a Company of each Regiment. As also several of the newest levies to be broke intire, of which Cololl Kane's Regiment, which then lay in the Cittadel of Dunkirk, was one.

The w'ch was first ordered to be drafted and the best of their men ordered to be disposed of in those Regiments designed for the Garrison of Dunkirk, they being oblidged to return them man for man of such as they supposed to be superannuated and unfitt for service. Of the which all those whose service intitul'd them to the benefitt of her Maj'tie's Royal Bounty at Chelsea for their more easier access thereto.

It was ordered that their Certificates should be sign'd by Sr James Abercrombie, the Comanding Officer, and Surjeon of the Regiment they respectively did belong to. All w'ch being performed according to order. After w'ch Colloll Kane's Regiment imbarqued for Dover where they were broke, with several other new Regiments.

The next reduction of the troops comenced the 25th of June with Colloll Lee and Colo'l Wyn's Regiments who were drafted as Cololl Kane's had been and imbarqued the next day but one for Dover where they were broke with two other Regiments that went by the way of Ostend, by those draughts as afore-mentioned. And a Company of each Regiment that was broke, those Regim'ts in Garrison at Dunkirk were compleated and in good order.[177]

The next motion of the Army was the transporting the Light Horse and Dragoons into Great Brittain and Ireland. The two Regiments of Dragoons imbarqued at Ostend for England and the Light Horse imbarqued at Dunkirk. Generall Lumley's and my Lord Winsor's came for England and the Marquiss of Harwich's, the Carbineers and Kollums went by long sea for Ireland.

The third reduction of the Army was made by Colo'l Newton's and Brigadeer Evan's Regiments which marched from Ghent and Bridges to Dunkirk where they were detain'd three days in order for those of the Garrison to entertain as many of them volunteers as they thought necessary to putt their Regiments in complete order. They being oblidged to return man for man in the same manner as to the other Regiments w'ch were drafted before. All which being performed, those Regiments imbarqued the day following for Dover where they were broke.

1714

After which the troops in the Netherlands remain'd without any further alteration untill the latter end of March, One Thousand

Seaven Hundred and Fourteen. At which time there came ord'rs from the Government for Collo'l Hans Hamilton and Colo'l Disney's Reg'ts to imbarque at Dunkirk and go by long sea for North Brittain. As also for Brigadier Preston's and Gen'll Primrose's Regiments w'ch were in Garrison at Newport to imbarque at Ostend and goe by long sea for Ireland, which Regiments imbarqued and sailed accordingly.

The next order in relation to the moving the troops was made upon the 11th of June w'ch was by the 2^d Battallion Royal and the Right Hon'ble the Earl of Hartford's Regiments w'ch marched from Dunkirk to New port. After which the Army continued without any alteration till after the 1st of August, upon w'ch day Her Maj'tie departed this life. Whereupon the Government sent orders for all the troops in Flanders to imbarque at Ostend for England with all expedition; the Lord North and Gray's, the Earl of Hartford's and Brigadeer Stern's except'd. The two former being in New Port and the latter in the Cittadel of Ghent, where they were to remain untill further orders.

Subsequent entries in Serjeant Wilson's Journal throw very little new light upon what we know already and he recounts events and campaigns in which he did not take part.

Although he tells the stories of the death of Anne and the arrival of George I, the Jacobite Rising of 1715 and the various struggles between the European powers and the Ottoman Empire, he does so as reportage and lacks the spark of first-hand experience or soldierly comment which typified his earlier entries and, to be truthful, made them interesting.

Wilson concludes with the death of George I in 1727 and the accession of George II, drawing his Journal to an end with the following paragraph:

His Ma'tie being thus proclaimed with all imagineable pomp & solemnity and the load acclamation of the populace, we also crown'd upon the 11th of October following at St Peter's, Westminster, King & Queen with great magnif'ence & grandeur. To whom I wish a long and prosperous reigne. As also that there may never be wanting one of His Royall Posterity to fill the Brittish Throne 'till Time return to it's latter urn.

To be more in confirmation of the sincerity of my hearty prayers and wishes, I say

AMEN

We have no date for the death of Serjeant Wilson.

Appendix I

Biographical Notes

No appendix note can do justice to a person's life. We seek here to give a brief sketch to enable the reader to gain an insight into the background of several of the important figures who appear in the Journal and as a prompt for further investigation. We do not list everyone mentioned in the text. We leave out many of the 'giants' whose careers are so well known, and we leave out those who play only 'bit parts' in the narrative although their military feats and achievements may warrant several pages. We also hope readers will excuse the necessity of reducing the greatest of men and their careers into a few lines of basic information. However, one 'giant' we cannot ignore is Marlborough who features so frequently in the text as to warrant an exceptional entry.

Marlborough, John Churchill, Duke of Marlborough (1650–1722) was the eldest son of Sir Winston Churchill, an old cavalier officer and MP for Lyme Regis in Dorset. John was appointed a page in the household of the Duke of York in 1666 and commissioned Ensign into the Foot Guards in 1667. He saw considerable service as a Marine officer with the Fleet and spent some time attached to Marshal Turenne in Flanders. He was the immediate choice of his patron James II to suppress Monmouth's rebellion in 1685, and although relinquishing command to Louis Duras, Earl of Feversham, he played a significant role at Sedgemoor. After service in Ireland at Cork and Kinsale for William III, Churchill commanded the English contingent in Flanders and was at Walcourt in 1690. He was accused of betraying plans to old companions still in French service and spent 1691 to the close of the century in disgrace, but close court connections with Princess Anne eventually led to his being restored to favour. He was subsequently deeply involved in negotiating The Grand Alliance and also appointed to command all the English troops in Holland in 1700. He was created Duke of Marlborough in 1702 and made Captain-General of Anglo-Dutch forces shortly after Anne's accession to the throne. The following nine years saw his greatest military achievements, winning the famous four battles of Blenheim, Ramillies, Oudenarde and Malplaquet. He fell from favour again in 1712 and lived abroad in exile until the death of the Queen in 1714. Restored to all his old offices by George I in 1715, he spent his declining years between London and Holywell, watching the gradual building of Blenheim Palace and trying to mediate in his family's quarrels. He died in 1722, revered as England's most able and most talented general.

Baden, Prince Louis (or Lewis) Guillaume, Margrave of Baden (1655–1707) was a distinguished Habsburg commander who had been taught his trade by Montecuccoli and the Duke of Lorraine. He served at the great siege and battle of Vienna in 1683 and in many other engagements against the Turks, including Belgrade in 1688, Nissa and Salankamen in 1691. He had been defeated by Marshal Villars at Friedlingen near Landau on the Rhine in 1702 and was past his best by 1704. His relationship with the older but less experienced Marlborough was very mixed. In 1705 he proved very unco-operative, resenting his deliberate exclusion from the battle of Blenheim and the resulting military glory. Nevertheless, over his military career he undertook twenty-six campaigns, and took part in thirteen battles and twenty-five sieges. He died from complications from a wound to his foot sustained at Donauwörth.

Boufflers, Louis-François, Chevalier, Marquis and Duc de Boufflers (1644–1711). One of the most experienced French soldiers of his day whose variegated service took him to Africa, the United Provinces and on many occasions thereafter to Flanders. He was promoted Lieutenant-General in 1681 and became a Marshal in 1693. His stalwart defence of Lille in 1708 was the crowning event of his distinguished military career.

Cadogan, William (1675–1726) was a burly Protestant Irishman who first saw action at the Boyne in 1690. He became a companion and trusted friend of Marlborough and rose through the ranks of responsibility, being entrusted with much of the organisation and administration of the Army. After Blenheim he was promoted Brigadier-General and became Lieutenant-General in 1709 after he was wounded at the siege of Mons. He made a major contribution to all Marlborough's ten campaigns, not least the last where he was instrumental in securing the fall of Bouchain. In 1712 he shared Marlborough's fall from favour, but was restored to all his posts by George I in 1714. He conducted the Barrier Treaties negotiations at The Hague between 1714 and 1718, interrupted by a short time repressing the 1715 Jacobite Rebellion. His reward was promotion to full General and then Master-General of the Board of Ordnance from 1722, as well as continued employment in diplomatic and military missions until his death in 1726.

Churchill, Charles (1656–1714) was the third son of Sir Winston Churchill, and the younger brother of Marlborough. He fought at Sedgemoor and in many of his brother's campaigns. He was a very experienced commander, becoming a General of Foot in 1703 and a full General in 1707. From 1706 to 1710 he was Governor of Guernsey and later became Governor of the Tower of London.

Coehorn, Menno, Baron van (1634–1704) nicknamed 'the Dutch Vauban', was the most distinguished Dutch military engineer of his time. He wrote treatises on fortification and gave his name to both a small grenade-mortar and to a type of defensive work. A Major-General in 1692, he was promoted Lieutenant-General and Director of Fortifications three years later. He ultimately became Master-General of the Ordnance of the United Provinces (1697).

Cutts, John, Baron Cutts of Gowran (1661–1707) was an Irishman who first saw service against the Turks in 1686. By 1688 he was a Colonel in Dutch pay and after fighting at the Boyne in 1690 he eventually became a Brigadier-General in 1695. He played a prominent role in the siege of Namur (being gravely wounded in the head) and was promoted Major-General in 1696. The next year he assisted in the peace negotiations at Ryswick. In 1702 he earned further fame in the Spanish War of Succession for storming Fort St Michel and, the year after, was promoted Lieutenant-General. He served with distinction at Blenheim in 1704 and, from 1705, was Commander-in-Chief and Lord Chief Justice in Ireland. He was nicknamed 'the Salamander' – a mythological lizard-like reptile supposed to live in fire – because he was always where the fighting was hottest.

Fitzjames, Michael James (1670–1734) was the bastard son of James II and Arabella Churchill, and hence Marlborough's nephew. Brought up in France he became Duke of Berwick in 1696. His military career included campaigns against the Turks and, during the Nine Years War, against William III in Ireland and then in Flanders as a French commander.

Made prisoner at Landen in 1693 he was freed by exchange. He was appointed a Marshal of France in 1705 after repressing the 'Camisard' revolt and capturing Nice. Thereafter he served with distinction in Spain, winning the battle of Almanza in 1707, and thereafter on the Rhine. He secretly corresponded regularly with his uncle, Marlborough, which was probably treasonable as he was the source of much useful intelligence. In 1733 he commanded French troops on the Rhine and was killed a year later at Phillippsburg.

Fagel, François-Nicholas (1655–1718) was a distinguished soldier in first the Dutch and then the Habsburg forces. He came to fame at Fleurus in 1690 and was promoted to Major-General in 1694. Eleven years later he became a Lieutenant-General and, as such, fought at Ramillies in 1706 and Malplaquet in 1709. He transferred to service with the Habsburgs and was appointed a Field-Marshal of the Empire.

Ginkel, Godart van (1630–1703) was born in Utrecht and carved himself a successful military and court career, becoming a favourite of William III. A highly capable soldier, he was promoted to Lieutenant General in 1683 and posted to Ireland as Commander-in-Chief in 1691 where he won the battle of Augrim. He was made full General in 1692 and created 1st Duke of Athlone. From 1692 to 1697 he had command of all the Dutch cavalry in Flanders and was very influential at court. However, Marlborough had a particular dislike of him, along with other 'Dutch favourites' who filled so many high positions in the English Army, which made matters difficult when he was ultimately promoted to Field Marshal and appointed as Marlborough's second-in-command in 1702. He died of apoplexy in his home town of Utrecht a year later.

Hamilton, George, Earl of Orkney (1666–1737) was a highly experienced Scottish soldier who reputedly served in every one of William III's and Marlborough's battles and sieges. After seeing action in Ireland at the Boyne and Aughrim, he was wounded at Namur and promoted Brigadier-General. In 1702 he was made Major-General and played significant roles in the Duke's quatrain of victories. He was credited with the saving of Liege in 1705 and was promoted again to General of Foot in 1711. He continued to rise, becoming Lord of the Bedchamber in 1714, followed, in 1715, by Governor of Virginia. His military career reached its pinnacle in 1736 when he was appointed the army's first Field Marshal.

Hostun, Camille d', Comte de Tallard (sometimes 'Tallart') (1652–1728) was a French soldier and diplomat of some note. He had been French Ambassador in London during the negotiation of the two Partition Treaties of 1698 and 1700 and was known to Marlborough. He received his baton in 1703 following his victory over the Prince of Hesse-Cassel at Speyerbach (sometimes 'Spirbach' or 'Spire') near the Rhine on 12 November, inflicting 6,000 casualties and thereby bringing the siege of Landau to a successful conclusion on the 15th. Following his capture at Blenheim he remained a prisoner in Lincolnshire until 1711, and is credited with having introduced the cultivation of asparagus into England. In later life he became a member of Louis XV's Regency Council (1717) and a Minister of State (from 1726).

Neufville, François de, Duc de Villeroi (1644–1730) was a brave but rather undistinguished French commander who, through his friendship with the King and other court influence, was made a Marshal of France in 1693. His military reputation, such as it was, was shattered by Marlborough at Ramillies.

Ormonde, James Butler Ormonde, 2nd Duke (1665–1745) first came to notice under William and Mary at the battles of Steinkirk and Landen. He was a Lieutenant-General in 1694 and was promoted to General of the Horse in 1702. He transferred to the Spanish theatre of the war but after abortive raids on Cadiz and Vigo, Ormonde was appointed Lord Lieutenant of Ireland, in which office he served three times. His military abilities were poor but his influence at court and in government was great, and he was appointed the new Captain-General, replacing Marlborough after his fall. His period in command was marred with difficulties, for most of the officers and soldiers deplored the disappearance of the popular Marlborough. A supporter of the House of Stuart, Ormonde was impeached under George I for Jacobitism in 1715 and forced to retire to France.

Ramsey or Ramsay, George (c. 1625–1705) was a man of noble Scottish descent who had become a Major by 1685. Three years later he had risen to Colonel and in 1690 was promoted Brigadier-General. In September of 1691 he became Colonel of the 2nd (or Scots) Guards and in 1694 was made Major-General. In 1700 he was appointed to Commander-in-Chief, Scotland. Two years later he was promoted Lieutenant-General and retired soon afterwards.

Salisch, Ernst Willem van, was a Dutch commander of high reputation. He was promoted Major-General in 1694 and was made Lieutenant-General three years later. In 1705 he was appointed General of Foot in the army of the United Provinces. In 1706 he distinguished himself at the siege of Menin from 22 July–22 August.

Seymour, Algernon (1684–1750) was a descendant of the Seymour family that rose to prominent power under the Tudors. Included in his ancestry are Jane Seymour, third wife of Henry VIII, who died giving birth to the future King Edward VI, and her brother who was Lord Protector to the young king. Algernon Seymour was created Earl of Hertford and first joined the Duke of Marlborough at Brussels in 1708 and fought at Oudenarde and Malplaquet. He was commissioned Colonel of the 15th Regiment of Foot on 23 October 1709 and relinquished it upon his appointment to command the Second Troop of Horse Guards (today's Life Guards) on 8 February 1715. He served in this post until he was promoted to the Colonelcy of The Royal Horse Guards (today's Blues and Royals) on 6 May 1740 for a period of two years. Like many of his contemporaries he also held other offices, some more lucrative than others. For much of this time he was General of Horse and Governor of Teignmouth (the period when Wilson wrote his dedication); and he also held the Governorship of Menorca, from 1737 to 1742.

He forfeited the Royal Horse Guards on 24 February 1742 to Field Marshal John Campbell, 2nd Duke of Argylle, but was rapidly re-appointed on 10 March 1742, just two weeks later. He received further honours in 1748, becoming the 7th Duke of Somerset and he remained in his military position until 13 February 1750, the year of his death. He was buried in Westminster Abbey.

Vaudemont, Charles Henri de Lorraine, Prince de Vaudemont (1649–1723) was the illegitimate son of Duke Charles IV of Lorraine. He served in the army of the Spanish Netherlands in 1674, and commanded its cavalry from 1688 to 1691 when he became its Governor until 1697, the year of his transfer to Milan. William III thought highly of him and often sought his counsel.

Villars, Claude Louis Hector, Duc de Villars (1653–1734) was the ablest of Louis XIV's latterday marshals. A Gascon by birth, he had a 'problematical' upbringing and went into the military where he rose steadily through the ranks to become a Colonel of Horse in 1674 and a Lieutenant-General in 1693. After serving as Ambassador to Vienna he earned his Marshal's baton by his victory at Friedlingen in 1702. He had the reputation of being temperamental and vainglorious and quarrelled with Louis' closest ally, the Elector of Bavaria, in 1703 and found himself replaced by Marshal Marsin in the Danube Valley. However, he distinguished himself and proved highly effective in suppressing the Camissard Revolt, and he was created Duc de Villars in 1705. He captured the Stollhofen Lines near Strasburg in 1707, and fought Marlborough to a bloody draw at Malplaquet in 1709 where he was gravely wounded. In 1712 he won Denain and recaptured several fortresses. In later years he was a member of the Council of Regency for the young Louis XV and became a Minister of State in 1724. He fought his last campaign as Marshal-General of France in north Italy in 1733. Only three other French soldiers have shared this higher distinction: Turenne, de Saxe and Soult.

Withers, Henry (d.1729) is rather an enigma. Certainly famous for his military reputation among his contemporaries, and meriting burial in Westminster Abbey, he does not appear to have commanded any English regiment although his early career was in the First Foot Guards, being promoted from Major to Lieutenant-Colonel in 1695 which carried with it the army rank of Colonel. He was promoted again in 1707 to Lieutenant-General and appears on the Malplaquet Roll. In 1709 he appears as second in seniority only to Marlborough as notional commander of companies in the First Foot Guards. Otherwise, except for his valued services mentioned here, his command of the nineteen battalions and ten squadrons 'from Tournai' on the Allied extreme right wing at Malplaquet, and his usefulness at the siege of Bouchain two years later at the head of twenty battalions and thirty squadrons, he remains a tantalisingly remote figure.

Wittelsbach, Maximilian-Emmanuel von Wittelsbach, Elector of Bavaria (1662–1736) had succeeded to that Electorate of the Holy Roman Empire in 1679. In 1691 he had been appointed Governor-General of the Spanish Netherlands in recognition of the support he had given the Austrian Habsburg Emperor against the French. In the succeeding war he would reverse his allegiance and opportunistically ally with Louis XIV in the hope that he might become the next Holy Roman Emperor after the anticipated French capture of Vienna. In fact he backed the wrong horse and, after sharing in Marshal Tallard's immense defeat by Marlborough and Prince Eugene at Blenheim in 1704, he would forfeit all his lands and possessions until 1714.

Württemburg, Charles Alexander, Duke of Württemburg, assumed the hereditary title after the death of his father, who had served William III in Ireland in 1690. He became a companion of Marlborough and served alongside him through most of his campaigns. He fought in the gory battle of Malplaquet in 1709.

Appendix II

Place Names

The place names below are the more difficult to 'translate' from phonetic spellings. We have not included those names where modern spelling is the same as that employed by Wilson, nor where only a letter or two is changed and the phonetic remains relatively unimpaired (such as Arrass for Arras, or Anderlacht for Anderlech). The modern names are derived by deduction from the sounds, experience with other documents and references to maps and a modern atlas. Where there is uncertainty a level of 'inherent military probability' has been employed – and noted with a question mark. Where Wilson uses two or three spellings for one place they are included on the same line. Unfortunately some small villages are impossible to find, being no longer extant, or swallowed up by urban development.

Wilson's spelling	Modern equivalent
Aith, Aeth	Ath
Arsche, Arsh, Ash	Assche-Asse
Audenarde, Audenard	Oudenarde
Boness	Boneffe
Bourchine, Bouchine	Bouchaine
Bridges, Bridgos	Bruges
Campheer	Kalmithoun
Chippley	St Dennis?
Clarken Wood	Wood of Clares?
Coblants	Koblenz
Danavert, Danawart, Donivert, Donewart, Donowart	Donauwörth
Doway	Douai
Dixmude	Diksmuide
Flans	Flawinau?
Ipre	Ypres
Jouvong, Judoigne	Jodoigne

Kizarswart	Kaiserwerth
L'Abesse	La Bassée
Landrassee	Landrecies
Lans	Lens
Lysle	Lille
Lewar, Leward	St Leau
Massy	Maeseick?
Newport	Nieuport
Newburgh	Neuburg
Newmegon, Nimeguen, Newmegen	Nijmegen
Notredam Hall, Notredam d'all	Hal
Perwys	Perwez
Shelinberg	Schellenberg
Sluice	Sluys
Waterlow	Waterloo

Rivers

We include some here from the full text to help future students understand Wilson's narratives.

Wilson's spelling	Modern equivalent
Ard	Asche
Buss	Beerze
Gheet	Gheete
Glem	Enz
Jamb	Sambre
Lays	Lyse
Leechs	Lech
Leyte	Lye
Maez, Maes	Meuse, Maas
Meyne	Main
Murtz	Murr
Rhino	Rhine
Schaldt, Sheld	Scheldt
Wall	Waal

Appendix III

Names of Regiments

Tracing the lineage of regiments can be difficult due to the frequent disbanding of units in peacetime and the early practice of calling a unit after its Colonel, or sometimes its Lieutenant-Colonel, who often commanded it in the field. If these commanding officers transferred to other, often more lucrative, regiments, then the new unit took their name. This adds to the research confusion, which is further complicated by the inconsistent and sometimes dual practice of using surnames and/or titles. We have chosen the more familiar (where known) – for example in the Royal Scots, when Archibald Douglas, Earl of Angus was CO the regiment is referred to as Douglas's, however when Lord George Douglas, Earl of Dumbarton takes command it was known as Dumbarton's.

Below is a list of foot units mentioned in this edited version of Wilson's Journal. Each is named after the commanding officer, with the names of those Colonels whose regiments are mentioned by Wilson in this text in **bold type**. They are arranged so the reader can discern the changes in name they went through until the numbering system was universally adopted in 1751. A later name for the regiment is supplied to help latter-day association but it must be remembered these names were mostly irrelevant in Wilson's day.

	Number	Later
1633 John Hepburn's – 1636 George Hepburn's – 1637 James Douglas's – 1645 Archibald Douglas's – 1655 Dumbarton's – 1688 Schomberg's – 1691 Robert Douglas's – 1692 **Orkney's** – 1737 Sinclair's – 1762 Erkine's	1st	Royal Scots
1665 Sydney's – 1668 Vane's – 1673 – Buckingham's – 1682 Stanhope's – 1684 Buckingham's – 1685 Oglethorpe's – 1688 **Charles Churchill's** – 1707 **Argylle's** – 1711 Selwyn's – 1713 Forfar's – 1716 Wills' – 1726 Pitt's – 1729 Tatton's – 1737 Thomas Howard's – 1749 George Howard's	3rd	Buffs
1685 Ferrers's – 1686 Berwick's – 1688 Beaumont's – 1695 **Webb's** – 1715 Morrison's – 1720 Hotham's – 1721 Pocock's –		

1732 Lenoe's – 1739 Onslow's – 1745 Wolfe's	8th	The King's
1685 Cornewall's – 1688 Nicholas's then Cunningham's – 1689 **Steuart's** – 1715 Campbell's – 1717 Cathcart's – 1718 Otway's – 1718 Kane's – 1729 Hargrave's – 1739 Reade's – 1749 Powlett's	9th	Norfolks
1685 Bath's – 1688 Carney's then Bath's – 1693 Granville's – 1703 – **North & Grey's** – 1715 Groves' – 1737 Columbine's – 1746 O'Hara's – 1749 Pole's	10th	Lincolnshires
1685 Norfolk's – 1686 Lee's – 1688 Carey's then Wharton's – 1689 **Brewer's** – 1702 – Livesay's – 1712 Philipps's – 1717 Stanwix's – 1725 Whetham's – 1741 Duroure's – 1745 Skelton's	12th	Suffolks
1685 Clifton's – 1686 Herbert's – 1687 Tufton's – 1688 **Leslie's** – 1695 Howe's – 1709 **Hertford's** – 1715 **Harrison's** – 1749 Jordan's	15th	East Yorks
1688 Archibald Douglas's then Hodges's – 1692 Derby's – 1705 **Godfrey's** – 1711 Durrell's – 1713 **Hans Hamilton's** – 1715 Ingram's – 1717 Cholmley's – 1724 Scott's – 1730 Handasyde's – 1730 Brudenell's	16th	Beds & Herts
1688 Richard's – 1689 St George's – 1695 **Courthorpe's** – 1695 **Bridges'** – 1703 Blood's – 1707 Wightman's – 1722 Ferrers' – 1722 Tyrell's – 1742 Wynyard's	17th	Leicestershire
1684 Granard's – 1686 Granard's (2nd Earl) – 1689 Edgeworth's then Meath's – 1692 Frederick Hamilton's – 1705 **Ingoldsby's** – 1712 Stearne's – 1717 Cosby's – 1732 Hotham's – 1735 Armstrong's – 1742 Mordaunt's – 1747 Folliott's	18th	Royal Irish
1678 Mar's – 1686 **Buchan's** – 1689 O'Farrell's – 1695 **Mackay's** – 1697 **Rowe's** – 1704 **Mordaunt's** – 1706 de Lalo's – 1709 Mordaunt's – 1710 Meredith's – then Orrery's – 1716 MacCartney's – 1727 Wood's – 1738 Argylle's	21st	Royal Scots Fusiliers
1689 Henry then Charles Herbert's – 1691 Purcell's – 1692 Morgan's – 1693 **Ingoldsby's** – 1705 Sabine's – 1739 Peer's – 1743 Huske's	23rd	Royal Welch Fusiliers
1689 Edward then Daniel Dering's – 1691 Venner's – 1695 Vasseur's – 1701 Seymour's – 1702 John Churchill's – 1704 Tatton's – 1708 **Primrose's** – 1717 Thomas Howard's – 1737 Wentworth's – 1745 Houghton's – 1747 Kerr's	24th	South Wales Borderers
1689 James Douglas's – 1692 Monro's – 1693 **Ferguson's** – 1705 Borthwick's – 1706 Dalrymple's then Preston's – 1720 Anstruther's	26th	Cameronians

1689 **Tiffin(y)'s** – 1702 Whetham's – 1725 Molesworth's –
1732 Archibald Hamilton's – 1737 Blakeney's   27th   Inniskillings

1694 Gibson's – 1704 de Lalo's – 1706 **Mordaunt's** – 1709
Windsor's – 1715 Barrell's – 1730 Price's – 1734 Bragg's   28th   Gloucestershires

1702 Lucas's – 1705 **Hans Hamilton's** – 1712 Chudleigh's –
1723 Hayes's – 1732 Cornwallis's – 1738 Cavendish's – 1742
Cholmondeley's – 1749 Conway's – 1751 Russell's   34th

1701 Caulfield's – 1706 Alnutt's – 1709 **Argylle's** – 1710
Disney's – 1715 Edgerton's – 1719 Hotham's – 1720
Pocock's – 1721 Lenoe's – 1737 Bland's – 1741 Fleming's –
1751 Manners's   36th

1702 **Meredith's** – 1710 Windress's – 1715 Fane's – 1717
Montagu's – 1722 Murray's – 1735 Ponsonby's – 1745
Munro's – 1746 Dejean's   37th   Hampshires

1705 **Wynne's**   disbanded
1703 **Evans's**   disbanded
1702 Stringer's – 1706 **Argylle's** – 1707 Orrery's – 1710
Sibourg's   disbanded
1663 Fitz-Gerald's – 1692 **Collingwood's**   disbanded
1702 **Temple's** – 1710 Newton's   disbanded 1713

Notes

Note to Introduction

1 Thomas Lediard was an important source on the histories of the first great Duke of Marlborough. Although there were several more attempts by other writers on the Duke's military career soon after his death on 16 June 1722, Lediard's three-volume *magnum opus* proved the standard comprehensive version for many years. The often hostile, long-living and very tough Duchess Sarah (1669–1744) was inevitably critical of some aspects of Lediard's history published in 1736 – for example his descriptions of young Churchill's mistresses – and above all she disliked his deference to royal bastards, and his description of Marlborough as having 'made a Considerable Figure among the Beau Monde.' 'That,' said Sarah, 'I interpret to be a fop. He was naturally genteel without the least affectation, and handsome as an angel tho' ever so carelessly dressed.'

It is important to realise that Lediard was present under the Duke on some occasions – 'myself been an Eye-witness of some of the Transactions . . . as I was at the Time of one of them, not the least among the glorious Number, in the Duke's Retinue', especially to meet Charles X of Sweden near Saxony in 1707. Lediard quotes the famous occasion when Count Piper deliberately snubbed the Duke, keeping his coach outside the Swedish minister's house. According to M. de la Mottraye (*pace* Thomas Lediard), the Duke 'came of his Coach, and, putting on his Hat, pass'd by the Count, without saluting him, and went aside, as if to make Water; and then, after having made him wait longer than was necessary for that Purpose, he went up to him, and address'd him with that Eloquence and Politeness, which every one knows was natural to him' (see Lediard, vol. 2, p. 165).

It is also likely that Lediard had been an attaché to the British Embassy at Hamburg, and was lent to the Duke as a foreign secretary – and was used again for some years. But Lediard was not only a secretary on military matters. He became celebrated for his knowledge of opera; rather later he became a specialist on *The Naval History of England . . . from the Norman Conquest to the occasion of 1734* (two volumes, 1735). Then came his famous three-volume *The Life of John Duke of Marlborough* (1733). He was able to copy many official documents, letters and papers. He also wrote on William III and Mary II and Anne to complete Rapin de Thyras (1737).

Earlier than this Lediard had settled in Smith Square in Westminster. He wrote *On a Historical Architecture* and the etymological parts of N. Bailey's *Dictionarium Brittannicum . . . A Compleat Universal Etymological English Dictionary* in 1736. The following year he wrote *A Scheme . . . for building a Bridge at Westminster*.

He had become Treasurer for Westminster Bridge in 1742, was made a JP and was elected a Fellow of the Royal Society. He died in June 1743.

Notes to Serjeant Wilson's Journal

1 See **Seymour** in Appendix I.
2 The 15th Regiment of Foot, later the East Yorkshire Regiment and currently The Prince of Wales' Own Regiment.
3 'Your Lordship'; elsewhere Wilson employs the term 'Lordspp' which reveals the origin of the diminutive form, 'Lopp'. The editors have decided to retain Wilson's erratic spelling, punctuation and grammar, preferring to retain the authenticity of the original manuscript. However, some minor alterations have been made to make passages clearer for the reader. These are mainly concerned with the addition of standard quotation marks around direct speech and are a far cry from 'correcting' Wilson's English which has been suggested.
4 'Martial fields'. Wilson often reverts to phonetic spelling of common words as well as the more usual interpretation of place names. We have retained most of these spellings as they appear in the Journal documents.
5 See **Ormonde** in Appendix I.
6 A considerable period to serve and survive in the ranks and as an NCO, especially as it included seeing action in both the Nine Years War (1688–97) and the War of the Spanish Succession (1702–13). Wilson's later service in the Life Guards was also far from 'easy'. He was evidently a tough, literate, 'old soldier'.
7 Lieutenant-General Henry Harrison succeeded Seymour as Colonel of the 15th Foot and remained in post from 1715 to 1749.
8 Colonel Sir James Leslie (or Lesley) commanded the 15th Foot from 31 December 1688 until 1 November 1695. He was cashiered by William III for concurring in the surrender of Dixmunde in July of that year. Never restored, it was the end of his military career.
9 Wilson was probably under sixteen years old at this time. Some boy soldiers were recruited as drummers but there is nothing to indicate Wilson served in that capacity. He was eventually accepted for service on 27 April 1695, after being held 'in pay' for some time. This is a strange arrangement; perhaps Colonel Lesley was beholden to his family?
10 Bijlanders – large flat-bottomed transport boats very similar to barges.
11 Like most writers of the period, Wilson spells most place-names phonetically. Where he mentions an important town and there is a

significant difference between what is written and modern spelling, the latter is placed in brackets in the body of the text.

12 See **Ramsey** in Appendix I.

13 See **Salisch** in Appendix I.

14 See **Coehorn** in Appendix I.

15 Water stock is a seventeenth-century term for a sluice or dam.

16 The counterscarp was the wall on the inner side of a fort's outer ring of a defence.

17 The covered or 'covert' way was a protected road that ran around the outside perimeter of a city's defences to permit the garrison to move rapidly from point to point while being sheltered from bombardment. It was often protected by a parapet or palisade on the outward side.

18 See **Wittelsbach** in Appendix I.

19 Cartridges were entering service with the majority of the infantry at this time. Here, however, our Serjeant Wilson is referring to 'partridge' or 'case-shot', serge bags filled with musket balls fired from cannon which were very useful in repelling a close-quarter attack.

20 A half-moon was a detached, free-standing fortification with an outer, semi-circular face and a straight inner wall; often placed within the ditch to protect a straight length of the main defences from direct enemy fire.

21 A demi-bastion was another form of defence-work, again often placed within the ditch, sometimes with cannon emplaced upon it. A bastion, on the other hand, was a major part of the 'enceinte' or inner ring of continuous defences, placed at the angles of the main fortifications and carrying the main artillery of the defenders, firing through embrasures.

22 See **Cutts** in Appendix I.

23 A cohorn is a defensive position with two curving horns standing forwards which from an aerial view would appear as a pair of cow's horns. It was named after its developer, the military engineer General Coehorn.

24 A 'forlorn hope' was a party of troops – almost always volunteers – who undertook very dangerous tasks. At sieges they led the storming of a breach or took up the most exposed forward position on a battlefield. Those who survived being placed in the utmost danger were invariably rewarded with promotions or money and were accorded great honour.

25 Serjeant Wilson gets a little confused here. These three regiments were in fact the 17th, 18th and 21st Foot (Courthorpe's, Hamilton's and Mackay's). Buchan had been Colonel of the 21st but had been deprived of his commission by William III for suspected Jacobite sympathies.

26 'Six fires' probably refers to fire being poured into them and can be a hint at Lord Cutts' nickname (see Appendix I). For three regiments to suffer fire from six sources would be very 'uncomfortable' but not disastrous, although then being charged in flank and rear would a disaster and call for prodigious efforts to get out of the situation! It is very doubtful that it means six 'blazes', although could it be a period expression akin to being 'at sixes and sevens'?

27 Again Wilson apparently is mistaken, this time he is confusing the General Hugh Mackay for the Hon. Robert Hugh Mackay. The latter was Colonel of the 21st Regiment of Foot from 1695 to 1697 not the General. Writing second-hand and at a some years distant it must have been easy to insert the name of the more famous Mackay, the one defeated by 'Bonny Dundee' at Killiekrankie in 1689, but he had been killed at Steinkirk in 1692.

28 The lower forward 'angle' or 'horn' of the cohorn fortification.

29 It was the contemporary practice to avoid stormings of fortresses to avoid great loss of life. Details of capitulation terms varied from the full 'honours of war' (drums beating, colours unfurled, matches lighted and ball in mouth) to unconditional surrender – the garrison marching out into captivity disarmed and 'hands in pockets' (their trouser ties or braces having been cut).

30 Translation: 'Capitulated, as it could not be captured'.

31 Nicholas Catinat (1637–1712) was a notable French soldier who distinguished himself in the Alps and North Italy. In 1689 he was promoted to Lieutentant-General and four years later received his Marshal's baton from Louis XIV.

32 See **Vaudemont** in Appendix I.

33 See **Ginkel** in Appendix I.

34 See **Württemburg** in Appendix I.

35 Although the rank of Brigadier-General was well established by this period, brigades, as such, were essentially *ad hoc* formations, put together at the outset of a particular campaign and rarely surviving the following winter season.

36 See **Boufflers** in Appendix I.

37 See **Villars** in Appendix I.

38 The river Grave is a tributary of the Meuse.

39 This was in fact Brigadier-General Charles Rowe who was later killed at Blenheim in 1704. See note 127 below.

40 To feed the tens of thousands of horses used by an army, turning them out to graze in the rich river valley plains became standard practice whenever possible. As shown here it did have its drawbacks, especially when speedy action was desired.

41 That is 'into units ready for battle' or 'battle formation'. What exactly was ordered at this time is not known, but generally the military practice of the period called for the troopers to draw up in line two ranks deep – the squadron being formed in line of troops (usually about three). The various squadrons were then arrayed in two or three lines on the flanks of the infantry, although Marlborough sometimes posted his Horse in other places in his overall deployment.

42 Rather than using couriers and/or drums, problems of passing urgent messages or those which required concerted action were overcome by giving loud and highly visible signals. Mérode-Westerloo (p. 167) tells us that

Tallard, before Blenheim, had arranged for the distinctive discharge of four 24-pounders to be 'the signal for the recall of the foragers'.

43 These are most probably light 'regimental' guns; mobile 1½- to 2-pounders. Marlborough made very good use of similar light pieces throughout his campaigns, attaching a pair to every battalion to serve very much in the equivalent modern role of a 'support company'.

44 The outer edge of the ditch, or counterscarp, was regularly augmented with a line of wooden stakes forming a palisade as an outermost line of defences along the top of the glacis. It was argued that such defences afforded an attacker cover once he had reached them.

45 Wilson possibly omits the word 'against' here, or he could mean 'defeat'?

46 The River Waal.

47 See **Fagel** in Appendix I.

48 That is, to remove the garrison and the more temporary structures erected to protect Nijmegen from the threat of a full attack.

49 Beating *chamade* denoted a wish to seek a temporary cessation of local hostilities in order to arrange a parley or the negotiation of terms. Such interludes could be, and were, unscrupulously employed by both parties to gain a closer look at the enemy's dispositions, morale state, etc.

50 Exhaustion through continued trench warfare, conducting repeated storms and repulsing frequent enemy sorties could cause what later generations would term 'battle-fatigue' and/or 'shell-shock', necessitating whole formations being withdrawn for 'rest and recuperation'.

51 In fact Marlborough was never given a clear position of authority over his Dutch allies. Some sources claim he was appointed Deputy Captain-General of the United Provinces, but although often mooted, it never took place.

52 See **Cadogan** in Appendix I. At this time he was only a major in rank although already holding the post of Quartermaster General and acting as Chief-of-Staff, although the post did not officially exist in the eighteenth-century army.

53 These were men charged with the task of laying out the camp. Part of their duties was to erect recognisable flags to delineate the various arms' lines at a camping site.

54 The River Meuse or Maas.

55 Wilson appears to have his genealogies confused. However, what is interesting is to see that members of the House of Hanover, candidates for the English succession if Queen Anne died childless, were already active in English affairs, and the reception accorded to them by Marlborough, obviously noting the political implications.

56 The 'Warrant for Holland', 14 March 1702, puts the main train at fourteen sakers (6-pounders), sixteen 3-pounders and four haubwitzers (howitzers or mortars). After reinforcements in 1703 and 1704 this became known as the Blenheim 'Train'.

57 Most probably both sides using drumming for psychological effect.

58 Marlborough was not known for his humour and this may well be one of his rare *bons mots*.

59 Fascines were bundles of sticks and thin branches tied together, varying in thickness and anything between one and two yards in length. They were used as lightweight material to improve badly cut-up roads, infill defensive ditches quickly during a storm or as temporary firecover to begin works. During sieges they were often slung across the saddles of dragoons who rode forward with them and threw them into any defensive ditch the infantry had to cross or into hurried piles ready to be stacked into makeshift and moveable walls. As the works progressed, fascines could be taken apart and retied and woven into gabions – barrel-like hoops, which, when filled with the trench spoil, would make more substantial defences.

60 This was obviously a fighting party and a slightly smaller pioneer party. The armed troops were there to prevent those digging the trenches falling prey to a sortie. The subsequent list of officers makes it clear which group was expected to take the heaviest casualties, especially among those responsible for command and control.

61 See **Withers** in Appendix I.

62 After the 'investiture', or sealing off, the 'opening of the trenches' was the next important event in a siege. It implied the digging of the first 'parallel' and the serious beginning of full operations.

63 Withers appears to have bullied the Governor of Gravenbock into unconditional surrender rather than allowing him to march out with full honours of war.

64 Camille d'Hostun, Comte de Tallard, was not a Marshal of France at this time; he received his baton in 1703. See **Hostun** in Appendix I.

65 See **Fitzjames** in Appendix I.

66 Morasse or marsh.

67 Bundles of hay, long grass or straw were trussed up and thrown across the saddle bow, while firewood was looped with thin ropes or cords and dragged back to camp. Clearly the horsemen had been foraging for some time and, nearly laden, abandoned everything in their haste to return to the ranks. It could always be gathered later if they won their fight; if they lost, it hardly mattered.

68 Wilson's use of the French term *non plus* for notwithstanding may show him to have received some boyhood education rather than a soldier picking up elements of a foreign tongue on active service overseas. This could be corroborated by his intricate, often Latinate phraseology and use sometimes of a grandiloquent style.

69 Karl, Landgrave of Hesse-Cassel (1654–1730), a Prince who ruled Hesse from 1670 and was actively engaged in the Empire's wars throughout his life. Marlborough's circle found him to be occasionally obstructive when the 'common cause' was in trouble.

70 This is an interesting decision when compared to that taken at Ramillies.

71 See **Hamilton** in Appendix I.

72 See **Churchill** in Appendix I.

73 This crossing of the Rhine at Koblenz on 26 May ended Marlborough's first strategic bluff in the campaign. Hitherto everyone, including the French, had anticipated an Allied move up the Moselle in continuance of the 1703 campaign; a perception the Duke fostered by the spreading of false information.

74 This is a graphic illustration of the problems involved in moving the train of artillery over hilly country in wet weather. The only consolation was that the problem was identical for the enemy.

75 Lee remains difficult to positively identify although the name is possibly linked to the Irish exiles who fought under the soubriquet of The Wild Geese and served all over Europe.

76 Jean Baptiste, Count d'Arco (d. 1715), a Piedmontese by birth, entered the Bavarian army and rapidly rose through its ranks, becoming a General of Cavalry by 1697. In 1702 he was President of the Bavarian Council of War and a Marshal, as well as unofficial Chief-of-Staff to the Elector. He survived the debacle of the Schellenberg on 2 July 2 1704, was present at Blenheim commanding the Bavarian infantry around Lutzingen, and commanded the Army of the Two Crowns' left wing at Ramillies in 1706.

77 The Schellenberg adjoining the town of Donauwörth is unimpressive as a feature today, being much overbuilt; however, in 1704 it was more daunting. The eminence was an encampment of Gustavus Adolphus from the Thirty Years War and its steep slopes had been 'improved' by three lines of entrenchment constructed before the Allies appeared before the position.

78 Wilson uses the old style of dating and makes the day of the battle 21 June. The new style date is 2 July.

79 In fact both battalions of the Royal Scots were involved, as becomes clear later. At the time the regiment was known as Orkney's and was the only one in the English Army of this period to have two battalions.

80 Johan van Goor was an experienced, Dutch officer and, as a Lieutenant-General, became the most senior rank to be killed at the Schellenberg.

81 This elite force of 5,850 grenadiers was formed by brigading all the grenadier companies in the army. There was no regiment of grenadiers in the English service at that time.

82 Wilson makes an interesting point here – the use of fascines (see note 59 above) by the front rank of the storming party as a form of rudimentary body armour. Perhaps this could comment upon the poor penetrating power of musket-balls of the day, but it was probably more of a psychological encouragement than a practical protection. It did, however, get the fascines carried into action.

83 Three enemy ditches had to be crossed in this storming of the Schellenberg feature. The Bavarians were much impressed by the fury of the Anglo-

Dutch attack against the wood on their right flank and weakened their left to reinforce it – with dire consequences.

84 Donauwörth's importance was that it possessed two bridges, one of stone, across the Danube. Upriver, the bridge at Ulm was too strongly protected for the Allies to take, bereft as they were of heavy artillery, while downriver the nearest one was thirty-five miles away at Ingolstadt, and the two pontoon bridges at Dillingen lay under the guns of the entrenched Bavarians. In addition to this, the Allies were drawing supplies from the River Main by way of Nüremberg and Nordlingen, and they needed a forward depot for their lines of communication. Donauwörth was the only suitable location.

85 Major-General Pallandt's force of Habsburg infantry attacked the central sector of the Schellenberg's defences and, finding them almost undefended, poured over to take d'Arco's main body in the flank, cutting them off from Donauwörth. This caused a panic.

86 See **Baden** in Appendix I.

87 Most probably a variant of Hompesch.

88 According to most contemporary maps there were four bridges (two of them pontoons). It was the stone bridge that collapsed. The action ended about 8.30 p.m.

89 The English regiments took some 1,500 casualties. In all the Allies lost 5,474 of which 1,423 were killed. No fewer than eight generals were killed and seven wounded, eleven further senior officers were fatally wounded and another seventeen injured, and there were seventy-nine dead and 296 wounded among the regimental officers. According to Deane, the First Foot Guards suffered 311 casualties (50 per cent) but Lediard counts only 229 as he most probably ignored the lightly injured. The Bavarians are estimated to have lost some 8,000.

90 Prince Lewis of Baden received an injury to his foot which soon became referred to as 'the Margrave's toe'. It was generally thought that he made a great deal out of his wound and used it to avoid tasks which he disliked but it was, in fact, a serious wound which contributed to his death in 1707.

91 It is strange to see how Wilson freely moves from the description of Bavaria as the Duke de Bavar's to the Elector of Bavaria's country, without any apparent reason.

92 This is surprising. Most British accounts blame Baden for the order to burn 300 to 400 villages over the next three weeks in an attempt to force the Elector to come out and fight (the Allies' shortage of heavy cannon made it impossible to besiege Augsburg) or to negotiate a peace settlement. In fact he did neither, but stuck out the devastation of his country awaiting the arrival of Tallard's French army. This was in a sense calling Marlborough's bluff – and the initiative duly returned to the Franco-Bavarians for the time being.

93 A jolly phrase for what was, no doubt, a major binge for all ranks!

94 The Allies could besiege this small town, whose possession (just south of the Danube) would strengthen their bridgehead.

95 Count Vehlen (*fl.*1704) was commander of the Palatinate Horse, forming part of the force of 15,000 men left to shadow the main French army at Strasbourg and give notice of its approach to the Danube theatre.

96 See **Hostun** in Appendix I.

97 See **Neufville** in Appendix I. In fact, after shadowing Marlborough's long march from the west bank of the Rhine, Villeroi's force was only in support of Tallard, guarding his lines of communication.

98 Fort Kehl was to the south of the undermanned Allied lines of Stolheim. Most sources place Tallard's strength at 45,000 men at this juncture and Villeroi's at about 20,000.

99 In fact the Elector was being given an ultimatum: 'Fight or surrender.' The Elector's resistance to these blandishments was strengthened by receiving news of Tallard's long-delayed approach apparently in a message smuggled through the Allied lines concealed in a button.

100 The courtly forms of expression in the early eighteenth century should be taken at face value. The Elector had allied with Louis XIV with an eye to the main chance of becoming a French puppet Holy Roman Emperor; the stakes were as high as that. In the event he would lose all his lands after Blenheim, and only recover them at the end of the war.

101 Hussars were, at this time, largely indisciplined light cavalry of Hungarian origin. The Bavarian, Colonel de la Colonie, described them as 'little more than bandits on horseback'. They were thus well suited to ravage Bavaria – an estimated 400 villages being put to the torch in the (vain) hope of making the Elector more compliant.

102 This conference took place at Schrobenhausen on 6 August (NS). To get rid of the cautious and prickly Baden, he was sent off with 15,000 men to besiege Ingolstadt on the Danube to the east, while the 'Twin Captains' set about dealing with Tallard and the Elector, whose armies had joined on 4 August at Augsburg before crossing north of the great river near Lavingen in an attempt to sever the Allied communications with Nüremberg. Although Baden never forgave being deprived of a share in Blenheim, the siege of Ingolstadt was justified; it was the next bridge below Donauwörth, now in danger of being retaken by the French, and was full of supplies and martial stores. Marlborough had no wish to find himself trapped south of the Danube.

103 An error: Wilson should have written 'Danube'. Marlborough was marching as fast as he could to cross that river, via Lech and Rain (which had surrendered on 28 July, providing the under-gunned Allies with twenty-four brass cannon which would prove vital at Blenheim a few days later) in order to join Prince Eugene's covering force on the north bank. Jointly they commanded 52,000 men and sixty guns; Tallard 56,000 and ninety guns.

104 Telescope or 'perspective-glass'. They inspected the French encampment from the spire of Tapfheim church.

105 The River Nebel and its marshy banks – today little more than a ditch.

106 Wilson makes no mention of the dense fog which both complicated this advance (made in nine columns) and achieved surprise; Tallard believing that the Allies were retiring towards Nordlingen. This impression was fostered by spreading 'rumour in the countryside' and by sending handpicked 'deserters' into the French camp with the same story. Tallard's pre-battle despatch to Versailles reveals how totally he was fooled by these methods; a classic instance of Clausewitz's 'fog of war'. Wilson's regiment formed part of Rowe's Brigade under Lord Cutts on the Allied left. Note his use of 'we' and 'our'.

107 Eugene, also held up by wooded hills, was finally in position a little after midday. Tallard's torpidity in wasting the whole morning in bombarding the Allied left and centre (whose troops were ordered by Marlborough to lie down in their ranks) can only be explained by surmising that he wanted the Allies to attack over the Nebel inviting a Franco-Bavarian counter-stroke.

108 Eugene's force on the Allied right comprised twenty-eight battalions and ninety-two squadrons, facing Lutzingen and Oberglau villages. The centre was (unusually for the time) drawn up four lines of units deep under Charles Churchill – seventeen battalions in the first line, seventy-two squadrons of Horse in the next two with a reserve of eleven more battalions to their rear. The Allied left under Lord Cutts comprised twenty battalions and fourteen squadrons. Facing them was Tallard's army on the right – a brigade of dismounted dragoons on the Danube's bank, nine battalions in Blenheim with a further eighteen in the rear, sixty-four squadrons and ten battalions forming his centre. The Elector's and Marsin's command consisted of fourteen battalions occupying Oberglau, with sixty-seven squadrons on its left and sixteen battalions on the extreme left.

109 Hochstadt was a town on the bank of the Danube, about three miles west of Blenheim. In due course the Franco-Bavarian left wing fell back upon it in full retreat.

110 The French, in fact, only developed firing by *peletons* after 1709. This is another indication of Wilson writing many years *post facto*.

111 To 're-order' his formations and calculate their losses.

112 In fact five squadrons, under Colonel Palmes, had routed seven squadrons of the elite *Gendarmerie* early in the battle – an event that shook Tallard's composure as he admitted after the battle. The three (not four) attacks by Cutts on Blenheim itself served to contain all of twenty-seven French battalions crowded within the defences by order of Clerembault (the sector commander) until the close of the day.

113 In fact the cavalry battle went as follows: Tallard launched his squadrons towards the Nebel when he saw Charles Churchill's troops floundering in the marshes. An Allied counter-charge was defeated but there were sufficient infantry present to permit them to rally, while Eugene selflessly sent over Fugger's cuirassiers to help stabilise the situation. Then, when

120

all of Tallard's cavalry were blown, Marlborough launched his reserve line of squadrons which shattered the French horsemen and the line of only nine battalions placed to support them, whereupon Tallard's centre collapsed.

114 Tallard was captured as he tried to make his way into Blenheim, whose inflated garrison had been mere spectators for several hours.

115 The twenty-seven battalions were leaderless as Clerembault had also fled, only to be drowned attempting to swim the Danube on his horse.

116 Orkney was, in fact, bluffing but in the growing dusk and with smoke from some fired cottages blinding them, the French decided to capitulate.

117 To 'surrender at discretion' meant unconditional laying down of arms. Coxe tells us that a little later Marlborough agreed that their officers should not be 'searched' (i.e. robbed) and allowed them to retain their swords.

118 They had had no contact with Cutts nor any agreement and therefore feared they would be shot at as presumed combatants.

119 This paragraph of incidental detail is not to be found in most other narratives and indicates that Wilson was an eye-witness – as indeed he should have been as part of Rowe's Brigade. It was 8.00 p.m.

120 A wise precaution in case the twenty-seven battalions and twelve squadrons of dismounted dragoons attempted to escape from their midst overnight.

121 Sheathed his sword.

122 Although the *Letters of Lord Orkney* give much of this story, it is quite possible that Wilson heard it first-hand. The Orkney correspondence was not published by 1732.

123 The Franco-Bavarian left wing had left the field by about 6.00 p.m. and headed for Hochstadt. The pursuit was slow – but after ten hours' marching over broken and mainly hilly ground, and five hours of hard combat, Eugene's troops had performed well by any standard.

124 Franco-Bavarian losses are put at 20,000 killed, 14,000 taken prisoner and another 6,000 deserters. Some sixty cannon, 300 colours and standards and the entire camp were also taken.

125 The precise casualties of Marlborough's force would seem to have been 190 officers and 3,102 other ranks killed and 264 officers and 4,927 rank and file wounded. Prince Eugene's losses were some 4,200. Wilson's estimates are pretty close.

126 The Prince of Holstein Beck (sometimes Holstein Plon) fell commanding the attack on Oberglau in Tallard's centre.

127 Brigadier-General Charles Archibald Rowe (also 'Rue' or 'Row') (d. 1704) was a gallant officer who personally led the first (ultimately, abortive) attack on Blenheim village. He ordered his men to hold their fire until he could strike the outermost palisade of the defences with his sword. Advancing with 'an unparalle'd intrepidity' (Lediard) he made his stroke and at once fell, shot dead. His brigade lost a third of its strength before falling back, but so impressed was the Marquis de Clerembault, commander of Blenheim, that

he packed all Tallard's infantry reserve into the village's defences – with ultimately fatal effects.

128 For '1400' possibly read '14,000', but the total loss, in fact, would seem to have been some 13,000.

129 This is a rare example of Marlborough's liberality. A *pistole* was an out-of-date Spanish gold coin then worth approximately 18 shillings (90p).

130 The first intimation (written in pencil on the back of an old tavern bill) was carried by Colonel Parke to Duchess Sarah. She took it to the Queen who read it in an alcove in Windsor Castle Library. Her reaction was to reward Parke with a miniature of herself and 1,000 guineas.

131 Marlborough was created Prince of Mindelheim, a very small Imperial enclave. He never visited it.

132 This pillar used to stand near Sonderheim, where the French cavalry tried to swim the Danube. There is a modern memorial near Blenheim itself but it has little to commend it in artistic terms.

133 It was rare for a regiment to be actually commanded by its colonel because the rank was ascribed to the 'proprietor commander' who was not always a soldier. If he was, then his social station often took him to other duties such as one of the general officer ranks or onto the staff, away from regimental command of his unit. Hence this comment by Wilson.

134 Irish Roman-Catholic exiles, many of whom went into voluntary exile in France in 1691 after the fall of Limerick; the famous 'Wild Geese'. Most of these Irish mercenaries carried colours featuring the Cross of St George on a variety of coloured fields and embroidered with *In hoc signo vinces*. In the early 1700s the Regiment Walsh (Roth) actually carried what we today would call the English Flag of a red cross upon a white field (with a lion surmounting a crown in gold in the centre).

135 Wilson's tactical detail appears to be first-hand. His estimate of enemy casualties is probably vastly exaggerated.

136 This is a unique recital of this verbatim story concerning the levelling of the French lines near Courtrai. Marlborough was notorious for his meanness where money was concerned – as his troops well knew. However, he was as careful with their lives as with his guineas, which they fully appreciated.

137 Engineer officers belonged to the Board of Ordnance and were relatively few in number – hence the comment here. Wilson may be making a snide comment of the sort used in the American Civil War by the infantry: 'Whoever saw a dead cavalryman?' On the other hand, Vauban once referred to his engineers as 'Martyrs to the infantry'.

138 This was probably the occasion when an unnamed British sergeant swam the moat and let down the drawbridge single-handed.

139 Deane says Howe's lost 144 in all, but estimates equivalent losses to Temple's Regiment – a point Wilson challenges claiming Temple's only lost twenty men. The effect of wounds is of interest; by Wilson's account only approximately 15 per cent ever returned for further duty.

140 A tent-party usually numbered eight men.

141 Note the use of empty bread waggons as ambulances, averaging out at about four wounded to each vehicle for both Howe's and Temple's regiments. This would suggest that the bread waggons were two-wheeled.

142 According to a military dictionary of 1702 a 'blind' was either a canvas screen 'stretched to take away the sight of the enemy', or bundles of branches set up between stakes. It was also used in the seventeenth century to describe a defensive wooden screen, sometimes improvised about a cart to make it mobile – they were used as mobile shields in attacks upon towns or fortified places. In Wilson's case it is probably the branch barricade.

143 It is interesting to speculate whether these words from Orkney are, or were, accurately reported. They have a rhythmic ring and could well have been 'worked upon' in the retelling. The lines at Seclin and Ennetieres were held from 5 to 17 September.

144 This was the only known occasion when Marlborough entrenched his battle position and thus, presumably, chose to fight defensively.

145 Fortunately it was an almost expended musket-ball. Eugene himself bandaged up the wound and suffered only a mild concussion. He only agreed to leave the lines at Marlborough's personal entreaty.

146 The 'attacks' were the trenches dug facing the sectors of the enemy's fortifications that were selected as being most vulnerable.

147 The new campaign opened very late in the year; throughout Europe many people and animals had died of famine in the bitter winter and this effectively delayed all negotiations. Louix XIV was ready to agree to all of the Allies' demands except one; the dethronement of Philip V of Spain. Rumour had it that Louis XIV had offered a secret 'gift' of more than a million livres to Marlborough but this had been rejected.

148 Very small Dutch mortars carried by individual soldiers.

149 The Allies often combined several Grenadier companies and used them as 'special forces'.

150 Wilson's use of the term 'sword in hand' when describing the storming of breaches or works may be dramatic licence but at this time, despite being musket-armed, many soldiers still carried swords used by the 'hatmen' to chop wood, spit-roast meat or threaten civilians. The Grenadiers were encouraged to draw swords, or hangers, when fighting their way across obstacles where a one-handed, close quarters, stabbing and slashing weapon would be of more use than a bayonet on the end of a musket.

151 How could Serjeant Wilson have known what was in these documents of war? One answer must be that he was writing later and was able to consult them – although such documents were occasionally published to the troops at the time.

152 General de Surville-Hautfois, the French garrison commander, had 7,700 troops, with which he defended the fortress for a further sixty-nine days before surrendering to the Allies. The Governor, M. de Mesgrigny, was a skilled mining engineer who prolonged the bitter and expensive operation by

his siting of the saps and mines beneath the fortress. The Allies lost 5,400 troops as a result and these casualties were much commented on.

153 It was a custom of the period to compel peasants – of both sides – to dig trenches without payment. Troops did not like digging works and often had to be cajoled with money to undertake it.

154 The reason for the movement of the Grand Army to Orchies was to acquire new foraging areas. Apart from the obvious foodstuffs and animal fodder which ran into supply troubles if an army stayed in one place too long, wood was quickly consumed as it was used for cooking and keeping warm as well as making fascines, gabions, palisades, blinds, duck-boards and all the other siege and camp impedimenta. An army on the march could strip an area of trees within days.

155 Marshal Villars, aided by Marshal Boufflers, had two days to prepare for the battle of Malplaquet near a village called Camp Perdu. Calculating that the Allies would be the stronger, Villars prepared his defences and positions with great care. At this juncture the French Army, numbering some 80,000 men, was the weaker one and faced 110,000 Allied soldiers (they were the largest armies of this war). Villars' cunning preparations almost redressed the balanced.

156 The States (or Dutch) forces were commanded by the young Prince of Orange, with thirty regiments (including a number of hired Scots).

157 The Allied army consisted of 128 battalions, 253 squadrons and 100 guns (including the British contingent of 15,000 men, including ten battalions, fourteen squadrons and forty guns). The French placed ninety-six battalions, 183 squadrons and sixty guns on the field.

158 The Allied left wing of thirty battalions was placed facing the Wood of Lanieres, where the French had hidden twenty cannon which would inflict great damage, particularly upon the Dutch. In the centre was the small coppice called the Wood of Tiry, around which were placed the fifteen battalions commanded by Lord Orkney, and the masses of Allied cavalry. They were opposite the Forest of Sars, defended by Villars. On the Allied right, their seventy-seven battalions faced the woods of Taisnieres, Blaugies and of Dour in the north-west.

159 The centre attack developed into an intense battle by Lottum's and Orkney's thirty-four battalions to penetrate the thick forest of the Triangle. After a long and bloody fight amongst the bushes and tangled undergrowth they eventually defeated Albergotti's twenty-one battalions and twenty guns. Once this was completed, Orkney's best British units swept forwards and occupied the French redoubts in support of the massive Allied cavalry which ultimately broke through.

160 The Allied forces broke through the Wood of Sars and swung southwards through the Wood of Blaugies, led by Schulenburg and assisted by Miklau's and Withers' nineteen battalions and ten cavalry squadrons. This turned the French left wing.

161 Marshal Villars was seriously wounded in the heavy fighting in the centre, leaving Marshal Boufflers to carry on without him. The French prevailed in the fighting on their right, but the Allies carried the centre and the other wing.

162 The twenty well positioned French guns almost defeated the Dutch. De Guiche's eighteen battalions and guns held on to the French right wing.

163 The generally accepted casualties at Malplaquet are as follows: the Allies lost at least 24,000 men alone; the French lost just 12,000 men (including 3,000 prisoners-of-war) and sixteen cannon. Thus Serjeant Wilson undercalculated considerably. Serjeant Millner gives the following figures (killed and wounded): British – 1,783; Germans – 5,231; Prussians 1,694; Hanoverians – 2,219; Dutch – 8,680 (by far the worst). The total came to 19,696 Allied soldiers (only 1,963 being horse and dragoons). These were the worst casualties of these wars.

164 There was no question of any pursuit; the Allies were exhausted.

165 Wilson is incorrect here. Villars was, by this time, out of action; Boufflers and de Guiche carried out the negotiations with Marlborough.

166 The Siege of Mons began on 9 September and the garrison capitulated on 10 October.

167 These were 'field signs' often worn by soldiers to distinguish one side from another in an age when polyglot armies shared no common language or uniform (Dutch, Imperial and French troops all wore white/grey coats). The Allies were often known to wear sprigs of greenery or tie in green ribbons, so this was a deliberate deception by the French. Whether Wilson means bows of ribbon or boughs of greenery is a moot point – the word 'bower' should help explain why we pose the question.

168 Although Wilson was not a witness to these events, it can be expected that what we have is the 'full story' complete with quotes as it went round the Allied camp fires. It is interesting to note, in this account by an NCO, how the NCO of the guard does everything correctly and the junior officer makes the mistakes.

169 Serjeant Wilson usually praises French fighting abilities and describes their killing Englishmen as 'vigourous' and 'valiant'. Because of the nature of the action, here he calls it murder.

170 The low-lying nature of the country made the breaking of dikes a serious option for quick results. Canal waters would empty into the fields and make the area impassable. It was, however, devastating for local agriculture.

171 A partisan was described in a military dictionary of 1702 as follows: 'A good Partifan is an able cunning Soldier, well skill'd in commanding a Party, who knows the country, and how to avoid Ambufhies, and furprize the Enemy.' Wilson clearly admires this unusual irregular attack carried out by a Dutch raiding party in which most of the men who were involved had divested themselves of their military uniforms. It is worth comparing Wilson's attitude here to that expressed when describing the surprise of the camp near Arleux.

172 This issue meant the men could have a pint of beer to quench their thirst and a thick slice of white bread for their hunger, presumably to go with the cheese mentioned earlier. The 'quatern' of brandy poses more of a problem. This old word means 'being four' or 'a set of four'; Wilson could mean they had a quarter pint or a quart! If it was the latter then two pints of brandy; it could have been some to drink for 'Dutch courage' and the rest to carry along with them both for 'medicinal purposes' and to sustain them on the necessarily fast return. Peninsular veterans kept pints of Spanish brandy in their canteens in preference to the wine and the water, both of which could give crippling dysentery.

173 The 'barrier' was probably a moveable *chevaux de frise* and would have been close to the gate but on the far side of the drawbridge. Although a minor obstacle, it could look fearsome and distract horses so such things were often used as controlling devices.

174 He was asking the sentry if he would use his tinder and steel to light his pipe. Most people carried a small box in which they kept a small quantity of black, baked linen, a flint and steel to strike it. The sparks produced fell upon the dry material and smouldered. Blowing upon the glowing material encouraged flame. It was the period equivalent to a box of matches.

175 The sentry had abandoned his guard and allowed the Dutchmen to capture the Governor and Commanding Officer and thus his complete fortress.

176 It is a pity that the Serjeant has not written more 'soldier stories' of this kind. Details of individual soldiering feats are difficult to find.

177 It is interesting to note all the details listed by Serjeant Wilson concerning the reductions to and changes in the Regiments of Foot. In 1713 the custom of numbering Regiments was commenced, against much opposition.

Bibliography

(All books published in London unless noted otherwise)

Contemporary memoirs (British sources)

Ailesbury, Thomas Bruce, Earl of, *Memoirs* (2 vols, 1890)

Bishop, Matthew, *The Life and Adventures of Matthew Bishop of Doddington in Oxfordshire* (1744)

Blackadder, Lieutenant-Colonel John, *The Life and Diary of Lieutenant Colonel J. Blackadder*, ed. Andrew Crichton (1924)

Cadogan, William, 'Correspondence' (British Library Add. Mss 28918, 42176, 2196)

Churchill, John, *The Correspondence 1701-1711 of John Churchill, First Duke of Marlborough, and Anthonie Heinsius, Grand Pensionary of Holland*, ed. B. van'T. Hoff, (The Hague, 1951)

—— *The Marlborough–Godolphin Correspondence*, ed. H.L. Snyder (3 vols, Oxford, 1975)

—— *The Letters and Dispatches of John Churchill, 1st Duke of Marlborough, from 1702 to 1712*, ed. G. Murray (5 vols, 1845)

Cranstoun, Colonel, 'Letters' (Report of the Royal Commission on Historical Manuscripts, Vol. 1, 1904)

Deane, Private John Marshall, *A Journal of the Campaign in Flanders in A.D. MDCCVIII*, ed. J.B. Deane (Edinburgh, 1846)

—— *A Journal of Marlborough's Campaigns during the War of the Spanish Succession, 1704–11*, ed. D.G. Chandler (Society for Army Historical Research Special Publication no. 12, 1984)

Drake, Captain Peter, *Memoirs* (Dublin, 1755)

Hare, Chaplain-General Francis, 'Journal' (Appendix and Part I, Report XIV, Royal Commission on Historical Manuscripts, 1895)

Jefferyes, Captain James, *Captain James Jefferyes' Letters to the Secretary of State, Whitehall, from the Swedish Army, 1707–1709*, ed. Raghnhild Hatton (Stockholm, 1954)

Kane, Brigadier-General Richard, *Campaigns of King William and Queen Anne* (1745)

Lediard, T., *The Life of John, Duke of Marlborough* (3 vols, 1736)

Millner, Serjeant John, *A Compendious Journal of all the Marches, Famous Battles, Sieges, and Other Most Note-Worthy, Heroical, and Ever Memorable Actions of* the Triumphant Armies of the Ever-Glorious Confederate High Allies in Their Late and Victorious War against the Powerful Armies of Proud and Lofty France . . . begun A.D. 1701, and ended in 1712 (1733)

Noyes, Dr Samuel, 'Diary of 1705 and 1706' (privately owned)

Orkney, Field Marshal George Hamilton, Earl of, Letters (English Historical Records, 1904)

Parker, Captain Robert, Memoirs of the Most Remarkable Military Transactions from the Year 1683, to 1718. Containing a More Particular Account, Than Any Ever Yet Published, of the Several Battles, Sieges, &C. in Ireland and Flanders, During the Reigns of K. William and Q. Anne (1745)

—— and Comte Mérode-Westerloo, The Marlborough Wars, 1702–1712, ed. D.G. Chandler (1968), reprinted as Military Memoirs of Marlborough's Campaigns, 1702–1712 (1998)

Pope, Captain Richard, 'Letters' (Report of the Royal Commission on Historical Manuscripts, 1952)

Richards, Major-General John, 'Journal' and 'Letters' (British Library, Add. Mss, Stowe 474 and 475).

Sterne, Brigadier-General Robert, in Richard Cannon, Historical Records of the British Army (1835)

Swift, Jonathan, The Conduct of the Allies and of the Late Ministry, in Beginning and Carrying on the Present War (1712)

Contemporary memoirs (continental sources)

Colonie, J.-M. de la, Chronicles of an Old Campaigner (1904)

Corvisier, André, La Bataille de Malplaquet, 1709 (Paris, 1997)

Dutems, J.F.H., Histoire de Jean, Duc de Marlborough (Paris, 1806)

Eugene, Prince of Savoy, Feldzüge, two series (Vienna, 1876–81)

Goslinga, Secco van, Mémoires (The Hague, 1857)

Klopp, O., Der Fall des Hauses Stuart (14 vols, Vienna, 1875–88)

Legrelle, A., La Diplomatique française et le succession d'Espagne (4 vols, Braine-le-Comte, 1895–1900)

Mérode-Westerloo, Comte de, Mémoires (2 vols, Brussels, 1840)

Puysegur, Maréchal de, L'Art de la guerre (2 vols, Paris, 1748)

Saint-Simon, Duc de, Mémoires (40 vols, Paris, 1881–1907)

Sautai, M., La Bataille de Malplaquet (Paris, 1904)

Schulenburg, J.M., Keben und Denkwürdigkeiten (2 vols, Vienna, 1834)

Villars, Claude L.H., Le Maréchal le Duc: Mémoires (Paris, 1887)

General

Ashley, Maurice, Marlborough (1939)

—— The Glorious Revolution of 1688 (1966)

Atkinson, C.T., Marlborough and the Rise of the British Army (1921)

Barnett, Correlli, *Marlborough* (1974)

Barzun, Jacques, *From Dawn to Decadence: 500 Years of Cultural Triumph and Defeat, 1500 to the Present* (2000)

Baxter, S., *William III* (1966)

Belloc, Hilaire, *The Tactics and Strategy of the Great Duke of Marlborough* (1933)

Black, Jeremy, *European Warfare, 1660–1815* (1994)

—— *The Cambridge Illustrated Atlas: Warfare: Renaissance to Revolution, 1492–1792* (Cambridge, 1996)

Burton, I., *The Captain-General: The Career of John Churchill, Duke of Marlborough, from 1702 to 1711* (1968)

Butler, Iris, *Rule of Three: Sarah, Duchess of Marlborough and her Companions in Power* (1967)

Chandler, David G., *Marlborough as Military Commander* (1973)

——*The Art of Warfare in the Age of Marlborough* (1976)

—— *Sedgemoor, 1685* (1985)

—— *Blenheim Preparation* (Staplehurst, 2004)

—— and Beckett, Ian, *The Oxford Illustrated History of the British Army* (Oxford, 1994)

Chidsey, Donald B., *Marlborough: the Portrait of a Conqueror* (1930)

Childs, John, *The Army of Charles II* (1976)

—— *The Army, James II and the Glorious Revolution* (Manchester, 1980)

—— *The British Army of William III, 1689–1702* (Manchester, 1987)

—— *The Nine Years War and the British Army, 1688–1697: The Operations in the Low Countries* (Manchester, 1991)

—— *Warfare in the Seventeenth Century* (2001)

Churchill, W.S., *Marlborough, His Life and Times* (4 vols, 1933–8)

Clark, Sir G., *The Later Stuarts 1660–1714* (Oxford, 1955)

Cowles, Virginia, *The Great Marlborough and His Duchess* (1983)

Coxe, William, *Memoirs of John, Duke of Marlborough*, new edition rev. by J. Wade (3 vols, 1847–8)

Dalton, C., *English Army Lists and Commission Registers, 1661–1714* (6 vols, 1892–1904)

Earle, Peter, *Monmouth's Rebels: The Road to Sedgemoor, 1685* (1977)

Falls, Captain Cyril (ed.), *Great Military Battles* (1964)

Foot, Michael, *The Pen and the Sword* (1957)

Fortescue, Sir John, *History of the British Army*, Vol. 1 (1899)

—— *Marlborough* (1932)

Francis, David, *The First Peninsular War, 1702–1713* (1975)

Fuller, Major-General J.F.C., *The Decisive Battles of the Western World and Their Influence upon History*, Vol. 2 (1955)

Geikie, Roderick and Montgomery, Isabel A., *The Dutch Barrier, 1705–1719* (Cambridge, 1930)

Green, David, *Blenheim Palace* (1951)

—— *Queen Anne* (1970)

—— *Blenheim* (1974)

Guy, Alan, *Oeconomy and Discipline: Officership and Administration in the British Army, 1714–63* (Manchester, 1985)

—— and Spencer-Smith, Jenny (eds), *1688: Glorious Revolution? The Fall and Rise of the British Army, 1660–1704* (1988)

Hastings, Max (ed.), *The Oxford Book of Military Anecdotes* (Oxford, 1985)

Hattendorf, J.B., *England in the War of the Spanish Succession: A Study of the English View and Conduct of Grand Strategy, 1702–1712* (New York, 1987)

Hatton, Ragnhild, *Charles XII* (1968)

—— *George I* (1978)

Henderson, Nicholas, *Prince Eugen of Savoy: A Biography* (1964)

Houlding, J.A., *Fit for Service: The Training of the British Army, 1715–1795* (Oxford, 1981)

Hugill, J.A.C., *No Peace without Spain* (Oxford, 1991)

Jones, D.W., *War and Economy in the Age of William III and Marlborough* (Oxford, 1988)

Jones, J.R., *The Revolution of 1688 in England* (1972)

—— *Marlborough* (Cambridge, 1993)

Kearsey, A.H.C., *Marlborough and his Campaigns, 1702–1709* (1931)

Leslie, N.B., *The Succession of Colonels of the British Army from 1660 to the Present Day* (Aldershot, 1974)

Macaulay, Lord T., *History of England from the Accession of James II* (6 vols, 1849–61)

McGuffie, T.H. (ed.), *Rank and File: The Common Soldier at Peace and War, 1642–1914* (1964)

McKay, D., *Prince Eugene of Savoy* (1977)

Macmunn, G.F., *Prince Eugène: Twin Marshal with Marlborough* (1934)

Malleson, G.B., *Prince Eugène of Savoy* (1888)

Ogg, D., *England in the Reigns of James II and William III* (Oxford, 1955)

Parnell, A., *The War of the Succession in Spain during the Reign of Queen Anne,, 1702–1711* (1888)

Petrie, Sir Charles, *Bolingbroke* (1937)

—— *The Marshal Duke of Berwick: The Picture of an Age* (1953)

Rogers, Colonel H.C.B., *The British Army of the Eighteenth Century* (1977)

Rowse, A.L., *The Early Churchills: An English Family* (1956)

Scouller, Major R.E., *The Armies of Queen Anne* (Oxford, 1966)

Sturgill, C.C., *Marshal Villars and the War of the Spanish Succession* (Lexington, KY, 1965)

Taylor, F., *The Wars of Marlborough, 1702–1709* (2 vols, Oxford, 1921)

Thomson, G.M., *The First Churchill: The Life of John, 1st Duke of Marlborough* (Oxford, 1979)

Trevelyan, G.M., *England under Queen Anne* (3 vols, 1930–4)

—— *The English Revolution, 1688–1689* (1965)

Wace, Alan, *The Marlborough Tapestries at Blenheim Palace* (1968)

Walton, C., *History of the British Standing Army, AD 1660–1700* (1894)

Watson, J.N.P., *Marlborough's Shadow: The Life of the First Earl Cadogan* (Barnsley, 2003)

Wills, John E., *1688: A Global History* (2001)

Wolseley, Field Marshal Viscount, *The Life of John Churchill, Duke of Marlborough* (2 vols, 1894)

Part II

Captain Hon. William Leslie (1751–77)
His Life, Letters and Commemoration

Edited by
MARIANNE M. GILCHRIST

Acknowledgements

With sincere thanks to the Earl of Leven and Melville and the staff of the National Archives of Scotland for permission to publish extracts from the Leven and Melville Papers (GD 26); Philip R. French, Leicester City Museums Service; Lieutenant-Colonel S.J. Lindsay, Museum of the Black Watch (Royal Highland Regiment), Balhousie Castle, Perth; John Mills, Princeton Battlefield State Park, Princeton, NJ; Edith Philip, Librarian, National War Museum of Scotland, Edinburgh; the staff of New Register House, Edinburgh; the Special Collections Department, Library of the University of St Andrews; Cupar Public Library.

Abbreviations

NAS   National Archives of Scotland
OPR   Old Parochial Registers

Introduction

The Hon. William Leslie was born on 8 August (Old Style) 1751, at Melville House, near Monimail in Fife. He was the second son of David Leslie (1722–1802), 6th Earl of Leven and 5th of Melville, and his wife Wilhelmina Nisbet (1724–98), posthumous daughter of William Nisbet of Dirleton. No exceptional distinction attached itself to his life and military career: both were cut short on the morning of 3 January 1777, in the battle of Princeton, New Jersey. He has left behind no portrait. His only significant legacy is a handful of letters in the Leven and Melville Papers (GD 26/9/313), housed in the National Archives of Scotland, and published here, with supporting documentation from the collection, by kind permission of the present Earl of Leven and Melville. The manuscripts are in good condition, although some have damage from opening, where the seals have been cut around. In most cases, context makes it easy to restore the sense.

William Leslie's letters from America have attracted attention in the United States because of the circumstances of his burial. His body, in the back of a captured baggage cart, was unwittingly removed from the field by the enemy. He was buried by them in Pluckemin with full military honours, because a letter in his coat pocket revealed his family's friendship with Dr Benjamin Rush, a signatory of the American Declaration of Independence, and a prominent surgeon with the Continental Army.

American emphasis on Rush's involvement meant that earlier writers (Butterfield (1947) and Cohen (1990)) have paid scant attention to Captain Leslie's earlier letters from Ireland. Cohen misread some personal and place-names, and interpreted character and tone according to established American stereotypes of redcoat officers, describing William as 'a somewhat callow, extremely conformable young man' (p. 76). A non-American might take a less patronising view of his youthful naivety in its bruising first contact with real action. Cohen also cited some comments as proof of 'disdain of the rebels' (p. 64), ignoring the natural tendency of soldiers on active service to play down the threat posed by the enemy to protect anxious relatives at home. Captain Leslie had already displayed such concern for others earlier in his career, when he asked his brother to spare their mother news of attacks by the 'Hearts of Steel' in Ireland.

The letters' chief value is in providing a glimpse into the social life and experiences of a young officer from a cultured and influential Scots family while serving in Ireland and in the rebellious Colonies. They also demonstrate the networking of information and influence within a large extended family. The Leslies, Websters, Erskines and Carnegies – all cousins of varying degrees – kept an eye on each other, circulated news within the family, and gave support in the face of loss.

William's own letters are presented here in full, with extracts from supporting documentation from the same collection. For the sake of clarity, the usage of 'Y' for 'th', inconsistently employed in the manuscripts, has been amended. Two deleted passages have been reinstated.

1 Home and Ireland

The Leven and Melville family combined a tradition of military service with one of devout Presbyterianism, both traceable back to the first Earl, General Alexander Leslie (d. 1661), veteran of the armies of Gustaf Adolf of Sweden in the Thirty Years War and of the Covenant in the British Civil Wars. Captain Leslie's father, David, Lord Balgonie, served in Handasyde's Regiment of Foot from 1742 until 1755, a year after succeeding his father as Earl. While embracing many artistic and scientific aspects of the Scottish Enlightenment, and Freemasonry – he was Grand Master of Scotland, 1759–61 – his family did not share the era's religious scepticism. He and his Countess were both closely associated with Evangelical trends. Lord Leven, a Commissioner of the General Assembly, was President of the Society for the Propagation of Christian Knowledge. The Countess, like her mother, was a disciple of the Rev. George Whitefield, and, like her friend Selina, Countess of Huntingdon, was noted for piety and charitable works.[1] Alexander, Lord Balgonie, Captain Leslie's older brother, later married Jane Thornton, a member of the Hull merchant family related to William Wilberforce and at the centre of the 'Clapham Sect', devoted to Evangelical Christianity and the abolition of slavery.[2]

The Leslies' chief residences were Melville House, near Monimail in Fife, and a townhouse in the north-west corner of Nicolson Square, Edinburgh. Both of these are still standing. Melville House, now in private hands, was for many years a residential school, while the Nicolson Square house, much altered, is divided into flats above a shop.

William Leslie was the 6th and 5th Earl's second surviving child. He seems to have been close to his older brother, Alexander (1749–1820), Lord Balgonie, later 7th Earl of Leven and 6th of Melville, whom he generally addresses as 'Bal'. Next came Jane, or 'Jeany' (1753–1829), of whom he also seems to have been fond. The younger children – David (1755–1838), Mary (1757–1820), John (1759–1824), Charlotte (1761–1830) and George Melville (1766–1812) – receive only passing mentions in his surviving correspondence. His first surviving letter, undated, from Perth, is a playful note to 'Bal' about servants and home life.

139

William entered the Army as an Ensign in the 42nd Foot (Black Watch) on 3 May 1770, three months before his nineteenth birthday. The regiment was then stationed in the north of Ireland. He described violent attacks by the 'Hearts of Steel', Protestant tenant farmers protesting against evictions and economic hardship, and riots in the Dublin Parliament caused by the depression in linen manufacture. His letters from Ireland are dominated by his social activities: not only taking tea with young ladies, but also compassionately sitting up all night to watch over the dying Alexander MacKay.

In June 1773, frustrated by lack of promotion in his own regiment, and by what he believed to be the dilution of its national character, William Leslie purchased a lieutenancy in the 17th Foot. His commission was dated from 12 July that year. The 17th had arrived in Ireland only four months previously, after two years in Scotland. Leslie made friends with the younger officers, especially Sir Alexander Hepburn-Murray, Bt, of Balmanno and Blackcastle, and William Armstrong, both of whom he seems to have known from Edinburgh, and Marcus Antony Morgan, a young Irishman.

1
William Leslie to his brother Lord Balgonie

To Lord Balgonie
Melvill   Perth thurs 2 °Clock

D[r] Bal:
Papa has sent back Paterson[3] to wait on the stables in which
employment he is [to] wear his livery coat & to appear every way
as a gentleman servant, if you will order him to wash the open
Chaise, he will drive it with one of the old mares, so I think as to
Chaise, Driver & Horse you will be very well equipped, & in no
danger of breaking your neck; we have got a droll genius in his
place, about 4 foot high, he does not appear to be much older than
Paterson. He will tell you we had a good journey as far –
Remember me to all with you; tell Jeany[4] not to go to my room
with a candle as there is a good deal of scattered powder on the
floor I wish you would see if rover would make love to Maggs a
fine breed[5]

   Ever yours my D[r] Bal –
    With love & regard
     W[m] Leslie, 42[d] R[t].

Grandmama[6] was here all last night went away before 5 this
morning excuse haste –

Leven and Melville Papers, NAS, GD 26/9/513/2

2
William Leslie to his brother Lord Balgonie

To The Right Honble
The Lord Balgony
Edinr
[via] Port Patrick[7]   Belfast Feb[ry] 16th
                                                               1771

My Dearest Bal,
Now I am in a settled habitation I intend to write punctually & to
answer every letter as I receive it, please peace free of all debts of

that kind at present only W^{lie} Sinclairs[8] which I will answer very soon. Nothing extraordinary going on here. The Hearts Steell[9] are all come back to the Country, it is thought they will kick up a Dust again, but dont speak of that as it will make mama uneasy; they fired 4 days ago at a sergeant of ours & a constable walking together & wounded the constable. I go to one Mr. Knox's house the beginning of the week to stay two or three days along with C^t. Murray[10] our commanding Officer; Mr. Knox[11] is a great friend of Col^l. Monnypenny,[12] by that means we got acquaint at a Fandango[13] he was very civil to me, invited me to his house about ten Miles from Belfast & promised me the lend of a horse to hunt whenever I chose; We dont think half so much of going 10 or a dozen miles here, as of going to Musselburgh or Dalkieth from Edin^r. Was at Carrick Fergus on Monday saw Scotland from the top of the tower & my heart leapt for joy, I daresay papa has been there. Tireing much to hear from some of my Friends, it is ten days Since I received a letter, but have the consolation to think you are all well or else somebody would have had the compassion to write. Was at Church last Sunday, heard Mr. M^claggan[14] our Parson he is a good honest Man, not the best best Preacher in the world; him & I mess together – at Breakfast, he is to learn me Earse.[15] Campbell[16] will tell you how he cheated him out of the room which I have in the Barrack. I was very near being genteelly humbugg'd, last night I had been invited to drin[k] tea with a young lady; after I was dr[essed] & ready to sally, rec^d. a card from the [lady] with an excuse that she could not see me that night, I sat down to write a letter, a very short time after, a gentleman who had promised to shew me the house called for me, & I shewed him the card, he said it was certainly a hum, for he had seen the Lady just before & she said nothing about it, so away we went & got Miss Hambleton[17] with six or seven more young ladies just beginning to tea, having rec^d. a card in my name that it was not in my power to wait on her; Found out next day that it was some of the rest of the Belfast ladies who envied her the happiness of having me to drink tea with her.

my Kindest Love wait on my Dear Father, Mother & all the rest of my Dr Friends God grant you all, health & happiness. As I go to Mr. Knox's, probably can't write again till thursday or friday, wrote Jeany[18] on tuesday or Weden: write me how Campbell is, if he is arrived &c. Best Comp[ts] to our Sunday night friends Mr. & Mrs. Hogg[19] Granny Erskine[20] &c.

Yours most affect[ely] W[m] Leslie

I intended to have wrote 3 or 4 letters with this, but could not get it done –

NAS, GD 26/9/513/24

3
William Leslie to his brother Lord Balgonie

To
The Right Honble
The Lord Balgonie
Edinburgh
[via] Port Patrick[21]
                                                        Belfast March 1st
                                                        1771

My Dear Bal,

I had the pleasure of your long letter from H. House.[22] how happy should I have been to have popt in, some day while you were at Dinner or running up & down with the Children – Very sorry to hear of poor Bel's[23] being so ill, hope he is quite recovered by this time, I will write him in two days. If you dont send me franks,[24] it will cost you fifty times more than my letters are worth, Irish Franks don't pass in Scotland – The Parliament[25] has met & the ministry have 25 of majority. There was a riot at Dublin, pulled the members out of their Chairs broke noses, gave blue eyes[26] & tossed their wigs in the air &c.[27] How does D[d] Home do after his ducking, it was an excellent story; I wonder if He has said the Creed since.[28] I wrote my Father that our quarters were to be at Killough, but they are altered since to Carrick Fergus. C[t]. Murray who brought the two Companies from Drogheda, will be obliged to pay for the mens quarters here, out of his own pocket as the Government have refused it. It seems the G[t]:[29] never allows quarters when troops are sent to quell riots. will be very hard on Murray about 40 £ –

hope all my Dear friends are well, remember me affec^{tly} to them all r^d. Mama's letter yesterday will answer it whenever I hav[e] any thing worth writing. I g[ot] one Newspaper ~~yesterday~~ [. . .] night ago but never anothe[r] be much obliged to you if [? you could] get them sent regularly [. . .] you heard of Burgess —³⁰

> Believe how much I am my
> Dear Bal's most faithfull
> and affe^{ct}. Brother
> Wm Leslie 42^d R.

NAS, GD 26/9/513/23

4
William Leslie to his brother Lord Balgonie

To
The Right Honble
The Lord Balgonie
Cupar Fife
Scotland
[via] Donaghadee   Galway Novr. 24th
                                                            1772

My Dear Bal,

I had the pleasure of a short Epistle from you since your arrival at Melvill, hope you feel no bad effects from your fall; suppose before this reaches you, Nicolsons park³¹ will enjoy your Company – I am in very low spirits at which you won't be surprised when you hear the reason; In a letter I wrote my Mother some Posts ago I mentioned being much with Capt Mackay³² who was not very well, little did I think then how near he was to his end; how uncertain is the fate of us poor Mortals: On tuesday last he went out in a Chair for Exercise in order to promote sleep of which he had none for some nights, I sat with him till nine °Clock, about twelve he was taken very ill with a raging fever, obliged to be held down by four Men. I went in to him about 10 on Wedensday forenoon, he was then a little Calmer, he said, Son (he always called me his son) take the key of my Scritore [*sic* escritoire] & give it to my Wife; after that he never was sensible, raved without intermission; I stay'd with him mostly, till three next morning; it was equally affecting to see him & his wife; I came to him again at ten, he had been worse; staid with him most of the day, and till seven saturday morning when he expired. He has left a widow without anything, luckily no Children; Miss Winepress, who I daresay my Father remembers,[33] showed a great deal of Compassion & goodness of temper; after staying with her most the whole time of his illness, she carried her to her fathers, who is a very respectable old man & liked by everybody. I have lost my friend & companion, one who realy behaved as a parent to me. How affecting it is to see a man hurried out of the world without a moments warning, and how much more so to see one for whom you have a real esteem; it is an awefull lesson to those left behind. He was buried yesterday. Pardon this letter I can write of nothing else while I think of it –

May God grant you, my Dr Mother many many happy returns of this m[onth][34]

It may be said that Officers feed on one anothers bodies. You may tell my father that L^t. Robertson[35] of whom I wrote him lately will probably get the Capt. Lieut^{cy}, the oldest Ensign, (Graham)[36] his Lieut^{cy}, in which case the next Ensign[37] & myself will have purchases immediately, there are already two Ensigns in view –

I have got my mare in pretty good order & ride every good day –

Believe me yours, My Dr Brother,

with sincerest Affection Wm Leslie 42nd R^t.

Don't forget Kindest Love to all with you.

NAS, GD 26/9/513/22

5
William Leslie to his father Lord Leven

To
The Right Honble
The Earl of Leven
Melvill House
by Edinburgh
[via] Donaghadee[38]
[In Lord Leven's hand: 'Willie's Lt.cy June 73']   Dublin June 8th
                                                                      1773

I hope my Dear Father will not be displeased at my accepting a
Lieutenancy in the 17th Regt., without first consulting him, as
there was not time granted for writing & receiving an Answer, the
Regt. does not go abroad for a long time, it has the name of being a
very good Corps & I know a number of the Officers, all which
considered I hope will plead my Excuse. No doubt you will be
surprised at this; Our memorial was to have been presented at the
Kings Birth day,[39] that morning before the Levee the under
secretary sent for me & told me that it was the Lord Lieut.s[40]
intention to give me a Lieutcy in a Regt. then vacant, that the Regt.
would not go abroad for many years and begged immediately to
know if I would accept, which I did – Coll Blacquiere, secretary for
Ireland[41] sent for me yesterday, & told me the same thing, only he
mentioned the 17th Regt., said he was very glad to have it in his
power to show any civility to Lord Leven's son, with whom he was
very well acquainted some years ago & desired to be particularly
remembered to you –

I am very sorry to leave the Highlanders, don't expect to be ever
in so good a Corps of Officers again; I fear it won't be long a
national Corps unless a war happens, for now they put in English
& Irish without Distinction; Our Colonel has not the smallest
Interest & is disliked by the whole – For this exchange I will need
about fifty pounds for Regimentals, accoutrements, Commission
Fees, to carry me clear out of this Regt. & put a little money in my
pocket of which it is perfectly empty at present; I did not chuse to
draw for it till I got your consent; hope by the time I get your

answer the Commission will be arrived. The purchases in the Reg^t. go on as before, Lord Balcarres's[42] Ensign gets the first; the other is not yet fixed but Major Murray[43] say's he will give a final Answer in ten days at farthest –

By report the 5th R^t. has had a Shocking Affair on their march at Longford, a Grenadier who had kill[ed a] man there was taken up & confined in the goal [*sic* gaol], the rest of the Grenadiers attempted to rescue their Comrade & attack'd the goal [*sic*] with their arms, they repulsed their officers who came to quell them; at last the Officers were obliged to get the Battalion companies & fired upon the grenadiers two or three of whom were killed, before they would desist. I don't doubt but it is represented much worse than it happened – We hear Lord Rosebery is to be married to Miss Barbara Montgomery;[44] Miss Montg: is to be married immediately to a rich Mr. Gardiner,[45] so you may tell Mary,[46] that M^r. Montgomery[47] will get quit of three plagues in a very short time.[48] –

Kindest Love where due. In haste my Dr Father

Your most affec^{te} Son

W^m. Leslie 42^d R^t.

NAS, GD 26/9/513/21

2 America

The 17th Regiment was inspected in Kilkenny in May 1774, before marching to Clare Castle. By June the following year, it was in Galway, and then marched to Athlone.[49] However, William Leslie's hopes that the regiment would not be going abroad for some time were confounded by the outbreak of hostilities in the American colonies in April 1775. The 17th sailed from Cork on 3 October 1775. Contrary winds hindered the voyage, but at New Year, the 17th arrived in Boston, where William was reunited with his father's half-brother, Lieutenant-Colonel Alexander Leslie,[50] 64th Regiment, commander of the garrison at Castle William in Boston Harbour. As Colonel Leslie wrote to Lord Leven on 7 January 1776:

> Willie is at last arrived after being 14 Weeks at Sea, he looks thin, but we must fatten him with Salt Pork and Pease, for he must have starved on board.[51]
>
> Major Goodenough[52] tells me he is by this time a Captain, I wish it may be so, at all counts he must soon, for he is Eldest Lieutenant, and promotion may soon be rapid amonst us – I expect the next summer will bring those people to their duty by <u>force</u>, for if they don't get a Bleeding, they'll ever be insolent, I know them from near eight years experiency –[53]

In March 1776 the 17th was withdrawn, with the rest of the British troops, from Boston to Halifax, Nova Scotia, until June. It was there that William Leslie was promoted Captain.[54] The regiment was included in General Howe's expedition against New York. On 3 July the troops landed on Staten Island. The 17th, 40th, 46th and 55th Regiments formed General Grant of Ballindalloch's 4th Brigade. Since Lord Balgonie was now on his Grand Tour, Captain Leslie related his experiences on campaign to his parents.

The battle of Long Island on 27 August seems to have been Captain Leslie's first experience of a major action. Writing to his father, he did not hide his distress at encountering the corpse of his friend Sir

Alexander Hepburn-Murray, 'tore by a cannon ball'. He also wrote of the fire in New York and of the capture of Fort Washington. A couple of remarks criticising the performance of Hessian allies at White Plains were deleted. It is impossible to be certain whether this was self-censorship, external censorship imposed by a superior officer before the letters were sealed, or perhaps the work of the recipients, for the sake of posterity.

On Christmas Day, Captain Leslie wrote to his mother with news of an old friend Dr Benjamin Rush (1745/6–1813) of Philadelphia. As a medical student in Edinburgh in 1767, Rush had been introduced to the family by Thomas and Colin(a) Hogg. A frequent visitor to the Leslies' Nicolson Square home and to Melville House, he became infatuated with William's adolescent sister Lady Jane, through her singing Mallet's *The Birks of Endermay*. They conducted an innocent romance, nicknaming each other 'Edwin' and 'Angelina', after characters in Goldsmith's poem *The Hermit*.[55] Rush was a close friend of Lord Balgonie, who gave him, before he returned to the Colonies, a ring with the Lord's Prayer on the bezel, and the date on which he had left Melville House inside the band. Now they were enemies: Rush had signed the American Declaration of Independence and was serving as a surgeon with the Rebels' Continental Army.

6
William Leslie to his father Lord Leven
Bedford Long Isl^d

Septr 2nd 1776

My Dearest Father

Now that we have got a little Revenge I can write with more Satisfaction than when the Rebels were insulting us on all hands with Impunity; My last letter mentioned I believe that we soon expected to take Field. On the 22^d. of Augt. the whole Army, except 3000 Hessians who were left to defend Staaten Island, made a Descent upon Long Island in Flat Boats & landed on the South Side without opposition, encamped at Denises [*sic* Denyse], Gravesend, Utrecht &c – On the 26th Our Brigade (viz the 4th) commanded by Major Genl. Grant[56] & the Brigade on our Right (the 6th) commanded by B. Genl. Agnew[57] rec^d. Orders to be in readiness to March at night in one Division, marched at ten o Clock pm. Denises along Shore as marked in a small Chart which I send by way of Explanation. The rest of the Army marched I believe at the same time in the two Colomns some miles on our right, but they were at such a Distance and a Private Officer has so little opportunity of knowing the Particulars of any Action that does not happen under his own eye, that I shall mention nothing but what I saw.

Our Reg^t. marched in the front by files the advanced guard consisted of a Capt. 2 Sub^{ns}. & 50 Privates; on our right we had 2 Comp^{ys} composed of People who made their escape f^m. New York, they scoured the Woods & hedges; the Sea secured our left; about 12 °Clock they fell in with the Rebels advanced Piquet, out of which 7 were killed & several wounded, a few of our Men & Yorkers were wounded; a little after, our Reg^t. was detached round a Wood where a Party of the Rebels were supposed to be lurking, we were challenged by a Sentry and upon not answering rec^d. a smart fire without doing us much harm we return'd the fire but with what success is impossible to know, for it was quite dark; We took a number of Prisoners amongst the rest a Major & some Officers all Riffle Men, joined the Brigades and lay on our Arms till Day Light. I never wish to be concerned in a night attack a second time, of all things I think, it is the most to be dreaded when the Nature of the ground, & the number & disposition of the Enemy are not known, if we had had a regular Enemy to deal with every man of the two Brigades must have been cut off or taken – At 5 °Clock we began our March again, and about 7 perceived the Rebels within Musquet Shot drawn up to a great Extent on the top of a rising Ground with every advantage they could wish; their Right extended to a Marsh over which they could retreat under some Cannon, their left was covered with a very thick Wood in which were innumerable Riffle men; it is supposed there were two Lines in the Rear to support their main Body; in their Front were two Field Pieces, and all the Bushes, Hedges, Trees and Hollows were lined with Rifflers. Our Disposition was very soon made, Genl. Grant ordered the 6th Brigade to form up on a rising Ground on the Right, during their forming two field Pieces & a Howitzer fired incessantly at the Rebels, some Grape Shot dislodged them from the Bushes &c next our Front & from which they fired at our Reg^t. at a few Yard's Distance; The 17th was ordered to advance to a house 70 or 80 Y^{rds} in our Front, the other three Reg^t.s of the 4th Brigade took up the Ground betwixt our Reg^t. & 6th Brigade; when we took Possession of the Ground at the House my Comp^y. was sent as a Reinforcement to the advanced Guard who were much incommoded by Rifflers from behind the hedges; During all this time Showers of Grape were tumbling among us which wounded some of our men. Thank God neither myself nor one of my Comp^y. were touched the whole Day, altho in the direct line of Fire. A few Minutes after I joined the advanced Guard I was told Sir Alex^r. Murray[58] was killed & Lieut. Morgan[59] wounded, my two most intimate Friends! I never was so shock'd in my Life, but at that time was too much engaged to give way to it After the Action when I saw the Corps of my beloved Friend lying on the Ground tore by a Cannon Ball, it is impossible to describe my own anguish or the melancholly appearance of the whole Reg^t., for he was every Man's Friend, the darling of the Soldiers, respected & regretted by those even who did not know him personally. The joy of a complete Victory did not throw off the Gloom & I feel a Blank which will take a long time to fill up; excuse this melancholy Subject, but imparting what ones heart is full of, whether Grief or Joy, to a friend who I am sure will sympathise certainly eases the mind of some part of its Burthen; what will his poor Mother & Sisters feel![60] – But to return to the Battle, a little after poor Murrays fate the Fire ceased by Degrees & the Rebels began to retreat in pretty good Order across the Marsh on their right, at last a CompY of Grenadiers appearing in their Rear a Panick siezed them & they took to a precipitate Retreat without the least Order; Shoals of them run over the Marsh, vast numbers took to the Woods. During this Engagement the 17th and part of the 40th only were engaged of the 4th Brigade; of the 6th Brigade the 23rd & 44th only; the 17th S.A.M.[61] & 2 Men were killed, 20 Wounded;[62] 40th L[t] Col[l] Grant[63] killed & two or three Men wounded;[64] 23rd 16 Men wounded;[65] 44th Cap[t]. Brown[66] & L[t]. Brown[67] & 2 or 3 Men wounded[68] – We took in the Course of the Day 370 Prisoners 2 L[t] Col[ls]., 1 Major and a great number of other Officers, 2 Field Pieces & Amunition Waggon; Their <u>Gen[l]. Lord Stirling</u>[69] was also taken – So much for Gen[l]. Grants Victory; When we had time to breath and rest ourselves a little after being on foot for 12 Hours, we heard by the noise of Cannon & small Arms that another Part of the Army were engaged at Brookland about three Miles from us, & had the pleasure to learn soon after, that the Rebels were forced behind their Lines with great Loss – The Loss of the Rebels it is confidently said amounts to about 3,000 killed wounded & Prisoners; Ours at the Most to 30 killed, 300 slightly wounded & 30 Prisoners. Gen[l]. O'Sullivan is likewise taken, once Pres[t]. of the Continental Congress.[70] The Rebel Lines at Brookland are so strong that the General thought it necessary to make regular aproaches; accordingly on the night of the 28th Inst. the Trenches were opened, but they did not think proper to wait the issue of a regular attack, so took the advantage next night of a thick Fog to retreat to New York and left us in Possession of all their Works & cannon on this Side. The Day after their Retreat we had orders to March to the Ground we are now encamped on, near the Village of Bedford; It is now a fortnight we have lain on the Ground wrapt in our Blankets, and thank God who supports us when we stand most in need, I never enjoyed better health in my Life, My whole Stock consists of 2 Shirts 2 p. of Shoes, 2 Handcurchefs, half of which I use, the other half I carry in my Blanket, like a Pedlars Pack. Gen[l]. L – in good Health; I saw ~~Roschill~~[71] on Staaten Island; I suppose Uncle has wrote you of him; W Carnegie[72] was in good health on board Lord Howes Ship[73] when we came here. The Chart is so small that I'm afraid you will not be able to make anything of it; when I made it I never thought of putting it to this use or should have done it on a larger Scale – I had to beg a Sheet of paper from several People, as you may see by the difference of Size & Sort, not quite certain if I can procure as much wax as will seal it –

Kindest Love to my D[r]. Mother, Brothers & Sisters God bless you all –

Ever believe me my D[rest] Father with the sincerest Affec[n].

Your dutifull Son

W[m] Leslie

Sep[r]. 3rd.

NB Instone who you remember was married to a Lathem [*sic* Letham] Girl beg'd I would let her Friends know that she was dead.[74]

NAS, GD 26/9/513/16–17

7

A Chart of the Entrance to New York from Sandy Hook (drawn by William Leslie, with key)

a –   The place where our Reg.[t] landed Aug.t 22.nd

B –   The Road the 4th & 6th Brigades marched on the night of Aug.t 26.th & where we fell in with the advanced Piquet of the Rebels.

C –   The Wood to which our Reg.[t] was detached & where we were fired upon –

D   The Spot from which we first perceived Rebel Army drawn up on a rising Ground.

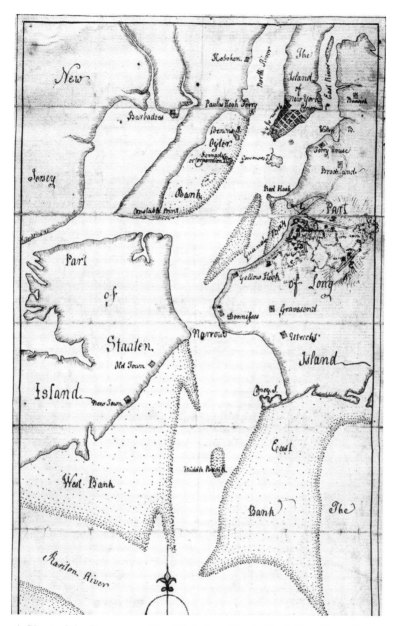

A Chart of the Entrance to New York from Sandy Hook (detail), as drawn by William Leslie. (National Archives of Scotland)

E The rising Ground on which Gen[l] Grant formed the 6th Brigade with 2 Field Pieces in their front –

F The Rebel army drawn up on a hill two field Pieces in their Front –

G Where my Comp.[y] was sent to reinforce the advanced Guard –

H The Houses to which the 17.th were sent to in front of which we drew up –

I The Ground which the other three Reg.[ts] of the 4th Brigade took up betwixt the right of the 17.th & left of the 6.th Brigade.

L Morass over which the Rebels retreated –

o A Piece of Cannon from which they fired at us often –

–

——

–

D Our Field Pieces & Howitzers planted on a small Eminence above our Reg.[t] –

–

——

–

–

——

–

Red Hook is strongly fortified & their lines run all along from the Marsh to Brookland; Governors Island is also very strong, but all these they have abandoned and our Victory is as complete as could be wished & with much less loss than could possibly have been expected –

Key: NAS, GD 26/9/513/1; Chart: RHP 85408

8
William Leslie to his father Lord Leven

To
The Earl of Leven
Edinburgh
N. Britain[75]
[stamped: Portsmouth Ship]

Septr 25th 1776
York Island

My Dear Father

In my last I gave you an account of our success on Long Island, and have now the Satisfaction of telling you that we have taken the Town & greatest part of the Island of New York, we landed under cover of the Shipping, without opposition, altho the Rebels might have made a very great Defence as they had high Grounds, Woods, and strong Breastworks to cover them, but they scoured off in thousands when the ships began to Fire; Indeed they are so outgeneraled that it is impossible for them to know where to prepare for Defence. From Genl Howe's Motions, they thought he would attempt to land at a Place call'd Harlem, & there threw up strong Redoubts & entrenched themselves up to their Chins, but he gave them the Slip & landed two Miles farer down the river, even there they were infinitely superior to us in Numbers, but the Rogues have not learnt manners yet, they cannot look Gentlemen in the Face altho we give them a Lesson now & then; this happy Event happened on the 16th ^{76} Inst., next day the Light Inf^y. had like to have suffered severely, for some companies inadvertantly pursued a Party of the Rebels too near their Works, from whence vast numbers sallied out, (8000 as we are told since by Deserters) Genl L.^{77} who commands the Lt Inf^y went immediately with two of his Battalions to assist them, the Grenadiers & 42^d Reg^t were sent to support them and the whole Army was on the March in case of Need, but it was all over befor we got half way, they were beat into their Lines; on our Side about 70 or 80 killed and wounded, some Officers wounded; The poor infatuated wretches we took were most all drunk, even the Officers; One of Genl L.^{s} Servants was killed near him; The Rebels have still possession of

157

the strongest ground on Long Island, viz, the north End, about 5 miles in Length; Gen[l] Amherst passing over Kings Bridge last War[78] observed that it was the strongest piece of Ground he had ever seen; Kings Bridge joins York Island to the Continent; upon the most commanding Spot they have erected a regular fortification (Fort Washington) which they think impregnable; on every hill and Hillock there are Redoubts & Lines, so you may suppose if they make any Defence, we will have a very tough p[iece] of work to take it; Gen[l]. Howe has [*torn*] Lines opposite to theirs, as soon as they are finished I suppose he will attack some where else – To shew what an infamous set the Rebels are, they set fire last night to the Town of New York in a number of places at once, as it must have been [a] concerted Plan; several People were seen with lighted Torches, the Soldiers threw one man into the Fire; the most elegant Part of the Town was quite consumed, in all about one third;[79] we are encamped four miles from the Town. Our Friend N. Balfour[80] goes to Britain with the News of our having taken York which will be either a majority or 500 £ in his way, he has been very kind & civil to me. I daresay he will winter in Scotland.

I had one Letter from you dated in April a Duplicate of which Gen[l]. L got, as to [*seal damage*] purchase. I hope you have rec[d]. thoro' Satisfaction on that head as I have wrote twice fully & mentioned it in several Letters besides, I have wrote <u>Mother Jane</u>[81] by this opportunity. I will write mother an Account of next battle.

God bless you all. Kind Love,

Yours my Dr[est] Father w[t]. sincere Aff[n] W.L

NAS, GD 26/9/513/15

9
William Leslie to his father Lord Leven

To
The Earl of Leven,
Edinburgh
North Britain[82]

Kings Bridge
Nov 22nd 1776

Late as the Season is my Dear Father we are still in the Field, carrying on our Successes with more Spirit than ever. Since my last, Gen[l]. How with the greatest part of the Army made a Descent on the Continent up the East River, and landed with very little Loss at a place called Rochelle; our Brigade & two more were left on York Island under the Command of Lord Percy[83] to defend our Lines, for the Rebels were still in Possession of Fort Washington and the north End of the Island, the Fort lies on the North River, opposite to it on the Jersey Shore is Fort Constitution & Fort Lee, all these Forts command the north River, which makes it dangerous for shipping, consequently the General did not chuse to risque the Troops that way; upon landing he marched to white Plains (about 5 miles up the Country) the Light Infantry had a skirmish in which Major Musgrave[84] was wounded, Cap[n] Evelyn[85] killed, & several men killed & wounded; the Army encamped near the Rebels who were in possession of very strong ground, for the tract of Country which is called white Plains is by far the most hilly, rocky ground I have seen in America; the two Army's were divided by a rivulet called Brunx [*sic* Bronx] with high ground on each Side, so that whoever made the attack had the River to pass & the Hills to scramble up; on the 28th Oct[r]. Gen[l] Howe thought proper to attack them, he ordered a Brigade of Hessians, the 2nd Brigade of British (of which Gen[l] Leslie has now the Command) and a Detatchment of Light Horse, to drive them from the nearest Hill, our Artillery played on the Rebels at the same time; [the Hess: after passing the Brunx (whether they thought it a Desperate Attack or what other reason we dont know) did not go on as they ought to have done],[86] upon which G[l] L, with his Brigade, passed them and mounted the Hill with considerable Loss; the Rebels retreated to the Hills much stronger than those they had left, where they entrenched themselves immediately – Col[l] Carr[87] of the 35th Cap[t]. Gore[88] of the 49th and several more were killed and many wounded, 150 or 60 men killed & wounded; my good Uncle escaped unhurt altho always in the thickest fire, the Light Horse behaved vastly well, lost 5 or 6 Horses; the intention of this attack was to get Possession of the Brunx, without which a general engagement could not be attempted with any sort of Safety; to give the Rebels a Diversion on the other Side Lord Percy was ordered to make an attack from his Lines on Y. Is[d].[89] the same Day; he took out 4 Reg[ts] & some Artillery; the Hessians advanced at another Place; on our Artillery playing on their Lines & making a Disposition to attack them, they retired from their lowest Lines; we might have taken Possession of them, but that was not intended, Lord Percy's Orders from the Gen[l] only extended to drawing the attention of the Rebels, during his Attack at White Plains; we kept Possession of Harlem Plains which lie betwixt our & the Rebel lines till next Day & then retired to our old encampment; we lost 5 men. Two days after our Brigade was ordered to join Ge[l]. How immediately, we embarqued in flat Boats next morning at 9 °Clock, about 4 we landed at Rochelle & the same night joined the Army after dark, at 10 °C. we rec[d] orders to be ready for a General Engagement next morning at break of Day; it rained excessive hard the whole night so that we who lay in the open air had most of our amunition spoil'd & ourselves driping wet, notwithstanding w[h] the men were in high spirits eager for the attack; after being under Arms some time waiting for orders, we were desired to dismiss, but to be ready at a moments warning; however there was no attack made & very lucky it was, for the Rebels retreated bag & baggage next night from the Ground we wanted to possess; it is reported that several of the General Officers were against the Attack thinking it too desperate & of too little consequence to risque losing a number of men; most People seem to think that Gen[l]. How's intention was to endeavour to bring the Rebels to a general Engagement in Order to disperse their Army, which if once dispersed will be very difficult to bring together, at least this Season. The Hessians under Gen[l]. Kniphausen[90] before this time had taken possession of the Country betwixt white Plains

& Kings Bridge & stormed Fort ~~Constitution~~ Independance (this commands Kings Bridge); they were ordered to invest Fort Washington which lies on a Hill, the Sides of which are almost perpendicular & if properly defended must cost the Lives of thousands; [During the stay of the Army at White Plains it was thought the Hessians went on very slow.][91] Gen[l]. How brought his Army before Kings Bridge; On Friday the 15th Inst. he summon'd the Fort to surrender, or he would storm it next Day & put every man to the Sword, they returned for answer that they were determined to defend themselves to the last Extremity; the Army immediately received Orders to be ready next Morning for the Attack, the Disposition for which is as follows: Two Brigades of Hessians to attack in one place, the Light Inf[y] & Guards in a second, Grenadiers & 33rd Reg[t] at a third, the 42nd, at a fourth, and lastly Lord Percy was ordered to attack them from his lines on York Island, the rest of the Army to be under Arms; Every thing was ready for the important Event At Day break; About 9 °Clock the Signal was given and the Attack began from all Quarters; the Rebels kept a constant fire with Grape & musquetry from behind rocks and Trees in Spite of which our troops gained the top of the Hill & drove all the Rebels into the Fort; preperations were now making to storm it, during which Gen[l] How again sent to them to surrender, which after some Consultation they did, the only terms they got were their Lives & Officers Baggage; The Prisoners amount to near three thous[d]. The Hessians behaved nobly, I saw their Attack, they advanced in two Colomns and kept the same order altho three six pounders with Grape fired upon them while they scrambled up the Rock; they had 300 Men killed & wounded; You may be sure the British did not behave with a Bit less Spirit; the 42nd had 84 killed and wounded; these were the two most desperate attacks; I have not heard what number the other Troops have lost, but altogether cannot exceed 30; it adds greatly to our Spirits on this happy Affair that we have not lost one British Officer, two or three slightly wounded. By this Victory we have entire possession of York Is[d]. which opens a Communication with the Continent, of the utmost consequence to us, as the Communication by water is froze up in Winter & the Troops would be in want of Forage; besides there is quiet winter Quarters for most of the Army & the Campain finished with Eclat; John Bull would not have been pleased if some great Stroke had not been atchieved – Fort Washington is for the Future to be called Kniphausen in honor of the Hessian General, who advanced at the head of his Troops to within a very short way of the Fort.

24th. We have this instant rec^d orders to march to the Jerseys – On the 20th Inst. about 6000 Troops were sent over to that Shore & performed wonders, they landed without opposition, marched a great way up in the Country, took 30 pieces of Cannon, a vast quantity of military Store, 400 Tents standing, as much Flour as will serve our Army above four Months & plenty of Live Stock; the most valuable part of this Conquest is having Possession of a plentifull Country; I ought to have mentioned that they took Fort Lee the same night – It is probable this will finish the Campaign in this Part of America, but there is an Embarkation of 4 or 5000 Troops now at New York; It is not publickly known where they are destined, but is generally thought for Rhode Island, a very rebellious Province, will be usefull to us on account of the safe Harbours as the Shipping cannot lie here for Shoals of Ice – We March tomorrow Morning at 7 ^{o}Clock for the Jerseys, I suppose to remain there for Winter Quarters – I must finish very abruptly in case the Packet sails tomorrow & I must mount Picket instantly & unexpectedly –

Kindest Love to all
your most affec^{te} Son
Wm Leslie

A respite of two Minutes, if the Packet does not sail in two Days I will write again – As to our Friends, Genl Leslie is in perfect Health & gained a great [deal] of Credit on the 28th of Octr when his Brigade was engaged,[92] is esteemed by every one; I dined with [him] two days ago, he desires kindest Love to you all, if he has not time to write. Genl. Prescot[93] also desires Love, & kisses your hands &c &c John & James Webster & Wife[94] are all in good –

Once more called, so God bless you all –

NAS, GD 26/9/513/13, 14, 12

10
William Leslie to his mother Lady Leven

To
The Right Honble
The Countess of Leven,
Nicolson Square,
Ed^r.
North Britain[95]   Hilsborough Decr. 25th 1776

My Dearest Mother,
I had the Satisfaction of receiving yours & Fathers kind Letters of
July 13th & hope you have forgiven any rash Expression in a Letter
you mention. I can say from my Heart I never intended it as any
reproach on our Indulgent Parents, nor did I ever think it a wrong
Step to stop our Intercourse & only regretted it as the Loss of a
Pleasure we had long enjoyed.

In my last I think was mentioned the taking Fort Washington &
the Excursion into the Jerseys commanded by Lord Cornwallis,[96]
taking an immense quantity of Stores &c &c; Soon after that, our
Brigade & the 2nd, viz G^l L^s.[97] had Orders to Join his Lordship; on
the 27th we crossed over & joined his army, on which he marched
immediately and the Rebels retreated as we advanced; they cut
down the Bridges & gave us all the Molestation they could,
(except fighting) notwithstanding which we were within two
Hours of coming up with the rear of their Army, crossing the
Delaware at Trenton; they took Post on the other side & anoyed us
a little with their Cannon; we took Possession of Trenton which is
only 30 miles from Philadelphia, but the Delaware stoped our
Course, for we had not one Boat nor was there one on our Side for
8 Miles up or down the River; this obliged the Genl. to send us to
winter Quarters; the Hessians have Possession of Burlington
which is only 18 Miles from Philadelphia; it is the general opinion
that as soon as the River is froze up, we shall proceed to Phil: the
Object of our present wishes, and for all the lateness and coldness
of the Season, I believe there is not an Oficer or Soldier who is not
sorry, and much disappointed at not passing the Delaware; We are
quartered here for Winter Quarters, but hope we shall pass parts

of the Winter there. I'm afraid Rush[98] has not only joined the American Cause, but likewise denied Allegiance to his King – Mr. Witherspoon[99] who was President of the College at Princetown is obliged to fly for the same Crime – That famous College is now turned into a Barrack, In short my Dear Mother the Desolation that this unhappy Country has suffered, must distress every feeling heart, altho the Inhabitants deserve it as much as any set of people who ever rebelled against their Sovereign; they lived in plenty even to Luxury, every man was equal to his neighbour & not one beggar in the whole country; but now too late they feell the ravages of war, every day pres[ents] objects of Distress; Protection is offered [by] Lord & Gen[l]. Howe[100] to every individual in Amemerica [*sic*] who comes in, in a certain time; Great Numbers are come in – I must finish this Letter with a piece of good news, the famous Gen[l]. Lee[101] is taken Prisoner by Col[l]. Harcourt son to our good friend my Lord,[102] his Fate is not as yet known, many Conjectures but mine is that Gen[l]. Howe will send to England for Instructions; nobody would begrudge him the Highest Tree in America.[103]

This small town is in the County of Somerset New Jersey, 40 Miles from York –

Thank God I have escaped sickness during a severe Campaign & trust in his goodness that you are all in perfect Health, my best wishes attend you all, praying you a happy new Year & many many of them

> Ever my Dearest Mother
> > with the sincerest affection Your W[m]. Leslie

NAS, GD 26/9/513/11

3 Death and Burial

The same Christmas night that William Leslie wrote to his mother from Hillsborough, Washington and his Continental troops crossed the Delaware. In the early hours of Boxing Day, they launched a surprise attack on the Hessian garrison at Trenton. They captured the post, mortally wounding the commander, Colonel Johann Gottlieb Rall. A week later William Leslie too was dead.

On the morning of 3 January 1777, the 17th Regiment, with part of the 55th, and a troop of 16th Light Dragoons set out from Princeton to join up with General Alexander Leslie at Maidenhead, before heading for Trenton, where Cornwallis had established himself. They did not realise the proximity of the Continental troops, and in the morning mist, the enemy's blue uniforms were initially mistaken for Hessians. Much of the Battle of Princeton took place around Clark's Orchard, south-west of the town. The majority of British killed and wounded were from the 17th Regiment, who fought their way back on to the road. General Leslie learned of the death of the nephew with whom he had dined the previous day.

Dr Benjamin Rush reached Princeton only on 5 January, and found the snow-covered battlefield 'still red in many places with human blood'.[104] He helped tend the wounded of both sides in the town. From prisoners he learned of Willie's death: Captain John McPherson, who had commanded the left of the 17th, and whom he was treating for a lung wound, said, 'Oh! Sir, he loved you like a brother,'[105] and 'that he had heard his friend Leslie say a thousand times that he forgot in me the political enemy in the personal friend.' 'I wept, for the first time, for a victory gained over British troops',[106] Rush wrote on 7 January.

It was the end of February before the Leslies received the first reports of their son's death. As more information gradually reached him from friends and family, Lord Leven compiled a diary paper, *Progress of the Accounts of My Sons Death*. His half-brother, General Alexander Leslie, had felt unable to break the news directly to him. Instead, the General wrote to a distant cousin, Captain John Webster, whose father, Rev. Dr

Alexander Webster, was a well-respected Edinburgh minister and former Moderator of the Kirk. He apologised for this in a letter written from Brunswick on 18 March:

> My D[r]. Brother,
> You must not abuse me for not writing you by the last opportunity, I could not prevail on myself to attempt the melancholy task, I employed M[r]. Webster[107] and Lady Northesk[108] to execute that disagreeable duty.
>   I hope by this time from your own good sense, and desire to acquiesce to the will of Providence, you have in some degree got the better of your Grief, your loss everyone must allow was great, but he fell in a Glorious Cause. My Grief for him, and my feelings for you, my Lady and family is still <u>high in my Mind</u>. I wish it was less, but I must have done on this Subject. a State of his Affairs and of purchase Money due, I shall transmit next opportunity his Watch is in my Possession and his Letters and some other things are to be sent in from the Enemy by the first Flag of Truce.[109]

He was able to furnish him with more information later, from Peter MacDonald, William's regimental servant, in whose arms he had died, and from Dr Rush.[110] He wrote from Staten Island, New York, on 7 July:

> My D[r]. Brother,
> I am honored with yours by the last packet dated 27th March. Yours by the highland drafts not yet come to hand, when it arrives I shall get Dr Rush's Letter forwarded.
>   Our D[r]. friend had 2 Gun shot-wounds in the body, the one in the heart and the other in the same side, but lower down, he had no signs of Life when they were ordered to retreat, this I had from Peter M[c]Donald, who stayed by him the last of anyone, he does not seem desirous to leave the 17th Regiment, and is still an Officers Servant. from what I can learn a Gen[l]. Miflin[111] found the Cart the body was in, and hearing from some of the Prisoners, had great attention paid to his remains. Mifflin is a Philadelphia Quaker and much of the Gentleman, has seen most Courts of Europe. I dont find he was out of the Ranks when he fell, he was on the right of the Battalion, the Serj[t]. that covered him was not hurt, there were but 3 Caps that day under arms, Cap Tew[112] Com[d] in the Center, and the whole Battalion, D[r]. Willie on the Right, and Cap M[c].pherson on

the left, poor M[c].Pherson cant live[113] – Col. Mawhood[114] Com[d]. the
2 Batt[ns]. and some dragoons of the 16th Reg[t].[115]

The impact of his nephew's death also affected the General's response to
the death of another young officer, Captain Hon. John Finch,[116] 1st
Regiment of Foot Guards, killed at Westfield on 20 June. He described
Finch as 'a 2d. Willie . . . a pretty Youth'.[117]

11
Alexander Leslie to Captain John Webster

D.[r] Sir

Poor Willie is no more, his Body was carryed to Pluckimin,[118]
and there inter'd with all Military honors by order of Gen[el].
Washington.

I must beg you to write your Father[119] on this head, so that he
may communicate it in the most delicate Manner to his distressed
Parents.

Poor young man I cant get it out my head, when we parted the
day before, he little thought of what was to happen.

My best Respects to M[rs] Webster[120]
and believe me to be D[r] Sir
your most faithfull
humble servant
A Leslie.

Brunswick
7th Jan[y] – 1777

NAS, GD 26/9/513/10

12
Lord Leven's Diary Paper
Progress of the Accounts of My Sons Death

Friday, Febr. 28.th about 7 in the Evening, S[r]. Ad. Oughton[121] in
the most tender manner gave me reason to believe that my son had

fallen in the Jerseys. Saturdays post brought a Confirmation of it in the Gazette. No letters from my Brother for 10 days. In the greatest Anxiety for the particulars of His Death. The post of Friday March 7th brought a Letter from Archy Erskine[122] to David,[123] with the Accounts of his Body having been put into a Waggon before the Retreat, but in the Confusion of the Retreat the waggon was taken by the Rebels, and that he was interred the next day by orders of G[l]. Washington, with all the Honours of war. This intelligence came to our Army by an Officer & Flag of Truce who Archy Erskine saw & conversed with. No further particulars in that Letter.

On Monday March 10th. Lady O[n][?][124] had a Letter from my Brother, where he says That he fell amongst the first, was shot thro the Body, and did not survive above ten minutes and died in the greatest Composure, and without pain. That a Flag of Truce was ordered to go for the Body, but before he set out an Aid de Camp of G[l]. Washingtons arrived, who informed him that he had been buried at Pluckenheim, by the G[l].s Orders w[t]. all the Honours of War, attended by the provincial officers & our prisoner officers – He incloses a letter from Dr Rush to himself, who says that he had taken the most effectual method to secure what of his Effects His Family might esteem most, & was to give immediate directions to have a Tombstone with an Account of his Rank & merit placed over his Grave in the Country Churchyard where his Remains are deposited.

The same post March 10th brought a Letter from Cap[t]. John Webster to his Father, inclosing One from my Brother to the Cap[t]. desiring him to communicate The Accounts of his Death to M[r]. Webster[125] and says, His Body was carried to Pluckimin and there enterred with all military honours, by Order of G[l]. Washington.

A Letter from Colin Lindsay[126] to S[r]. Adolphus says that he had got leave to [go] along w. the flag of Truce for the Body, when Washingtons aid deCamp arrived. He says that he fell on the first Fire & expired instantly, & that one half of his Company was killed.

Letter from Genl. Leslie, in answer to a particular Enquiry made, 7th July 1777 – Our dear freind had two Gun Shot Wounds in his Body, the One in the Heart, & the other on the same side, lower down, from the first he had no Sign of Life, this I had from peter M^c.donald, his servant who stayed by him, the last of any One – A Genl. Miflin found the Cart the Body was in, and hearing who he was from some of the Prisoners, had great attention paid to his Remains.

I dont find he was too rash, as you seem to fear, or that he was out of the Ranks – He was on the right of the Battalion, The Serj^t. that covered him was not hurt, There were only 3 Capt.s under arms, Capt. Tew in the Center, Dear W^m. in the Right, and Capt. Macpherson in the left, poor M^c.pherson cant live –

NAS, GD 26/9/513/6

13
Lord Leven to Dr Benjamin Rush (draft)

~~My Brother Gl. Leslie having transmitted to me your letter~~ To Dr. Rush, March 1777 –

~~You will~~ Be so good as to accept of the very gratefull Acknowledgements of two persons, who you have laid under the greatest Obligations The parents of _____ of the 17th. by The friendly and generous Attention you have been pleased to show to The memory of their Dear Son. In the midst of our deep afliction, it has been a matter of great Consolation that you wer in a part of the Country where you had an opportunity of giving so strong a prooff of your Frindship to this Family. Lady L. & every ~~Individual~~ Branch of it join in assuring you of the Continuance of The great Regard they always had for you & I am w^t. Gratitude & much Esteem

Y^r. Most obliged humble Servt.

NAS, GD 26/9/513/4

14
Lieutenant William Armstrong,[127] 17th Foot, to his sister
(transcribed by Lord Leven)

Extract of a Letter
from Lieut. Armstrong,
17th Reg[t]. Foot

Lieut Armstrong after giving an acc[t]. of the Engagement of the 3rd. Jan[y], adds –
You will forgive my Dwelling so long on this Subject, But I own I am not a little vain of it, nor would I on any Consideration have been absent when the Reg[t]. was engaged – But my pleasure was not unmixt with pain – The Distress I felt on the Death of my much valued friend Capt. Leslie (who fell on the first fire) cast such a Damp on my Spirits that I was for some time insensible to every Object around me. A more amiable Young man never existed, Now that he and Sir A Murray[128] are gone, I have no particular Intimates in the Reg[t]. – Altho I am happy to say, that – with every one I am on the best footing.

But these were the Companions of my Early Years, my Schoolfellows – On their friendship I could depend, but they are now no more – ! – Nor need even a Soldier be accused of weakness in dropping a tear to the memory of such friends. They fell honourably – fighting for their King & country and if we may judge from the Conduct of their Lives they are now happy – Grudge not a tear my Dear Sister to the memory of two as worthy young men as ever breathed – who possesed every manly virtue that ever filled the human Breast – than whom as none ever lived more Beloved – so none ever died more regretted –

NAS, GD 26/9/513/5

15
John Belsches[129] to his father-in-law, Lord Leven

To The Earl of Leven
Melvill
Cupar Fife[130]   Edinburgh 21 May 1777

I have been made happy by being informed by Several letters to Lady Jane, that your Lor[h]. and all the family got safe home, & continued in good health. The enclosed, for Lady Leven, came today, I suppose it will inform that Lord B.[131] is in good health as his letter to me mentions nothing to the contrary she proposes making a trip to Portsmouth about this time: This good Town affords no news – Mr. Wardrobe[132] who was surgeon to the 17th is come here, tho' I have not conversed with himself yet I have had every information that he can give relative to the fall of our lamented dear freind his account exactly corresponds with what we have heard before, Wardrobe was not with him but at about a hundred yards distance in the rear & could be of no service, as he no sooner received the shot than he instantly expired without a groan, the only motion he made was to give his watch to his servant, who put the body on a baggage cart & conducted it for a considerable time in spite of a very heavy fire from the Enemy but at last he was obliged to abandon it & follow the regt. or must have given himself up as prisoner to the provincials which wd. have served no good purpose – Wardrobe's account of the affair is that the 17 & 56 [*sic* 55][133] were on their march from Princetown to join a detachment of the army at Trentown when they were about a mile and a half from the former the advanced guard discovered a body of Americans which tho' superior in number Coll. Mawhood had no doubt of defeating, however he went himself to reconoitre them & discovered their vast superiority in numbers w[h]. made him wish to retreat to the Town from whence he had come but this he found impossible as the Enemy were so near, Their was a rising ground which commanded the country about half a mile back & about a quarter of a mile off the road this he wished to gain & drew up the two regts with 50 light horse on one flank & (50,) who were dismounted), on the other; The Americans endeavoured also to gain this rising ground & their first Column reached the one side of it rather before the two regts. got to the other, so that first when the 17th reached the top they received the fire of this column composed of about 2000 men by which all the mischief was done. The 56 (who w^d not advance in a line with the 17th in spite of Coll. Mawhood frequently calling out to Capt. [134] who commanded them to mind his orders & come up) as soon as they saw such a slaughter among the first rank of the 17th, immediately run off, on their commanding officer saying it was all over with the others; The 17th returned a very well levelled fire ag^t. the provincial col.^m & instantly leaped over some rails which were bet[wixt] them & charged them w^t. their bayonets upo[n them] tho' ten times their number almost, they ru[n] off & retreated to the other col.^ms of the rebels four in number, & consisting of 2000 men each when the provincials first fired they were about 25 paces he thinks from the 17th & is certain they were not above 30. Upon the whole rebel army advancing, the 17th Regt. & the 50 light horse who were mounted, (& who behaved very well) retreated as fast as possible leaving their killed & wounded, when Washington came up he assured Capt. McPherson & the other wounded that their was not a private man in that regt. but should be used like an officer on account of their gallant behaviour – The 56th run off in the greatest confusion to Princetown – the 40th who were left to guard Pr.^{tn} never came up with the 17, Altho' Col. Mawhood sent for them as soon as he suspected the strength of the enemy. So far as to what relates to the 17 my paper will admit of no more.

All here are in good health & desire to be kindly remembered to all at Melvill.

I Ever am Yours most sincerely, Belsches

NAS, GD 26/9/513/8

4 Commemoration

Tributes to William Leslie from outwith the family were varied. As early as 12 March 1777, an unsigned letter of condolence was written to Lord Leven from Ayr:

> The Death of gallant Captt Leslie has been sensibly felt, by all his Acquaintances: & the manner of his Death, entitles his Memory to be embalmed in the breasts even of those who never saw him. Upon the first notice of so great a Price paid for the late signal Honour of the 17th Regiment; my Heart was deeply pierced for the Sufferings of his aged surviving Mother; & other anxious Friends.[135]

The Biblical tone and content suggest the anonymous author may have been a minister, possibly – given an allusion to God as 'that All-seeing Eye' – a fellow Mason. Alternately, the Ayr provenance may indicate a connection with John Webster's in-laws. The writer implied that William's early death had spared him future miseries:

> Not a Sparrow can fall to the Ground, without the Knowledge of our Father; and by him, the very Hairs of our Head are numbered. he knew, he ordained the seasonable Fall of the Man of Valour; the young, bold, righteous man, in his Countrys Cause; and though seasonable for him, yet most justly to be deplored by all the friends as a most promising Virtue. Who can say, what numberless & great Evils, by this early, easy stroke, the Mercy of Heaven may have removed him from? At any Rate, as dismission from this poor World, in the very Exercise of painful Duty; & after setting out to that Dismission, in such a manner as to be endeared to the most capable Judges both of Heroism and other Excellencies; could never be premature. Wisdom is the Grey-Hairs to a Man; & an unspotted Life is old Age. This single thought, of living much in a small Compass of Time; taken together with the glorious Gospel Assurances; are fully sufficient to extract the bitterness out of that late Cup.[136]

Samuel Martin (1740–1829), minister of Monimail parish and brother of the artist David Martin who painted several Leslie portraits, planned to publish verses on Captain Leslie's death. He wrote on 14 March 1778: 'I would have liked to have embalmed the Memory'.[137] He was dissuaded from publication by the family, although Lord Leven agreed to accept manuscript copies. As he replied on 17 March:

> The family is very much obliged to you for taking the trouble to committ to writing what you think most proper to say on that part of the subject where we are interested, but I must repeat, that it cannott be agreeable to Lady L—— to be desired to give her advice on so delicate a Subject . . . It will give us great pleasure to have a fair Copy of what concerns our poor son, to give Copies of to his Friends who will be very happy to have his memory recorded.[138]

What survives in the Leven and Melville Papers is a map, inscribed with a rhyming couplet.

16
Inscription by Rev. Samuel Martin

An Accurate Plan of the Country between New York and Philadelphia;
With the Disposition of the Forces
Extracted from the Gazette of Tuesday, Feb[y]. 25th [1777]

Here Leslie fell, the gentle & the brave;
And Rush, the generous Foe, wept o'er his grave.

S.M.

NAS, GD 26/9/515

17
Dr Benjamin Rush to Alexander Leslie
Philadelphia Augst 20th: 1778.

Sir/
I beg you would accept of my most grateful Acknowledgements for your polite Attention to my request in favor of Lieut. Hall.[139] You have laid me under the most lasting Obligations to you. But I cannot inform you of the happiness you have communicated to all his relations in any words so strong as those you will find in the enclosed letter written by Mr. Hall immediately After he reached his father's house. –

I am happy in being able to inform you that no expenses were incurred by the funeral honors that were paid to your nephew Capt: Leslie. They were generously given by General Washington upon hearing that he was my friend. I claim the privelidge of erecting a tombstone over him as a mark of my Affection for him & his worthy family. The following is a copy of an epitaph I have ordered to be inscribed upon his tombstone. –

In memory of the
Honble William Leslie Esqr
Second Son of the Right Honble
The Earl of Leven
He fell January 3rd 1777 in the 26th year of his age
at the Battle of Princetown.

Forbear, traveller, to insult his Ashes
Although his country and his profession
made him the enemy of America,
Yet his education, and disposition
made him the
Friend of Virtue

His political enemy, but personal friend
Benjamin Rush M.D. of Philadelphia
hath caused this Stone to be erected as a mark

of his esteem for his <u>worth</u>
and Affection for his
<u>Virtues.</u>

When you write to Lord Leven, I beg you would do me the honor of asuring his Lordship and all the branches of his amiable family of the continuance of my friendship for them.

Mr Hall will not fail of taking the most effectual Steps for refunding the money you so kindly advanced to enable him to pay for his board when he left new york. –

I am Sir with the greatest respect for your character, and the sincerest gratitude for your goodness to my kinsman your most Obed^t Hble Servant

B. Rush.

NAS, GD 26/13/678

As another well-wisher wrote to Lord Leven on 7 January 1779:

> the particulars of Dr Rush's attention to the memory of your very dear Son . . . do much credit to the tender feelings of Dr Rush as well as to the politeness of General Washington. Such strong proofs of respect from political Enemies cannot fail to be pleasing to your Lordship & family, tho they make your wounds bleed afresh for the death of so promising a youth.[140]

However, Rush's erection of the headstone was delayed until peacetime, lest the churchyard suffer any disturbance. It was finally raised in 1784, and still stands. With the end of hostilities, Rush modified the text to commemorate only their friendship:

In Memory of
the Honble Captn WILL^M. LESLIE
of the 17th *British Regiment*
Son of the Earl of Leven
in Scotland

The grave of Capt William Leslie at Pluckemin, New Jersey.
(Photo: Glenn Valis)

He fell Jan[y]. 3[d]. 1777 Aged
26 Years at the battle of
Princeton
His friend Benj[n]. Rush M.D. of
Philadelphia
hath Caused this Stone
to be erected as a mark
of his esteem for his WORTH
and of his respect for his noble family.

To Lady Jane, Dr Rush – like her, now married to another – sent a more personal memorial of her brother. In the back of a miniature portrait of his wife, Julia Stockton, he had set a picture in hair-work, depicting himself showing William's grave to Jane, beside a symbolic weeping willow. The figure of the doctor was made from his own hair, and that of the lady from the lock of her hair which he had kept for seventeen years since he had left Scotland.[141]

By the mid-nineteenth century, a romantic legend had developed in which Dr Rush, who did not, in fact, reach Princeton until two days *after* the battle, was present on the battlefield, and personally arranged and attended his friend's funeral. This myth was derived from John Trumbull's painting *The Death of General Mercer at the Battle of Princeton* (Yale University Art Gallery), which telescopes time and space to depict several incidents from the battle simultaneously: Rush and Washington gallop on to the scene just as Captain Leslie collapses at the right side of the canvas. Variants of the story even claim that Rush had arrived in time to tend his friend's wounds.[142] William Henry Leslie-Melville (1788–1856), third son of Alexander, the 7th Earl,[143] made the following note about his uncle's burial in 1844; again, it inaccurately places Rush with Washington on the battlefield, and makes him directly responsible for the burial.

18
Note by William Henry Leslie-Melville on his uncle's burial

Hon. William Leslie

Hon[ble] W[m]. Leslie 2[d] son of David.. Earl of Leven & 5th Earl of Melville Killed at . . . .

Just after he fell Genl. Washington & staff rode up & enquired what officers were killed. On Capt. Leslie's name being mentioned D[r]. Rush who accompanied Washington shewed great emotion having formerly received great kindness from Lord Levens family when studying medicine at Edinburgh. He caused the body to be removed to the rear had it interred & erected a monument with suitable inscription over it.

Last year (in 1843) I sent £10 to Professor Ogilvie of . . . College New Jersey to repair the monument which is at . . . in that State.

William Leslie Melville
17th. Sept. 1844

NAS, GD 26/9/513/3

Notes

1 See Fraser (1890), vol. I, p. 350.
2 General Alexander Leslie's support for raising Black troops in Charleston in 1782 (see Black (1991), pp. 33–4) may have been more than realpolitik, given the family's religious and moral affiliations. The Leslies' American friend Dr Rush was an early anti-slavery campaigner in Pennsylvania. The correspondence of Lord Balgonie's father-in-law John Thornton with the Black Bostonian poet Phyllis Wheatley is in the Leven and Melville Papers.
3 A servant.
4 His sister Lady Jane or Jean Leslie (1753–1829). After a teenage romance with American student Benjamin Rush, in 1775 she married John Wishart Belsches. See below for further references.
5 Family dogs or horses.
6 His paternal step-grandmother, Elizabeth Monypenny, Dowager Countess of Leven (1699–1783). She was the first cousin of his real paternal grandmother, Mary Erskine, daughter of Colonel John Erskine of Carnock, who had died in 1723.
7 There is some damage where the recipient has cut around the red wax seal, an allegorical scene of two doves perched on separate rocks, with the legend ABSENCE DRAWS IT CLOSER.
8 William Sinclair or St Clair: not identified with certainty.
9 The 'Hearts of Steel' was an organisation of impoverished Protestant tenant farmers who protested violently against evictions and economic hardship.
10 William Murray (1737–77), 42nd (Royal Highland) Regiment. Entered the regiment 1758. Major 1771. Lieutenant-Colonel 27th Regiment, 1777. He died of fever in Philadelphia, 2 November 1777. There is a polychrome wax portrait-relief of him in the Scottish National Portrait Gallery, Edinburgh.
11 Probably John Knox, Esq., of Waringsfort, Co. Down (1740–c.1791). His home at Waringstown, inherited from his wife, the heiress Anne Phyllis Waring, is further from Belfast than Captain Leslie believed. Knox's elder brother Thomas later became 1st Viscount Northland of Dungannon, and his nephew (Thomas's son) 1st Earl of Ranfurly.
12 Lieutenant-Colonel Alexander Monypenny of Pitmilly (1726–1801), 56th Regiment. Nephew of Elizabeth Monypenny, Dowager Countess of Leven, and cousin to Colonel (later General) Alexander Leslie. He had served in North America as ADC to General George Augustus, Viscount Howe, in the Seven Years War.

13 A dancing assembly or ball.

14 Rev. James MacLagan (1728–1805), 42nd (Royal Highland) Regiment, Chaplain 1764. Born in Ballechin, a graduate of the University of St Andrews, and later minister of Blair Atholl. A native Gaelic speaker and prominent scholar in the language, he helped translate the scriptures into Gaelic for the Society for the Propagation of Christian Knowledge.

15 Erse, i.e. Scots Gaelic.

16 Colin Campbell (d. 1814), 42nd (Royal Highland) Regiment. Ensign 1771. Lieutenant, 44th Regiment, 31 December 1772. He died a Lieutenant-General.

17 Probably 'Hamilton'; unidentified.

18 His sister, Lady Jane.

19 Thomas Hogg (1722–84), banker, and his wife Colin or Colina Campbell (b. 1729), of Kinloch Close, Edinburgh. Colina was the daughter of Colin Campbell and Katherine Nisbet, Lady Leven's half-sister. It was the Hoggs who introduced the American medical student Benjamin Rush to the Leslies. See Butterfield (1951), vol. I: 1761–1792, p. 40, and Corner (1948), p. 47.

20 Mary Stuart (d. 1772): as fourth wife of Colonel John Erskine of Carnock, stepmother of William's long-dead paternal grandmother.

21 The red wax seal depicts the head of an African in profile.

22 Hopetoun House. Lady Elizabeth (Betty) Leslie (1737–88), Lord Leven's half-sister, was Countess of Hopetoun. She had married the twice-widowed John Hope, 2nd Earl of Hopetoun in 1767. The children mentioned in the sentence are Lady Betty's step-children and her own. She was at this time expecting her fourth child, Charlotte.

23 Alexander Belsches of Greenyards (1746–77): a friend of Lord Balgonie; member of Faculty of Advocates (1768).

24 The precursors of postage stamps.

25 The Irish Parliament in Dublin.

26 Black eyes, in modern parlance.

27 These events are described in greater detail in an anonymous 'Extract of a letter from Dublin, Feb. 27', *The Scots Magazine*, vol. XXXIII, March 1777, pp. 164–5:

> when the House should have proceeded on the usual business of the day, a desperate mob, armed with clubs, cutlasses, &c. surrounded the parliament-house, and attempted to swear several of the members; who very spiritedly refused the proposed oath. Upon which, they insulted some, and beat others, selecting with great nicety the supporters of government, from the members in opposition. The Bishops of Ferns and Corke were both beat and otherwise much abused, Lord Chief Justice Annely and Lord Tyrare were also very roughly treated. Lord Loftus was particularly searched for: he is marked by the mob, for joining government and deserting from the patriots.
>
> Whilst free access to parliament was thus interrupted, the Lord

Chancellor sent an account of these proceedings to the Lord Lieutenant. Soon after a detachment of the military was requested by the Mayor and Sheriffs, who had returned to the castle. The Lord Lieutenant first asked them, whether they could quell the riot by the aid of the civil power alone; on their answering in the negative, the troops were sent. On their appearance, the mob dispersed, and peace was soon restored. – When lo! the storm arose within doors; for the patriots largely expatiated on the terrors of an armed force surrounding the house, and had been debating, whether the troops should be removed or not, before they proceeded to business, and whether there really had been a riotous mob assembled, though several members stood up, and declared they had been insulted and threatened; when luckily, just as the celebrated Mr. Flood was proving the only danger to be apprehended was from government, and a mercenary soldiery, and not from a mob, the door behind the Speaker's chair was suddenly forced open by some rioters, who broke into the house. This accident, notwithstanding that gentleman's eloquence and abilities, convinced the House of the actual existence of the riot.

Two of the ringleaders, armed with cutlasses, who attempted to swear the Bishops with a Manual (or Popish Prayer-book) were taken, and lodged in Newgate, by order of the House of Lords.

Their confession was taken down by the Lord Mayor: it is said they have made some material discoveries. This mob consisted of the weavers, for whom a charitable contribution was carried on by our patriots for some months past. The Speaker subscribed one hundred pounds to this scheme, two days before the opening of the sessions.

28 While crossing between the Old Town and the New, David Hume (1711–76), philosopher, historian and religious sceptic, had slipped from the causeway into the mud left by the draining of the Nor' Loch. An elderly woman, recognising 'Hume the Atheist', refused to haul him out unless he recited the Creed. Hume complied. The devoutly Presbyterian Leslies clearly found the incident entertaining. See Mossner (1954), p. 563, citing William Mure, ed., Caldwell Papers, vol. II, part II, p. 177.

29 Government.

30 The final paragraph of this letter is damaged from cutting around the seal.

31 The vicinity of the family's Edinburgh home on Nicolson Square.

32 Alexander MacKay (d. 1772), 42nd (Royal Highland) Regiment from 1757. Captain-Lieutenant 1770.

33 Unidentified. Lord Leven had served in Ireland in 1753, as an officer in Handasyde's Regiment, hence his son's speculation that he may have been acquainted with the local families.

34 Lady Leven's birthday: she was born and baptised on 8 November 1724 (Old Style) in the Canongate Parish, Edinburgh.

35 John Robertson, 42nd (Royal Highland) Regiment from 1758. Half-pay 1775.

36 James Graham (d. 1784), of the family of Airth. Ensign 42nd (Royal Highland) Regiment, 1770. Lieutenant, 42nd Foot, 1773; Captain, 57th Foot; 1777. Died as Major.

37 Colin Campbell, who instead went to the 44th Foot.

38 The red wax seal depicts a Classical deity, possibly Hermes or Mercury, the Messenger.

39 4 June.

40 Simon Harcourt (1714–77), 1st Earl and 2nd Viscount Harcourt. Governor to the Prince of Wales (1751–2); FRS and diplomat; Lord Lieutenant of Ireland (1772–7).

41 John de Blaquiere (1732–1812), Lieutenant-Colonel 17th Dragoons 1763–73; Chief Secretary to Lord Harcourt as Lord Lieutenant of Ireland, 1772–7. Blaquiere, of London Huguenot family, had served as Chief Secretary to Harcourt's legation in Paris, 1771–2, and accompanied him to Ireland. He served as an MP in both the Irish and United Kingdom Parliaments. He was made a Knight of the Bath (1784), and, as a reward for his support for Irish parliamentary union, 1st Baron de Blaquiere (1800).

42 Alexander Lindsay (1752–1825), 6th Earl of Balcarres (1768), de jure 23rd Earl of Crawford (1808). Ensign, 53rd Regiment, 1767. Captain 42nd (Royal Highland) Regiment, 1771; Major 53rd Regiment, 1775; Lieutenant-Colonel 1782. He served in Burgoyne's campaigns in America and was wounded at Ticonderoga, 1777. He later became a General and Colonel of the 63rd Foot. Civil Governor of Jersey (1793) and of Jamaica (1794). He returned to Britain in 1801, and was made full General in 1803.

43 Captain William Murray had been promoted Major on 11 September 1771.

44 Either by slip of the pen or from mishearing, William Leslie mistakenly writes 'Rosebery' for 'Beresford'. Barbara Montgomery (d. 1788), daughter of William Mongomery of Magbiehill, married Hon. John de la Poer Beresford (1738–1805), second son of the Earl of Tyrone, in June 1774.

45 The eldest of the Montgomery sisters, Elizabeth (1751–83) married Luke Gardiner, later Viscount Mountjoy (1745–98), in Dublin on 3 July 1773.

46 Lady Mary Elizabeth Leslie (1757–1820), one of William Leslie's sisters. She married her cousin Captain James Ruthven (after 1783, 4th Baron Ruthven) in 1776.

47 William Montgomery of Magbiehill, Peebleshire (1717–84). He had long been settled in Ireland, with two successive Irish wives, Hannah Tomkyns (m. 1750), and Anne Evatt (m. 1761, d. 1777). Member of Irish Parliament for Ballynakill (1769–84); Baronet (1774). Agent for several regiments in Ireland.

48 This reference encompasses the recent marriage of Anne Montgomery (d. 1819) to George, Lord Townshend, on 19 May 1773 – all three daughters of William Montgomery's first marriage thus being married or engaged in a short time. In commemoration, Reynolds depicted the sisters, who were known as 'the Irish Graces', as *Three Ladies Adorning a Term of*

Hymen (Tate Gallery, London, N00079), commissioned by Luke Gardiner in 1773.

49 Webb (1911), pp. 64–5.

50 Alexander Leslie (1731–94), son of Alexander, 5th Earl of Leven, 4th of Melville, by his second wife Elizabeth Monypenny. He joined the Army in 1753, with a brief period of service in the Marines. In 1760 he married Mary Tullidelph, but she died in childbed the following year, leaving a daughter, Mary Anne. He never remarried. By 1768 he was Lieutenant-Colonel of the 64th Regiment, stationed in Boston. As Major-General, he served extensively in the Southern Campaigns and supervised the evacuation of Savannah and Charleston towards the end of the war. He returned home in poor health. Major-General of the Army in Scotland 1782. An encounter with violent rioters following the arrest of mutineers from the Breadalbane Fencibles seems to have brought on a heart attack, from which he died on 27 December 1794. (See Kay (1991 [1877]), no. CXCVII.) The Leven and Melville Papers contain a number of documents and letters relating to his life and career (NAS, GD 26/9/509, 512, 518, 523).

51 The 17th Foot arrived in Boston on New Year's Day. The crossing usually took only two months, but the winter of 1775–6 was especially severe: not a single supply ship reached Boston for 148 days. Convoys moved slowly, threatened by privateers, and the food on board ship was often rotting. Small wonder Lieutenant Leslie had lost weight.

52 Edward Goodenough: Major 17th Regiment 1773. Previously Captain 67th Regiment 1769.

53 NAS, GD 26/9/512/8.

54 His commission as captain was dated 9 July in *The London Gazette*, vice Charles Lyons. Ensign Matthew Anketell, 55th Regiment, replaced him as Lieutenant, 30 July.

55 In the poem, Angelina describes her lover thus:

> In humble, simplest habits clad,
> No wealth or power had he;
> Wisdom and worth were all he had,
> But these were all to me.

See Goldsmith (1901), pp. 385–9.

56 Brigadier-General James Grant of Ballindalloch (1720–1806), Colonel, 55th Regiment, 1775; Major-General, 1777. He entered the Royal Scots as Ensign in 1741, serving in the War of the Austrian Succession and the Jacobite Rebellion. As Captain in 1747, he was ADC to General St Clair on his embassy to Vienna, with David Hume as secretary. He also served in the Seven Years War in North America (77th Foot), and was Governor of East Florida, 1764–71. In command of British posts in New Jersey over the winter of 1776–7, he did not anticipate Washington's offensive at Trenton and Princeton – William Leslie being one of the resulting casualties. In December 1778, he led a detachment to the West Indies, capturing and

defending St Lucia against French attack. In his later years, he served as MP for Wick Burghs (1773–80) and for Sutherland (1787–1802). The Edinburgh barber-cartoonist John Kay caricatured him in his old age: see Kay (1991 [1877]), no. CLXXVIII.

57 James Agnew (d. 1777), 44th Regiment. Lieutenant-Colonel by 1768, with Provincial rank as Brigadier-General from May 1776. Son of Major James Agnew, 7th Dragoons, of Bishop Auckland, and grandson of Sir James Agnew of Lochnaw, 4th Baronet, Hereditary Sheriff of Galloway. His sister Mary was the first wife of Alexander McQueen, the judge Lord Braxfield. Agnew was killed at Germantown, Pennsylvania, 4 October 1777. He is buried with Lieutenant-Colonel John Bird, 15th Foot, in the De Benneville family cemetery, Philadelphia.

58 Sir Alexander Hepburn-Murray, Bt of Balmanno and Blackcastle (1754–76), 17th Regiment. Ensign, 1771; Lieutenant, 1773; Captain, 1775. An only son, he inherited the baronetcy aged seventeen months on the death of his father, Sir Patrick (or Peter) Hepburn-Murray, in 1756. Not yet twenty-two when he was killed on 27 August 1776, his title died with him.

59 Marcus Antony Morgan (b. 1756, Dublin), 17th Regiment. Ensign, 1773; Lieutenant, 1775. After 1777, he ceases to appear in *The Army List*.

60 Sir Alexander Hepburn-Murray's mother, Anne Hay (d. 1807), of the Drumelzier family. She had married Archibald Stirling of Keir as her second husband in 1762. Of Alexander Hepburn-Murray's two sisters, Anne married John Stirling of Craigbarnet, and died without issue, and Mary married, in 1777, Colonel John Belsches of Invermay, a kinsman of Lady Jane Leslie's husband. On the death of Mary's son Alexander Hepburn-Murray-Belsches, the family's property devolved upon Lady Jane's grandson, Sir John Stewart Forbes of Pitsligo, Bt (1804–66).

61 Sir Alexander Hepburn-Murray.

62 According to General Howe's official returns, twenty-one were wounded: Lieutenant Morgan, one sergeant, and nineteen rank and file.

63 James Grant had served with the 40th Regiment since 1760, and was Lieutenant-Colonel by 1768. Some newspapers confused him with General James Grant, and reported the latter's death in error.

64 Besides Lieutenant-Colonel Grant, one rank and file was killed, and five were wounded.

65 One sergeant, six rank and file killed; Captain Grove, one sergeant, and twenty-six rank and file wounded.

66 Andrew Browne (d. 1776), 44th Regiment. Ensign, 1758; Lieutenant, 1772; Captain-Lieutenant, 1772; Captain, 1776. He died from his wounds.

67 Thomas Browne, 44th Regiment. Ensign, 17th Regiment, 1771; Lieutenant, 44th Regiment, 1773. He was still a Lieutenant in 1785.

68 Ten rank and file were killed, and besides the two Brownes, Lieutenant Archibald Kennedy, one sergeant and seventeen rank and file were wounded.

69 William Alexander (1726–83), Colonel, 1st New Jersey Regiment, November

1775; Brigadier-General, Continental Army, March 1776. A New York merchant of Jacobite parentage, *soi-disant* Earl of Stirling (his claim to the peerage, extinct since 1739, had been rejected by the House of Commons in 1762). A member of the New Jersey Provincial Council, he served throughout the war. He was exchanged in September 1776 for Montfort Browne, Governor of New Providence, and Major Cortlandt Skinner. For all their republican principles, his Rebel colleagues always referred to him as 'Lord Stirling'. He personally surrendered to the Hessian General von Heister.

70 John Sullivan (1740–95), Major, New Hampshire militia 1772; Brigadier-General, 1775; Major-General, Continental Army, 9 August 1776. He succeeded Nathanael Greene in command on Long Island on 20 August. As prisoners, he and General Alexander were invited to dine on Lord Howe's flagship *The Eagle*. William Leslie is mistaken: although Sullivan had a seat in the Continental Congress, he was never its President. In September he presented the Admiral's proposals for a negotiated peace to the Congress, and was exchanged for General Richard Prescott. In 1779, on Washington's orders, he notoriously commanded a campaign of mass destruction against the Iroquois Nation, who, like the majority of indigenous peoples in the war zone, remained loyal to Britain. (The Rebels resented the 1763 treaty restricting westward expansion by whites: indeed, it was among the causes of the war.)

71 The name has been deleted, probably by Lord Leven or another family member. David Carnegie, Lord Rosehill (1749–88): cousin of William Leslie, eldest surviving son of George Carnegie, 6th Earl of Northesk, and his wife Lady Anne Leslie. Formerly an Ensign in the 25th Foot, he seems to have become the 'black sheep' of the family. According to *The Scots Peerage*, vol. VI, p. 503, and vol. IX, p. 144, he married Mary Cheer in Maryland in 1768, but in 1770 was accused of having married Christian Cameron, daughter of Captain Alexander Cameron of Dungannon, at Fort William in 1767. He died in Rouen without lawful issue.

72 William Carnegie (1758–1831), younger brother of Lord Rosehill, cousin of William Leslie, the second surviving son of Lord and Lady Northesk. As Rosehill had predeceased their father, he succeeded as 7th Earl in 1792. He had a long career as a naval officer, including service under Nelson at Trafalgar.

73 *The Eagle*, Admiral Lord Howe's flagship.

74 Samuel Instone, 'Soldier in the 17th Regiment of Foot', had married Elizabeth Russell in the Leslies' home parish of Monimail (which incorporates the village of Letham) in July 1772 (Old Parochial Register, Monimail, OPR 448/2). She was evidently one of the regimental wives travelling 'on the strength'. 'Friends' is used in the Scots sense of kindred. Cohen (1990), p. 63, has misread the place-name as 'Lothian'.

75 The red wax seal is identical to that used on NAS, GD 26/9/513/21, depicting a Classical god.

76 Marginal correction by another hand, possibly Lord Leven's: '15th'.

77 General Alexander Leslie.

78 The Seven Years War.

79 While there is no firm evidence regarding the cause of the New York fire, contemporary rumour strongly implied that, even if it did not originate with arson, its progress may have been assisted, or its extinction deliberately hindered. *The Scots Magazine*, vol. XXXVIII, November 1776, pp. 582–3, reports that a Rebel officer from New England, possibly a Richard Brown, had been apprehended and killed, and that several people had been arrested for refusing to help tackle the blaze. An officer aboard the *Phoenix* man-of-war claimed that 'About five or six rebels were caught setting fire to a fine English church, which was burnt, and the soldiers and seamen threw them into the flames, where they met their just reward'.

80 Nisbet Balfour (1744–1823), Ensign, 4th Regiment, 1761; Lieutenant, 1765; Captain, 1770. His father, Henry Balfour of Dunbog (1708–64), was laird of a Fife estate close to the Leslies'. Nisbet Balfour served through most of the American War. At Breed's or Bunker Hill in 1775, he was 'slightly wounded in the Belly, the ball having first pierced through his Cartridge box' (letter of Captain John Webster, 4th Regiment, to David, Earl of Leven, 21 June 1775, Boston Camp, NAS, GD 26/9/514). The Howes sent him back to London with their dispatches and instructions at the end of September 1776. He arrived on 2 November to find that his older brother, Major Henry Balfour, 1st Regiment, had been accidentally killed while fowling by another brother at Fort George, 1 October. As William Leslie anticipated, he wintered in Scotland, and returned to the colonies a Major, sailing on 28 March 1777. Lieutenant-Colonel, 23rd Regiment, 1778. Matriculated arms as Balfour of Dunbog, 24 April 1779. In 1780 he was appointed Commandant at Fort Ninety-Six, South Carolina, and then at Charleston. Brevet Colonel, 1781. He served as a commissioner for examining and processing Loyalist claims in the aftermath of the war. Burgess of Edinburgh, 1783; ADC to His Majesty, 1782–93; Major-General, 1793; Colonel, 93rd Regiment and 39th Regiment, 1794; Lieutenant-General, 1798; General, 1803; MP for Wigtown Burghs, 1790–6 and for Arundel, 1797–1802. He is buried in Dunbog.

81 Jane had married John Wishart Belsches, an advocate (later Sir John Wishart Belsches Stuart, Bt, of Fettercairn), at Melville House on 29 November 1775. William is referring to her pregnancy: she gave birth to her only surviving child, Wilhelmina or Williamina (1776–1810), later Lady Forbes of Pitsligo, in Edinburgh on 7 October 1776.

82 The red wax seal depicts a variant of the Leslie of Leven crest – an armoured arm wielding a sword – with the motto, PRO REGE ET PATRIA [For King and Country].

83 Brigadier-General Hugh Percy (1742–1817), later 2nd Duke of Northumberland. After a distinguished career serving in Germany during the Seven Years War, he was subsequently appointed ADC to George III. He

arrived in the colonies as Brigadier-General in 1774, and in April 1775 led troops to the relief of Colonel Smith and Major Pitcairn as they came under heavy fire returning to Boston after the outbreak of fighting at Lexington and Concord. Provincial and regular rank of Major-General 1775; provincial rank of General 1776. After commanding a division in the battle of Long Island, and, as this letter describes, the assault on Fort Washington, he participated in the capture of Rhode Island in December 1776. He returned to Britain in June 1777. Lieutenant-General, 1777; General, 1793, but played no further significant military rôle.

84 Thomas Musgrave (d. 1776) 64th Regiment. Entered Army 1759; Major 1774.

85 William Glanville Evelyn (1742–76), 4th Regiment. Born in Dublin, entered Army 1761; Lieutenant by 1769; Captain, 1772. He was wounded on 18 October, and died on 6 November, following the amputation of his right leg. He left his entire estate to Peggy Wright, a family servant who had accompanied him on the campaign as his mistress: see Holmes (2001), p. 297.

86 The text placed in brackets is heavily struck through in the manuscript. This happens again later in the same letter, suggesting an effort has been made to remove any derogatory references to the performance of the Hessian allies.

87 Robert Carr (d. 1776), 35th Regiment.

88 William Gore (d. 1776), 49th Regiment. Entered Army 1760; in 49th since 1770; Captain-Lieutenant and Captain.

89 York Island.

90 Wilhelm, Baron von Knyphausen (1716–1800): Prussian Lieutenant-General, in service since 1734, and a veteran of the Seven Years War. After the recall of von Heister in 1777, he became Commander-in-Chief of the German forces, commonly collectively labelled 'Hessians', but actually from several states. He served throughout the war, but his health began to fail in 1781, and he retired the following year. Returning to Germany, he became governor of Cassel.

91 Again, an unflattering sentence referring to the Hessians has been struck through in the original manuscript.

92 At White Plains.

93 Richard Prescott (1725–88), Lieutenant-Colonel, 7th Regiment (Royal Fusiliers), with provincial rank of Brigadier-General. A veteran of the Seven Years War, he had been taken prisoner at Quebec in 1775, and exchanged in September 1776 for the Continental General Sullivan. About the time this letter was written, he became full Colonel of 7th Regiment. He participated in the capture of Newport, Rhode Island, in December, and subsequently commanded its garrison. He was taken prisoner again in July 1777, and exchanged in May the following year for General Charles Lee, by which time he had been promoted Major-General. He returned to Newport, under General Pigot, and did not resume command there until a couple of months before the evacuation of the garrison in October 1779. Lieutenant-General, 1782.

94 Sons of Rev. Dr Alexander Webster. The Webster brothers, first cousins of James Boswell, were distant cousins of the Leslies. Their mother Mary Erskine (1715–66), of the Alva family, was a great-granddaughter of John, 2nd Earl of Mar, as were both Mary Erskine of Carnock and Elizabeth Monypenny, the two wives of Captain Leslie's grandfather, Alexander, 5th Earl of Leven.

John Webster (b. 1738) 4th Regiment. He had been in the Army since 1761, and Captain in the 4th Foot since 1769. His regiment had been in America since 1774. Despite William Leslie's syntax, the wife mentioned was his: Charlotte Kerr, whom he had married in Ayr in March 1771. The couple settled in Ayr after John left the Army in 1777, and had two children, Alexander (b. 1778), and Eleonora (b. 1780).

James (1740–81) had served in the 33rd Foot from the beginning of his military career in 1763. He was commissioned Lieutenant-Colonel in 1774, and distinguished himself after arriving in the American Colonies in 1776. Wounded in the battle of Guilford Courthouse, 15 March 1781, he died a couple of weeks later at Elizabethtown, North Carolina.

95 The red wax seal depicts a variant of the Leslie of Leven crest – an armoured arm wielding a sword – with the motto, PRO REGE ET PATRIA.

96 Charles Cornwallis, 2nd Earl Cornwallis (1738–1805). Having begun his military career as an ensign in 1st Foot Guards in 1756, Cornwallis was by this time Colonel of the 33rd Regiment and a Major-General. He opposed the American war, but served from 1776 onward, returning to Britain to attend Parliament and (1778–9) to be with his terminally ill wife. He took part in the battle of Long Island and in the operations against Fort Washington, both described by Captain Leslie; in the New Jersey campaign in which Leslie was killed; and in the Philadelphia campaign. In December 1779, he joined Sir Henry Clinton on his expedition to the south. Following the capture of Charleston and Clinton's return to New York (1780), he was left in command in the south. Ultimately, he surrendered his army to the alliance of the French and the Continentals at Yorktown in October 1781. He later engaged in controversy with Clinton over the conduct of the war. He served as Governor-General of Bengal, 1786–93, Master General of the Ordnance 1795–1801, and Lord Lieutenant of Ireland 1798–1801. 1st Marquis Cornwallis 1792. He died in Bengal after reappointment as Governor-General.

97 General Alexander Leslie's brigade.

98 Dr Benjamin Rush (1745/6–1813).

99 Rev. Dr John Witherspoon (1723–94). Born in Haddington, this hard-line Evangelical minister, formerly of Beith, then of Paisley, was elected President of the College of New Jersey (later the University of Princeton) in 1766, and accepted the post in 1768. His emigration was in part an escape from Enlightenment values: he had campaigned to have Rev. John Home expelled from the clergy for writing stage-plays, and lampooned him along

with David Hume and Lord Kames. He was a member of the Philadelphia Company, and played an instrumental role in the infamous voyage of the *Hector* to Pictou, Nova Scotia. He would have been known to the Leslies through Lord Leven's involvement in the General Assembly and the SPCK.

100 Admiral Richard Howe, Viscount Howe (1726–99), and his brother General William Howe (1729–1814). The brothers shared a joint command as Peace Commissioners and Commanders-in-Chief, to press for a negotiated settlement while securing key military objectives such as New York.

In 1758, Richard Howe succeeded his older brother, George Augustus, killed near Ticonderoga, to his Irish Viscountcy. He relieved Gibraltar in 1782. He last saw active service as commander in the Channel in 1793–4 at the beginning of the French Revolutionary War.

As Major-General, William Howe had supervised light infantry training camps in 1774. Although politically opposed to the American war, he served in the early stages of the conflict, 1775–7. He captured Philadelphia in 1777, but the following year resigned his command in favour of Sir Henry Clinton, and returned home shortly before the British withdrew from the city. He was Lieutenant-General of Ordnance 1782–1803, and full General from 1793.

101 Charles Lee (1731–82). A former British officer, he had also served in the Polish Army against the Turks before settling in the American colonies in 1774. Lee was taken prisoner at Widow White's tavern, Basking Ridge, New Jersey, on 13 December 1776, by a small force from 16th Light Dragoons.

102 William Harcourt (1743–1830): Lieutenant-Colonel, 16th Light Dragoons; Colonel (1779), later General. A younger son of the 1st Earl (see above, note 40), he succeeded his elder brother George Simon as 3rd Earl and 4th Viscount Harcourt in 1809. He left no issue, and the title became extinct at his death.

103 Having discontinued his half-pay, Lee could not be tried as a deserter. After being held in New York for over a year, he was exchanged in April 1778. While a prisoner, he had submitted a plan for ending the war by taking the middle colonies, but sadly, little attempt seems to have been made by the British to capitalise on his willingness to revert to his former loyalty.

104 Corner (1948), p. 128.

105 Ibid., p. 129.

106 Benjamin Rush to Richard Henry Lee, Princeton, 7 January 1777, in Butterfield (1951), vol. I, p. 126.

107 Rev. Dr Alexander Webster.

108 Lady Anne Leslie, Countess of Northesk (1730–79). General Leslie's sister and Lord Leven's half-sister, she had married George Carnegie (1716–92), 6th Earl of Northesk, in 1748.

109 Letter of General Alexander Leslie to David, Earl of Leven, 18 March 1777, NAS, GD 26/9/513/9.

110 This letter from Rush seems to be no longer extant.

111 Brigadier-General Thomas Mifflin (1744–1800), a Philadelphia Quaker businessman, member of the Provincial Assembly, 1772–73, and of the Continental Congress in 1774. He recruited troops for the Continental Army, in which he was elected Major. In 1775 he was appointed ADC to Washington, Quartermaster General, and Colonel. Brigadier-General, 1776; Major-General, February 1777; member of Board of War, 1777–8. He fell out with Washington, and in 1778 was investigated over his post as Quartermaster General. He resigned from the Continental Army in 1779. He became a delegate to Congress 1782–4, and President of Congress 1783–4. He was the first Governor of Pennsylvania, 1790–9.

112 Captain Francis Tew was later killed defending Stony Point, a fort on the Hudson, New York, on 16 July 1779. He had first been commissioned in the regiment in February 1757.

113 John McPherson, 17th Regiment. Entered Army in 1763; Lieutenant, 17th Regiment, 1769; Captain-Lieutenant and Captain, 1775. Wounded in the lung, he was tended by Dr Rush as a prisoner in Princeton. Despite being bled copiously – Rush was an extremely enthusiastic phlebotomist, even by the standards of the day – by August he was strong enough for the doctor to apply to have him paroled in order to be sent on a sea-voyage to recuperate. After recovering from his wounds, he was commissioned Major, 82nd Regiment, 1778.

114 Charles Mawhood (d. 1780), Lieutenant-Colonel, 19th Regiment, 1767; 17th Regiment, 26 October 1775, succeeding John Darby. Colonel in the Army, 1777; 72nd Regiment 1779.

115 'Gl. Leslie 7th July 1777'. Letter of General Alexander Leslie to David, Earl of Leven, NAS, GD 26/9/513/7.

116 Hon. John Finch (d. 1777), 1st Regiment of Foot Guards (Grenadier Guards), younger brother of Heneage Finch, 4th Earl of Aylesford. Ensign, 1772; Lieutenant and Captain, 1776. Killed at Westfield, 20 June 1777. He is commemorated on the Guards Memorial to casualties of the First American War, erected in 1880 in the Royal Military Chapel, Wellington Barracks, London.

117 A phrase which then implied 'a fine young man'. NAS, GD 26/9/513/7.

118 Pluckemin, New Jersey.

119 Rev. Dr Alexander Webster (1708–84), Minister at the Tolbooth Kirk, Edinburgh, and former Moderator of the General Assembly who, like Lord Leven, was heavily involved in the SPCK.

120 Charlotte Kerr, who had married John Webster in 1771.

121 Lieutenant-General Sir James Adolphus Dickenson Oughton (1719–80), illegitimate son of Sir Adolphus Oughton, Bt, of Tachbrooke, Warwickshire. Cornet, 1737, back-dated to 1734; Colonel of the 31st Foot, 1762; Major-General in North Britain, 1767; Lieutenant-General, 1770; KB, 1773, and Commander-in-Chief in North Britain, 1778. As a Freemason and a participant in many areas of Edinburgh cultural life, he would have been well

known to the Leslies. His career and interests are discussed in Stephen Wood's edition of Oughton's journal of 1758 (Wood, 1997).

122 Archibald Erskine of Venlaw (d. 1804): a first cousin of Lord Leven, being the fifth son of his uncle, John Erskine of Carnock and Cardross. An officer of the 42nd Foot (Black Watch) since 7 September 1771, he moved to the 22nd Regiment in 1778, and reached the rank of Major in that regiment. He later became Major of the Edinburgh Volunteers. In 1781, he married Margaret Maitland Barclay, a granddaughter of the 6th Earl of Lauderdale, and in 1794 became a Burgess of the City of Edinburgh.

123 David Leslie (1755–1838), Lord Leven's third son. Ensign, 59th Foot, 28 November 1775; later Brigadier-General. He married Rebecca Gillies in 1787, and died without issue.

124 Possibly Lady Oughton, née Mary Ross (d. 1793), widow of Captain John Dalrymple, 6th Dragoons (d. 1753), who had married the then Lieutenant-Colonel Oughton in 1755. However, the abbreviation may also be read as 'Or'. Since General Leslie, in his letter from Brunswick, NJ, 18 March 1777, quoted above, refers to his employing Rev. Dr Webster and Lady Northesk to break the news (see note 108 above), it may be a badly written 'A^n' for Anne, meaning Lady Northesk.

125 I.e. the preceding letter.

126 Colin Lindsay (1755–96), younger brother of Alexander, 6th Earl of Balcarres. Ensign, 4th Regiment, 1771; Lieutenant, 55th Regiment, 1773. In April 1777 – about a month after the above correspondence – he became a Captain. He transferred to 73rd Regiment in September 1778, seeing action with them as a Major at the siege of Gibraltar. Lieutenant-Colonel, 46th Regiment, July 1783 (Colonel in Army 1793); Brigadier-General, ADC to the King, and Commander of the West Indian Expedition of 1795.

127 William Armstrong, 17th Regiment; Ensign, 1774; Lieutenant, 1775; taken prisoner at Stony Point, New York, 1779. Captain-Lieutenant and Captain, 64th Regiment, 1781.

128 Captain Sir Alexander Hepburn-Murray.

129 John Belsches (after 1777 Belsches Wishart; after 1797 Stuart) (c.1752–1821). Advocate, husband of Lady Jane Leslie. He assumed his title as Sir John Belsches Wishart, Bt, by right of maternal descent in December 1777, and bought the estate of Fettercairn in 1783. MP for Kincardineshire, 1797–1806. Cohen (1990), p. 80, n. 47, has misread his signature on this letter, identifying him erroneously as 'Lord Balfour'.

130 The seal, in the black wax customary for mourning, shows the Belsches family crest, a sprouting oak stump with the motto REVIRESCIT.

131 Lord Balgonie, lately returned from his Grand Tour.

132 Andrew Wardrop served as surgeon to the 17th Regiment from 15 July 1772. On his return to his native Edinburgh in 1777, he was made a burgess of the city. John Horne replaced him as regimental surgeon.

133 Belsches mistakenly writes '56' throughout the letter, instead of 55th Foot.

134 The name is omitted in the manuscript.

135 'Anonymous Letter March 77. about William ayr postmark', NAS, GD 26/13/672.

136 Ibid.

137 'Mr. Martin & my Answer March 17.th 78 – about D.ʳ W.' [i.e., Dear William], NAS, GD 26/13/676.

138 Ibid.

139 Elisha or Elihu Hall, a maternal cousin of Dr Rush from Maryland, lately returned home on parole. He had been taken prisoner on Staten Island in August 1777.

140 Letter to Lord Leven from A. Hunter, Dumfries, 7 January 1779, NAS, GD 26/13/681.

141 Benjamin Rush to Lady Jane Wishart Belsches, Philadelphia, 4 July 1785, Butterfield (1951), vol. I, pp. 357–8.

142 Webb (1911), p. 70, erroneously claims that Captain Leslie died in Rush's care, en route to Pluckemin. Smith (1967), pp. 31–2, also mistakenly describes Leslie as a 'wounded prisoner' who 'died two days after the battle', and misidentifies him as General Leslie's son, not his nephew.

143 William Leslie-Melville was in the service of the Honourable East India Company from 1808, eventually becoming a Director (1841) after his return to Britain. He had strong antiquarian interests, and edited the correspondence of George, 1st Earl of Melville, for publication by the Bannatyne Club in 1843.

Bibliography

Manuscript sources

National Archives of Scotland
Leven and Melville Papers.

New Register House, Edinburgh
Old Parochial Registers for Ayr, Edinburgh, and Edinburgh Canongate (microfilm).

Public Library, Cupar, Fife
Old Parochial Registers for Dunbog and Monimail (microfilm).

Published memoirs and letters

Butterfield, L.H. (ed.), *Letters of Benjamin Rush*, vol. I: 1761–1792 (Memoirs of the American Philosophical Society, vol. 30, part I (Princeton, NJ: Princeton University Press, 1951).

Corner, George W. (ed.), *The Autobiography of Benjamin Rush* (Memoirs of the American Philosophical Society, vol. 25, Princeton, NJ: Princeton University Press, 1948).

Gruber, Ira D. (ed.), *John Peebles' American War: The Diary of a Scottish Grenadier, 1776–1782* (Publications of the Army Records Society, vol. 13, Stroud: Alan Sutton and Mechanicsburg, PA: Stackpole Books, 1998).

Wood, Stephen C. (ed.), *. . . By Dint of Labour and Perseverance . . . A journal recording two months in northern Germany kept by Lieutenant-Colonel James Adolphus Oughton, commanding 1st battalion 37th Regiment of Foot, 1758* (Society for Army Historical Research, Special Publications no. 14, London, 1997).

Articles and books

The Army List, 1769–1783.

Bill, Alfred Hoyt, *The Campaign of Princeton, 1776–1777* (Princeton, NJ: Princeton University Press, 1948, repr. 1975).

Black, Jeremy, *War for America: The Fight for Independence 1775–1783* (Stroud: Alan Sutton, 1991).

195

Boatner, Mark M. III, *Encyclopaedia of the American Revolution* (third edn, Mechanicsburg, PA: Stackpole Books, 1994).

Burke's Landed Gentry, *Burke's Landed Gentry of Ireland*, *Burke's Peerage & Baronetage*, various editions.

Butterfield, L.H., 'Love and Valor, or, Benjamin Rush and the Leslies of Edinburgh', *The Princeton University Library Chronicle* (Nov. 1947), vol. 9, no. 1, pp. 1–12.

Cohen, Sheldon S., 'Captain William Leslie's "Paths of Glory"', *New Jersey History* (1990), vol. 108, pp. 54–81.

Fraser, Sir William (ed.), *The Melvilles, Earls of Melville, and the Leslies, Earls of Leven* (three vols, Edinburgh: privately printed, 1890).

Goldsmith, Oliver, *Select Works of Oliver Goldsmith* (London: Macmillan and Co. Ltd, 1901).

Gruber, Ira D., *The Howe Brothers and the American Revolution* (Chapel Hill: University of North Carolina Press, 1972).

Holmes, Richard, *Redcoat: The British Soldier in the Age of Horse and Musket* (London: HarperCollins, 2001).

Kay, John, *A Series of Original Portraits and Caricature Etchings by John Kay, Miniature Painter, Edinburgh, with Biographical Sketches and Illustrative Anecdotes* (Edinburgh: Adam and Charles Black, 1877; electronic edition, Edinburgh: West Port Books, 1999).

McMicking, Neil (ed.), *Officers of the Black Watch (Royal Highland) Regiment 1725–1937* (Perth: Thomas Hunter and Sons, 1937).

Mossner, Ernest Campbell, *The Life of David Hume* (London: Nelson, 1954).

The Scots Magazine, 1770–1777

The Scots Peerage, ed. Sir James Balfour Paul (Edinburgh: D. Douglas, 1904–14).

Smith, Samuel Stelle, *The Battle of Princeton* (Monmouth Beach, NJ: Philip Freneau Press, 1967).

Webb, Lieutenant-Colonel E.A.H., *A History of the Service of the 17th (Leicestershire) Regiment* (London: Vacher and Sons Ltd, 1911).

Part III

The Diary of Private Robert Edward Cross
1st Battalion, The Leicestershire Regiment
September 1899–April 1901

Edited by
ROBIN JENKINS

Introduction

Robert Edward Cross

Robert Edward Cross was born on 26 August 1878. He was the fifth child of Joseph and Mary Cross, of 66 Aylestone Street, Leicestershire. By 1891, Cross was working for his father's joiners' and undertakers' business at 17 Infirmary Square, Leicester.

Cross cannot have found his employment in the family firm congenial however, for on 15 January 1895, following a spell in the militia, he enlisted in the regular army.[1] Although obliged to add two years to his age, Cross was in other respects a satisfactory recruit. He stood 5 feet 8⅝ inches in height, weighed 125 pounds and measured 34½ inches about the chest.[2]

The new no. 4285 Private Cross probably joined his unit, 1st Battalion, the Leicestershire Regiment, shortly after their arrival in South Africa in January 1896. The intervening period may have been spent with the 2nd Battalion at Chatham.

Cross served throughout the South African War, the medal rolls showing that he received the Queen's South Africa Medal, with clasps for Talana, Defence of Ladysmith, Belfast and Laing's Nek, and the King's South African War Medal, with both the 1901 and 1902 clasps.

Cross received his discharge from the colours at the end of the war and returned home to Infirmary Square, Leicester. On 8 April 1903 he joined the County Borough of Leicester Police. He served as a police constable in Leicester until May 1920, when he was forced to retire through medical unfitness.[3]

Cross had married Harriet Elizabeth Whitehouse, also of 17 Infirmary Square, at St Andrew's parish church, Leicester, on 4 April 1904. They lived at 60 Henton Road, Leicester, until 1932, when Cross supplemented his police pension by taking up the tenancy of the Lord Raglan public house at 55 New Bridge Street, Leicester. He died there on 6 March 1942 and was buried, on 10 March, in the city's Welford Road Cemetery.[4]

The Diary

The diary of Private Robert Cross is contained in a small exercise book, some 197 by 152 mm (7⅞ by 6½ inches) in size. The book lacks its cover and, to judge from the looseness of its three-hole stitching, had been used as a source for writing paper prior to Cross's adoption of it as a diary.

The paper is lined and has the mid-blue 'sprinkling' on its fore-edge typical of exercise books. On the first page, in ink, the book has the prominent title 'Amsterdam Cricket Club' and the reverse of the page has been ruled, in ink, probably to record the club's accounts. All other writing is in Cross's reasonably neat, right-sloping pencil script.

Cross's narrative is clear and legible. There are very occasional additions, indicated by a darker, blunter pencil. Generally they clarify or add details to the diary, such as the times, '8 a.m.', '11 a.m.' and '5 p.m.', added to the account of the retreat from Dundee on 22 October 1899.

Cross's punctuation and spelling are good, though by no means perfect. However, the mistakes that occur rarely obscure his meaning and so have been left. Where confusion may arise, clarification is given in square brackets or notes. Other errors, such as of fact or dating, have been indicated in the accompanying notes.

Private Cross's diary is still a cherished possession of his family. It came to light as a result of an appeal preceding a major exhibition held at the Record Office for Leicestershire, Leicester and Rutland, on the centenary of the siege of Ladysmith.

The diary is a comparatively rare and important account of the first campaign of the South African War from the viewpoint of a private soldier.

1 Talana Hill and the Defence of Ladysmith

Talana Hill and Yule's Retreat

Robert Cross began his diary on 24 September 1899. It must have seemed an auspicious moment to begin a journal. At 11 p.m. on that day Cross, with the greater part of the 1st Battalion, Leicestershire Regiment, entrained at Ladysmith and was carried north, via the railway junction at Glencoe, to Dundee. Few people with any awareness of events in South Africa in September 1899 could have doubted that war was imminent and that if it broke out, the troops steaming through northern Natal would soon be in the thick of it.

Plans for the defence of British territory had originally envisaged an advance to Laing's Nek, at the northernmost tip of a narrowing peninsula of Natal that projected perilously between the Orange Free State to the west and Transvaal to the east. The British force, under the command of Brigadier-General James H. Yule, was pushed north only as far as Dundee, at the base of that 'peninsula', where coalmines seemed to provide an object worthy of defence.

On 12 October, the day the Boer ultimatum expired and hostilities effectively began, Major-General Sir William Penn Symons succeeded Yule as commander of the Dundee force. Even Symons however, whose low opinion of the Boers is well attested,[5] must have had doubt about his new base. Not only was Dundee remote from any help, at the end of some forty-five miles of single-line railway, but the camp itself was undefended, virtually waterless and overlooked on three sides.

The doubts about the Dundee garrison were shared by Symons's superior, Sir George White, newly arrived in Ladysmith as commander of the Natal Field Force. Ultimately however political considerations triumphed over military. White, already loath to hazard his entire railway rolling-stock to bring Symons's troops back to Ladysmith, finally bowed to the view of the Governor of Natal, that a withdrawal, with its consequent jolt to British prestige, would have a disastrous effect on the black population, on loyalists in Natal and on Boer sympathisers, already prepared to rise in revolt.[6]

So Symons remained at Dundee. His force now comprised the four infantry battalions of the 8th Brigade, 18th Hussars, three batteries of field guns and detachments of the Natal Carbineers and Natal Police. The camp's routine reflected the increasing threat from the enemy, with Cross's 'outpost duty' (26 September) and 'a march or attack' (13 October) every morning.

On 20 October the inevitable happened. Inevitable, yet still a surprise. Shortly before dawn a Boer force, led by Lukas Meyer, brushed aside a picket of Royal Dublin Fusiliers[7] and two companies of Cross's battalion,[8] to seize Talana Hill, two miles from the British tents. The Boers waited for the sun to clear away some early morning mist and then opened fire, their two Krupp and one Creusot 75 mm guns bombarding Symons's camp, where the troops had been dismissed from parade to their tents for breakfast, or to fatigues and drill.

The battle for Talana Hill followed a pattern that was to become familiar. The 1st Leicesters were deployed with the Natal Police and Carbineers and 67th Field Battery to cover the camp, while Symons sent the rest of his infantry and guns against Talana Hill. The 18th Hussars under Colonel B.D. Möller, with mounted infantry in support, were despatched around the Boers' right flank.

Talana Hill was captured and the Boers driven off. Symons's gamble that a 'bloody nose', administered early enough, might bring the war to a satisfactory conclusion had, however, failed. The fight had cost the British dear. Symons himself was mortally wounded and his casualties, already high, were effectively doubled when Möller and some 240 officers and men, rather than cutting-off Meyer's retreat, were themselves cut off and forced to surrender.

The two succeeding days brought little comfort to Yule, once again commander of the Dundee force. The Boers gained in strength whilst a telegram from Sir George White brought word that no reinforcements might be expected from Ladysmith. Worse still, the Boers' superiority in artillery drove the British from their camp, to shelter on the bare hillsides to the south, in torrential rain. Having manoeuvred from Dundee to Glencoe Junction and back again, Yule determined on the inevitable – withdrawal.

Yule's retreat from Dundee began soon after dark on 22 October 1899. Supplies and forage for the march were gathered hastily from the abandoned camp by two companies of the Leicestershire Regiment, including Cross's, which then joined the main column as it hastened down the Helpmakaar road, guided by men of the Natal Police.

There followed a nightmare journey, through narrow defiles and along roads turned to quagmires by torrential rain, Yule believing that, at any moment, his path would be blocked by the more numerous and more mobile Boers. The last stage of the journey was the worst. On the night of 25 October, the exhausted column threw itself down to rest only to be roused again by news, received at last from Ladysmith, that the enemy was indeed close behind and that they should press on.

Having marched for twenty-two of the last twenty-eight hours,[9] the column reached the safety of Ladysmith at about 9 o'clock on the morning of 26 October.

'Mournful Monday': the battle for Ladysmith

While Yule's troops were struggling through flooded drifts and treacherous passes, Sir George White and the men of the Natal Field Force in Ladysmith had not been idle. Twice elements of the garrison sallied out. On 21 October, a Boer force, somewhat out on a limb at Elandslaagte, had been decisively beaten by Major-General John French. Three days later White had himself led a demonstration in support of Yule's column. There was an inconclusive engagement at Rietfontein, the artillery fire from which had been heard by Cross that morning.

With the Dundee force safely returned and rested, White was anxious to strike again before the Boer net closed too tightly around him. The resulting plan has been described as 'of the vaguest and most inadequate character'[10] and seems to have confused White's senior officers no less than it puzzles historians.

White's aim was to attack Boer forces believed to be occupying high ground to the north-east of Ladysmith. He assumed, or hoped, that if struck sufficiently hard, the unity of the Orange Free State and Transvaal Boers would disintegrate and the disparate commandos would withdraw towards their respective frontiers. To take advantage of such a withdrawal, White despatched the greater part of two battalions, with a mountain battery, to occupy Nicholson's Nek, behind the Boers' western flank.

The plan, as plans invariably must which rely upon the supineness and predictability of a foe scarcely noted for either, disintegrated into chaos and disaster. The Nicholson's Nek column was cut off some way short of its objective, a panic amongst the mule-train having already scattered much of their ammunition and the mountain battery across the veldt, and was forced to surrender.

The main striking force, Grimwood's brigade, including Cross's battalion, enjoyed only slightly more success. The brigade had left Ladysmith before midnight on 29 October but in the course of the march to its starting position south of Long Hill, not only its supporting artillery but two of five infantry battalions and all the mounted infantry managed to detach themselves.

As the sun rose, Grimwood's situation grew ever more precarious. Far from rolling up the Boers by attacking their flank on Long Hill, it seemed likely that the British would themselves be outflanked by Boers holding a line of hills along the eastern bank of the Modder Spruit. Grimwood's three remaining battalions made a scrambled redeployment as their line was hastily extended with reserve companies.

Little support came from the other British brigade, under Colonel Ian Hamilton, or from French's cavalry. The artillery, deployed around Flag Hill, at the centre of Sir George White's position, provided much needed covering fire. Indeed, the artillery proved to be the only arm to emerge from the battle with any credit. By 11.30 a.m., White, concerned at reports of a threat to Ladysmith, had decided to abandon his stalled attack. The six batteries then covered what became a confused, shambolic retreat.

The defence of Ladysmith

The cutting of the town's water-supply, telegraph links and, by 3 November 1899, the railway lines, all made inescapable the fact that the Natal Field Force was now beleaguered in Ladysmith.

A ring of high ground around the town was occupied and fortified with sangars and entrenchments. Although enemy artillery on more distant heights could bombard Ladysmith, the newly built defences, bolstered by long-range Royal Navy guns which had been hastened up from Durban on 30 October, would keep the Boers sufficiently far from the town.

Supplies of food and ammunition were adequate for many weeks. Indeed, the accumulation of such stores was one reason for White's reluctance to abandon Ladysmith. Moreover, White was by no means reconciled to the idea of a wholly defensive stance – as his retention of the cavalry, the daily parading, from 28 November, of a mobile column[11] and the manning of an armoured train, with steam up, testify.

Within a few days the lives of the garrison began to take on an air of routine. For Cross's battalion, holding a sector on the northern perimeter of the defences, there appear to have been alternating periods in and out of the front line: three days and four nights in the sangars and two days and one night sheltering in the hills closer to Ladysmith.[12]

Life for the beleaguered seems to have been generally quiet, though punctuated by the warning whistles or bugle-calls that preceded the detonation of Boer shells. Periodically, heavy gunfire from south of the Tugela would raise spirits, with the hope that Buller's relief force might break through.

There were also raids against the besiegers. On 7 December three sorties were made; the best known against the Boer siege guns on Gun Hill. Although the other raids failed to make contact with the enemy and raiders had to be content with the destruction of telegraph lines and shelters, the success of the Gun Hill attack prompted another sortie on 10 December. A howitzer was put out of action but the raiders had to fight their way back to Ladysmith.

On 6 January 1900, the besiegers made their only serious attempt to take Ladysmith by storm. The main attack fell on Wagon Hill and Caesar's Camp, high ground to the south of Ladysmith, generally known now as the Platrand. A diversionary raid, or feint, was made on the Observation Hill defences manned by Cross's battalion.[13] Although the feint was beaten off easily, fierce fighting to the south lasted all day, interrupted by torrential rain and thunderstorms. Ladysmith was held only with the commitment of all White's reserves and at heavy cost.

Despite the narrowness of the British victory on the Platrand the greatest threats to White's garrison were starvation and disease. While enemy action accounted for nearly 250 of the garrison, twice that number died of dysentery or enteric fever.[14] White had begun to cut his troops' rations on 25 November 1899.[15] By 26 February the garrison barely survived on a diet found from a quarter of their normal ration (where the supplies remained) supplemented with scavenged fruit,[16] bread from mealies and by-products of horse-rendering.[17]

Relief came on the evening of 28 February 1900. After ten days' battering, the Boers had abandoned their Tugela defences and, ever pragmatic, trekked away. The siege was lifted. Beyond an exploration of the besiegers' lines and the occasional shell sent over to make their withdrawal less comfortable, the garrison could do little to hinder the retreating Boers.

Buller's army made a triumphal entry into Ladysmith on 3 March 1900 but it was easy to see that neither Buller's nor White's troops were in a state to pursue the retreating enemy. The garrison was weak from starvation and sickness and had eaten or driven off, as useless mouths, its horses and other draught animals. There was little alternative to a period of rest and refitting.

Private Cross's diary, September 1899–April 1900

Sept. 24th **1899** Left Ladysmith at 10.30 p.m. for Glencoe equipped for active service. DF with us. No room for maxim.[18]

Sept. 25th Arrived about 5.30 am and camped at the foot of Impati mountain near Dundee where the Dublin Fus joined us. Cavalry joined 4 pm[19]

Sept. 26th We are busy pitching tents and unloading stores at the station and making them into stacks it looks as if we are staying here for some time. We are doing outpost duty at night and are allowed two pints of beer per day. Cavalry joined.

Oct. 12th On Outpost duty sleeping in the Dutch church[20] and wet through with rain when we got the news that the Transvaal and Orange Free State have declared war with Great Britain.

Oct. 13th We have to parade at 4 a.m. every morning and get dismissed after a march or attack for 2 or three hours.

Oct. 20th Stood to as usual at 4 a m[21] and were dismissed after standing on parade a quarter of an hour. As soon as we got into our tents the Boers opened fire from Talana Hill and the shells whistled over our camp and burst against the railway. Our Artillery were all going to water but the guns were soon in action and after 20 minutes shelling the boers guns 5 in number were out of action and the infantry advanced up the hill. Our Regt being on the left flank as another commando was expected in the direction of Impati. The firing was kept up till late and the boers retired with heavy loss. It was a very funny sensation the first time under fire with shells and bullets whistling round but we soon got used to it. The troops engaged were 13th 67th 69th Batteries Field Artillery 18th Hussars 1st Leic Regt 2nd RIF 2nd RDF 1st K.R.R.s with MI[22] of all except Royal Irish. Our casualties were 238 killed and wounded amongst whom was Major Gen. Pen Symons. Col Shirston DSO and Col. Gunning. Col Muller and Squadron of the 18th Hussars were taken prisoners.[23] The boers were reported to be 9000 under Lucas Meyer who was to wait for Joubert[24] but wanted to make a name and got as much as he could put up with.

Oct. 21st Boers reported in force near Glencoe junction. we were sent to hold some kopjes overlooking the railway but returned to camp in the afternoon. We started to move the camp to better positions overlooking Dundee Station and the enemy opened fire from Impati with long range 40 prs. and we had to retire out of range as the best guns we had were field gun[s]. It was during the retirement that Lieut. Hannah was killed and 2 men of the M I wounded by a shell near the colliery.[25] There was a large Geneva flag flying on the field hospital but the boers continued to shell it and it was a pitiful sight to see the wounded in the rain seeking shelter under a bridge some of them with their wounds not yet dressed. That night Sat. 21st was about the worst I ever passed we were wet through and got nothing to cover us and nothing to eat huddled together behind rocks expecting to get attacked I was pleased to see daylight that morning if ever I was. Smiths Hill

Oct. 22nd The transport tried to reach the old camp for provision but got shelled and had to return empty. We got the news of the victory at Elandslaagte[26] and Kelly[27] got wounded. Our grooms found a coffin filled with ammunition at Jagers Farm. We then started to retire towards glencoe but had to turn back as the road was held At dusk 250 of us were told off to go to the camp with 100 wagons[28] and pack them with provisions and forage we got them loaded by 10 aclock and started for the town leaving Talana on the left and got away safe but It was a very shaky job as we saw several suspicious looking persons riding about. We took the

Helpmakaar road and started to march to Ladysmith as we were too small a force to hold Dundee. We had to leave all wounded behind.[29]

Mon. Oct. 23rd We have been marching all night and halted at daybreak for breakfast between Helpmakaar at 8 a m and Beith and moved on again as soon as breakfast was finished 11 a.m. to Beith which we reached in the afternoon 5 p.m. and were told to get what sleep we could as there was a night march in front of us. We have got a few prisoners which we are taking with us.

Tues. Oct. 24th We started on the march again at 11 oclock last night and soon came to Dasfontein Pass which was very unpleasant with mountains on the left and the river right below us on the right every one was pleased to get out of it. We crossed Sundys River at daybreak and halted there firing could be heard in the direction of Modder Sp[ruit] and we were ordered out in the afternoon to cut off the enemys retreat, but were eventually withdrawn to our bivouac after waiting for two hours. We had a storm and the river is swelled a lot the boers are close up to us but cannot cross as the current is too strong it was lucky for us we camped on this side or we should have had to abandon our convoy. Waschbank 9: a m

Tintainyona Fight. Held position till 4 p.m.

Oct. 25th After another long march to Modder Spruit we got into helio communication with the Ladysmith force and just as we got settled for the night we got the order to march into Ladysmith as the boers were close behind this was where I started on the hardest march I have ever done. Started 3 a.m. halted Sundys R till 10 reached M.S. 5.30.

Oct. 26th Thurs. We have been marching all night and it was past nine this morning when we got in. the troops gave us a cheer but we could scarcely give one back. The Gloucesters gave us their breakfast and it was a treat to get a bit of bread and we devoured it like wolves.[30] We marched to our old camp at 3 p.m. and were very pleased to get in a barrack room again Camps are pitched all over the place and it looks quite different to when we left. The Queen complimented us on our hard march.[31]

Rum and coffee at 7 and a good sleep.

Sun. Oct. 29th A draft arrived from England at p.m. We fell in at 9 p.m.

Mon. Oct. 30th Battle of Lombards Kop. We fell in at 9.30 p.m. last night and marched with the 1st K.R. Rifles to some Kopjis on the left of Lombards Kop with the Artillery ready for action we waited for daylight. As soon as day broke the boers Artillery opened fire from Pepworths Farm. We were ordered to advance up the hill and when we got to the top we came under a terrible rifle fire from the boer trenches. The Rifles soon got their maxim in action and the Cavalry went by us to Charge them but got there just too late as the boers had gained another position and opened on them. We were now getting fire from three directions and the bullets were whistling by us in thousand [*sic*] and men were falling against us. About midday the boers got reinforced and tried to get round Lombards Kop and their pom-pom shells were dropping amongst us. The wounde[d] were lying about but we had distinct orders to leave them as there was plenty to look after them. It was getting later in the afternoon when General Hunter[32] gave us the order to retire on Ladysmith individually and it was while retiring that, we came under a very heavy shell fire and I saw what a battle field was like. Men and horses lying about dead and wounded and shells bursting bullets whistling and cracking and our own guns booming in front of us. I have often wished to see the sight but cannot say I enjoyed it. The Naval Brigade arrived in the niche [*sic*] of time with their long range guns or it might have meant us evacuating Ladysmith. Our casualties were about 100 Leic Regt 4 killed 23 wounded 4 missing.[33] We also had 6 companies R I Fusiliers and 4 guns of the 10th M.B. ambushed at Nicholsons Nek and captured by the boers.[34] We were pretty well worn out when we reached Ladysmith after 10 hours fighting under a hot sun and I thought it marvellous to escape so many bullets without getting hit but we have got pretty well used to being fired at now and take it as our luck.

Tues. 31st We are on outpost duty an armistace [*sic*] has been granted to enable both sides to bury the dead.

Wed. Nov. 1st The boers have surrounded Ladysmith and our communication cut off. Gen. French left here with the last train.[35] Boers started bombardment and our Artillery replied silencing them for a time.

Thurs. Nov. 2nd Boers shelling but doing little damage. The Manchester Regt. and Cavalry captured boer laager on Caezers Camp [*sic*].

Fri. Nov. 3rd We are told off to different parts on the hills and are entrenching ourselves ready for action[36] and expecting 14 days seige [*sic*].[37]

Sat. 4th Boers shelled Convent which was flying the red cross.[38] We had one killed and 3 wounded by a shell. had a brush with a party outside ladysmith and defeated them.

Tues. 7th The Boers shell us daily but we don't take much notice now only keep out of sight as much as possible. We are on outpost duty every other night they tried shelling by night but only knocked the ground about.

9th Royal salute 12 noon.[39] Boers attacked but were repulsed with heavy loss 1 killed 18 wounded.[40]

Fri. 10th Several spies captured conveying news to boers. Joubert sent in for food and medicine but got no food.[41]

Sat. 11th Gens. White and Joubert held a meeting which ended satisfactory as to sending all women and children to a neutral camp called Intombi under the boer position.[42] Several casualties in town today.

Sun. 12th Sunday is very quiet the boers do not fire unless they see a very good target it is very hot now and Enteric and dysentery is putting a good many in hospital.

Tues. 14th Several houses were wrecked by Long Tom on Umbulwana[43] the Royal Hotel was struck and a good deal of damage done to it and one Officer killed. Boers shelled at midnight doing no damage.

Thurs. 16th Enemy shelled railway Station killing 1 Civilian and wounding 9 also two of our Regt. who were doing duty on the Armoured train.

Fri. 17th Boers made a faint [*sic*] night attack but were drove back.

Nov. 18th Our Ration has been reduced to 1 lb bread and 1 lb meat but we can buy plenty in town we also get mealie but do not eat it. Boers mounted gun on Lombards Kop.

Mon. 20th We keep sniping at each other at 1000 yds but I don't think much damage is done as we don't make good targets for each other. Our Regt. has been put on flying column. Some of the I L H[44] have been arrested for carrying news to the enemy. Bestor[45] shot for trying to poison horses by putting poison in the forage. Rumoured that Gen Joubert has been wounded outside Ladysmith.[46]

21st A shell struck a barrack room killing 1 man.

Thurs. 23rd Forage is getting short and they are shooting all sick horses and mules. Our position is called Gordons post and the men of HMS Powerful on the hill with 1 4.7 and we get on very well together Lieut Hon Egerton was killed on duty he had his legs blown off but took it very easy smoking a cigarette.[47] Water is very scarce and what we get is khaki colour and not fit to drink. We are lucky if we get a wash every week. Boers have fired 2.500 shells and killed 9 and wounded 11.

Sun. 26th We are told that Gen Buller is on his way to us but we cannot see a paper or anything else. We were told we should be relived in 10 days but no sign yet. The boers have got search lights which they flash round our positions at night but I don't think they can see the time by them. We have a lot in hospital nearly 100.

Mon. 29th A shell dropped in Gen Whites quarters but did no harm all our field guns are placed in permanent positions on the hills as ammunition is not too plentiful.

Tues. 28th Victory at Mooi R. Frere occupied by British.[48]

Thurs. 30th The enemy are getting cheeky they signalled to know how we are getting on but we are not done yet. We are still getting bread but flour must be getting short. several deaths from Fever have occurred lately. The troops are all in good spirits and seem very little worse up to now after 1 months seige We have found some old papers of 82 and 84 and are reading about 10 years back. Boer gun on end hill knocked over.

Fri. Dec. 1st The boers shelled the town all day but with about the same result as usual.

Sat. 2nd Provisions are getting short in town it is roumoured [*sic*] that a convoy is trying to get through to us. Volunteers sports[49] and plenty of shells.

Tues. 5th No convoy came the flying column stood to ready to go out but nothing comes off unusual. News of Methuens successes near Kimberley.

Wed. 6th We are moved to a more advanced post on Observation Hill and have more sungars [*sic*] to build.

Th. 7th Boer gun blown up and Maxim Nordenfelt captured.[50]

Fri. 8th We heard of Methewens success[51] and that Buller is starting his advance which bucks us up a bit.

8th Sortie 3 guns destroyed 1 maxim captured.

Sat. 9th They shelled our outposts but did no damage. My Section only numbers eight out of twenty-one the remainder are all sick which makes duty hard.

Mon. 11th We went to bathe in the Klip River and the boers spotted us and started shelling some dropped very close but no one hit.

Tues. 12th We have no vegetables or Jam left now and are living on the Trek Oxen and bread.

Wed. 13th We saw a party of Boer outposts retiring and the Navy opened fire on them but the distance was too far to see the effect.

Thurs. 14th A reconnaissance party of I.L.H. and rifle brigade went out after dark and caught the Boer sentries by talking in dutch and managed to blow up three of their guns on Gun Hill.[52]

Frid. 15th Not a very pleasant day for us as we received the bad news of Gen Bullers reverse in his first attempt to cross the Tugela.

Sat. 16th Dingaans day heavy bombardment.[53]

Sunday 17th One killed and two wounded by a shell while digging trenches.

Dec. 18th We hear the Queen is sending a box of Chocolate for a Xmas Box. Also the death of Gen. Wauchope.[54] We have got 150 men in hospital with fever and dysentery.

Wed. 20th We have been receiving news from Gen. Bullers column by means of limelight flashes in the sky but they tell us nothing and it is come day go day God send Sunday.[55]

Thurs. 21st Our bread has been reduced to ¾ lb and tobacco is not to be had at any price so we are drying leaves to smoke which smell like Geranium leaves.

Fri. 22nd We have to parade for water now of which we are allowed 1 qt. per day and it is not fit to wash in. We are marched to the river once a week to do a bit of washing but we have not got much to wash and no soap so the bits of dirt with legs on are beginning to trouble us.

Sun. 24th Christmas Eve and on a bit of Mealie for breakfast but we get a little sugar with it so it is no so bad. We had 1 man wounded and two died of fever today.[56] Our clothes are all in rags and there is no sign of relief coming this year.

Mon. 25th Xmas day and stuck in a small shelter four feet high we have been building walls all morning to make some new Kraals and have just knocked off for our Xmas dinner which consists of Stewed Trek 1 tablespoonful of rum ½ oz. of Boer tobacco and a bit of what they call pudding made of Russian tallow which we use for greasing boots we only got a very small piece but it was too much for me. We are all talking of what we will do to make up for this when we get free and a Xmas in peace and the good things they will have The last draft are telling what they were doing last year at this time and this is how Xmas day of 99 passed in the Seige [*sic*] but not without long toms compliments.

Tues. Dec. 26th I have not got a fat head after Xmas day and don't expect many Xmas boxes unless they come from long Tom he has been firing at our Naval Gun on Cove Redoubt all day but has got nowhere near it yet.

Wed. 27th They are burying men at Intombi at the rate of 10 per day. Lieut C P Russel died today.[57] All sick animals are being shot.

Sunday 31st The last four days of the year passed uneventful but for a few shells which we get every day. We never see a bit of fat of any kind now and I would give anything for a bit of dripping.

Jan. 1900

Mon. 1st I saw the old year out on sentry on Cove Red[oub]t. I was on sentry from 11 to 1 and it was raining pretty hard. At 11.30 the boers started firing big guns and shells were dropping very close to me. they kept it up till after midnight and then quietened down again.

News of Lord Robert's arrival at Cape Town.[58]

Tues. 2nd We have had a heavy thunderstorm it is no use trying to keep dry as we have to lay in pools of water at night so we are getting used to water. There is a lot of men suffering from Jaundice the doctor says it is smoking tea leaves.

Thurs. 4th**Jan.** We are on duty every night now and it is too hot to sleep in the day the mosquitos rise lumps as big as peas. We can hear Bullers guns in the distance and are hoping for him to have better luck than last time.

Fri. 5th We can hear nothing of the guns today and our rations have been cut again so I don't know what will happen next. We are beginning to get weak.

Sat. 6th The enemy made an attack this morning at 3 a.m. they had taken two weak points in the night and about 7000 attacked Wagon Hill. Every man was in his place and shells and bullets whistling everywhere and it rained and thundered all day. The boers fought for all they were worth and gained the top of the hill but the Artillery stuck to the guns and gave them case shot and the Devons got a good charge in. Col Dick Cunningham[59] of the Gordons was forming his Regt. up in town to reinforce the Manchesters when he was struck by a spent bullet and died the same day he had just recovered from wounds received at Elandslaagte. It was night before the firing ceased and we had to stay on duty till morning in our wet cloths. Our Casualties were 400 including the Earl of Ava[60] Gen. Whites ADC killed. Leicesters 6 wounded[61] I think the boers have learnt half starved britishers can fight and if they try it on again will no doubt get a good reception.

Sunday 7th Came off duty to a bit of skilly a good thing after a hard day and night busy burying dead.

Mon. 8th We have had horseflesh issued to us as there is no more Oxen the men don't like the idea of eating it.

Tues. 9th Boers continue to shell us the Sergt. Major and QMS were sitting behind a big rock eating when a shell struck it and broke it up knocking them both over but they were only badly shaken.[62]

Thurs. 11th We do not reply to the boer fire now unless they give a good target as ammunition is getting short. They give us chevril now soup made of horseflesh it smells like socks and the troops parade at the station for the meat when it comes out of the coppers and eat it like wolves.[63]

Fri. 12th Got boots of all sorts issued that were found in town as a good many had none to wear. We saw some of the boers sheep a long way off it was the nearest bit of mutton for months.

Sat. 13th Saw shells bursting on Kranz Kloof.[64] ¼ Rations.

Sun. 14th Boers shelled town hall knocking down the tower and killed one of the balloon section and wounded nine patients.

Mon. 15th Heavy rifle fire last night among the boers but I don't think anyone belonging to us was near them the short rations are beginning to tell and it takes us all our time to walk from one post to another if anyone goes sick they get sent away.

Tues. 16th Arnold was sent away from hospital and died on his post.[65] We hear Buller is advancing again and we can see shells bursting in the direction of Acton Holmes [*sic*] I gathered some berries which the niggers call fomfoms and we are stewing them to fill our bellies they taste like quinine but go down just the same.

Wed. 17th It is pitiful to see the men going about nearly everyone has got dysentry and there is no medicine in the hospital. One of the 5th Dragoons shot himself.

Thurs. 18th We got some starch and boiled it goes down all right also green peaches. Served out with mealie bread a loaf as big as the palm of my hand weighs 1 lb and has to keep four men 1 day.

Fri. 19th I had an horrible night last night and every one was complaining of pains in the stomach through eating mealie bread.

at. 20th A shell from Surprise Hill killed 1 and wounded 2 H Coy.[66]

Wed. 24th Can still hear guns in the distance they keep bucking us up with rumours which never turn out true.[67]

Thurs. 25th They fired very hard last night but we can make out no reason they must fire at their own men.

Sat. 27th Our artillery fire star shells at night as it is so dark and we can see our front well with them. Gen. White is laid up with dysentry.

Wed. 31st Another month gone and no sign of relief. the Boers have placed an old Mortar gun on Surprise Hill which we have nicknamed Puffing Billy by the noise it makes we can see the shell at night.[68] We are beginning to think we shall never get out of this as the 10 days has got to 3 months and no sign yet.

Thurs. 1ˢᵗ Feb. The horses are dropping dead as they are being driven to the station to be killed and the men are about as bad it takes about 2 hrs. to go a mile.

Feb. 1900

Thurs. 2ⁿᵈ The boers seem contented to try and starve us out we hear that some have retired to help Cronje.[69]

Mon. 5ᵗʰ The men are getting more sick every day it is as much as we can do to stand on sentry for an hour at a time.

Sun. 18ᵗʰ Still going on the same we saw shells bursting 21ˢᵗ on Singola and Monte Cristo[70] this is the nearest we have been yet so are bucked up a bit.

Th. 22ⁿᵈ Got in communication with Bullers signallers and received the news that cronje was surrounded. I think the Boers had enough of the 6ᵗʰ Jan they don't seem to try again but keep the shelling up.

Fri. 23ʳᵈ Put on full rations.

Mon. 27ᵗʰ There is more rumours than ever now and we don't know what to believe we have been put on short rations again so I don't think there is any relief coming yet the troops are making bets on getting relieved by the end of the month.

Feb. 28ᵗʰ A dull morning everyone in a bad temper saying four months gone and still hanging on. but as soon as we had finished our bit of horseflesh the naval guns started shelling Bulwana which caused great excitement as they had not fired a shot for days everybody turned their glasses in that direction and is [*sic*] was soon seen that the boers were trying to take Long Tom away. About 4 pm Col. Rhodes[71] came galloping up and told us the boers were retiring and at 5 p.m. our Adjutant shouted Gen Bullers cavalry have entered Ladysmith under Dundonald.[72] Our feelings can be better imagined than described everyone who had strength gave a cheer and we went on duty that night with light hearts and stood in the pouring rain all night watching our guns shelling Surprise Hill. We have been continually on duty for 55 days and nights and not had a good rest or feed.

March

Tues. Mar. 1ˢᵗ We are more cheerful this morning we had a good feed of what was left at the boer laager and they had been living better than us by what we got. Supplies are fast coming in and we are free at last after a siege of 119 days which will long remain in history.

Mar. 1900

Wed. 1ˢᵗ Mar.[73] English mail of our months

Thurs. 2ⁿᵈ Expecting to go down the line to health camps it is quite a treat to get a feed and a night in bed. Lined the streets while the relief column marched in.[74]

Sun. 13ᵗʰ Left Ladysmith for Colenso halted at Onderbrook it is only a march of 8 miles but done us up.

Mon. 13ᵗʰ Marched into Colenso and passed the Railway bridge destroyed by the boers and the road bridge by Buller which only had 1 span destroyed.

Sat. 18ᵗʰ We do a parade every morning from 6.30 to 11 am without any breakfast we are allowed passes and go out for a day and see the positions Buller had to take to get to us and we don't wonder at him being so long it is wonderful to see the positions they held it would have took all the armies in the world to drive us out of them. The Army reserve men joined us also a Coy of Leic Volunteers[75] and things went on as usual till the end of the month.

Apr. 1900

Mon. 2ⁿᵈ Got the unexpected order to go up country again

Tues. 3ʳᵈ Marched to Onderbrook

Wed. 4ᵗʰ Marched into Ladysmith and camped at Sign Post Ridge against wagon hill where we stayed until 10ᵗʰ

Tues. 10ᵗʰ Marched to Surprise Hill an old position Volunteer Coy joined us

Thur. 12ᵗʰ Marched to Gun Hill where Gen Hunter blew up the boer guns in the Seige [*sic*] Gen Buller is at Elandslagt waiting for remounts the Boers are at Glencoe under Louis Botha.

26ᵗʰ See D joined at Gun Hill

Letter of Private R. Cross to his mother, reprinted in the *Leicester Daily Mercury*, 2 April 1900 and *Leicester Daily Post*, 3 April 1900

Private R. Cross, of 'G' Company, 1ˢᵗ Leicestershire Regiment, writing to his mother four days after the relief of Ladysmith, says:– 'This is the first time I have had a chance of writing, so I must now take advantage of it, after few months of worse than hard labour. It has been a very hard siege, as I suppose you have heard, but they have not told you what we are living on. We have not seen a bit of bread for two months, and the last month we have been on ¼ lb of biscuits, 3 ozs. of mealie (ground Indian corn), and 1 lb of horseflesh or mule per day. They put us on full rations on the 20ᵗʰ of February, and thought the relief column were coming in, but on the morning of the 28ᵗʰ they put us back on the quarter, so you can judge what a surprise it was at about 6 p.m. the same day when some of General Buller's cavalry rode into Ladysmith. The troops had not got much strength, but they found enough for a cheer. We had to line the roads yesterday while the relief column marched in, and they seemed to be as pleased to get here as we were to get relieved. I have been on the hills on outpost duty for the last 54 nights without a night off, and have not had a day's sickness, so I have been very lucky, but I am weak as a kitten and as fat as a match, but I hope to have a bit better time of it now. We have not seen a paper or letter all the time, so we don't know what has been going on at home. All we do know is just what we have been doing ourselves, so you know more about the war than us. But I expect we shall get the papers tomorrow, and then there will be a bit of excitement for about a week. We have a good many deaths from fever and dysentery, but considering the heavy fire we have been under at different times I think we are very lucky having such few casualties. I shall never forget Lombard's Kop, on the 30th of October, as long as I live. There is some sights to see in action. It is one thing to read about a battle, but nobody can realise the real thing until they see it for themselves. We were fired at from three different directions, and only got one way out of it, so it was lucky thing we retired in time, or I might have been in Pretoria now.'

2 After Ladysmith

Introduction

On 12 March the Leicestershire Regiment was evacuated from Ladysmith, first to Onderbrook and then to a camp beside the railway at Colenso. There the battalion was allowed nearly a month to recuperate. Much of the time was spent exploring the scenes of Buller's attempts to cross the Tugela; any resentment at the time it took the relief force evaporating as the strength of the Boer defences became apparent.[76] The battalion was reinforced by the arrival of 159 reservists, some of whom had served as stretcher-bearers with the 11th brigade.[77] On 24 March the battalion's strength was augmented further by the Service Company raised from the 1st (Volunteer) Battalion at home. A batch of 250 reservists also arrived on 21 April.[78]

At the beginning of April 1900 the Leicesters were recalled to duty, marching back to Onderbrook and then to a camp on Sign Post Ridge, two miles south-west of Ladysmith beside the main road to Colenso. Private Cross is silent for the next two months, during part of which his battalion was moved to a new camp north-east of Ladysmith and employed in the fortification of Lombard's Kop and other neighbouring hills. The exhausting labour, arduous enough to be considered worthy of comment in the battalion's history, may account for our diarist's reticence.[79]

At the beginning of May Buller's army began to move again. Whether the delay is blamed on his dithering and lack of vitality or upon necessary regrouping and re-equipping, coupled to interference from Lord Roberts, exercising his overall command,[80] there can be little doubt that Buller's next actions were decisive.

On 15 May Buller reoccupied Dundee, having outflanked a strong Boer force dug in along the Biggarsberg. Cross's battalion, though nominally part of Major General Howard's 8th Brigade, was detached to guard the advancing army's communications, with a squadron of the 18th Hussars and 19th Battery Royal Field Artillery. In the second week of June 1900, Buller pushed on over the Drakensberg, turning the flank of

223

Erasmus's strongly entrenched forces at Laing's Nek by seizing instead the pass at Alleman Nek, some eight miles to the north-west.

The Leicesters were again detached, with other elements of the 8th Brigade, to capture Wakkerstroom. The town proved to be more strongly defended than expected and fell only after several days' fighting on 17 June. On 19 June the battalion marched to Ingogo, where Buller was concentrating his army while awaiting the repair of the railway.

Cross's account begins again on 24 July 1900, with the culmination of an assault by troops under Howard and Major-General Brocklehurst on the Rooikoppies Ridge, which protected the town of Amersfoort. Cross's company was one of four detached from the Leicesters for the attack. Having driven the Boers back from the railway, Buller halted to concentrate his forces at Meerzicht, where the Leicestershire Regiment was reunited.

On 31 July, Cross heard the news of Sir Archibald Hunter's success in the Brandwater Basin, on the southern border of the Orange Free State. There over 4,300 of Marthinus Prinsloo's Free Staters, with three guns, two million rounds of ammunition and thousands of horses, cattle and sheep surrendered;[81] although Christiaan De Wet, with some 1,500 of the most determined fighters had already escaped the trap.

Buller was on the move again himself by 7 August, swiftly driving back a Boer force under Commandant D.J. Joubert which had reoccupied the Rooikoppies Ridge. Despite stiff opposition, the 4th Division supported by Brocklehurst's 2nd Cavalry and Dundonald's 3rd Mounted Brigades managed not only to capture Amersfoort but also far out-distance their transport. This necessitated another halt and the construction of defences.

The advance was resumed again on 21 August. That evening elements of Dundonald's brigade ran into the Boers at the farm of Van Wyk's Vlei. They were supported by four companies each from the 2nd Gordon Highlanders and Cross's battalion and a battery of guns. The Boers held their position until the arrival, the next day, of Major-General F.W. Kitchener's 7th Brigade. The advance was contested at each step but by now the armies of Lord Roberts, pushing on from Pretoria, and Buller were combining to crush the modest force of possibly only 5,000 men that remained with Botha against them.

Botha withdrew to a position along a ridge running for some twenty miles east of Belfast. The Boers were strongly entrenched and hopeful that their line might prove as hard to break as that along the Tugela had been six months before. Buller, who (despite the arrival of his superior,

Lord Roberts) directed the action, had learnt his lesson however and correctly identified a koppie near the farm of Bergendal as the key to the position. After a bombardment on an unprecendented scale, which clearly impressed Cross waiting with his battalion in support, the koppie was stormed by troops of the Fourth Division. The defenders, drawn from the Johannesburg police, contested every inch of ground but, as Cross witnessed, suffered terribly for their stubborn courage.

With the vital koppie in British hands, the Boers – never ones to show any sentimental attachment to mere features of the landscape – abandoned their entrenchments and withdrew towards Machadodorp, which was temporarily the seat of the Transvaal government. The British advance continued, hampered but never stopped by Botha's rearguard. At Badfontein, on 5 September, the 7th Brigade was driven from its own camp by long-range fire from a 'Long Tom'. An attempt by the Boers to occupy high ground nearer the camp was forestalled by Cross's battalion, supported by the rest of the 8th Brigade, though sniping continued until dark.

Lydenburg was occupied on 6 September. The town remained under sporadic fire from Boer artillery near the Paardeplaats farm, until 8 September when a major move by three brigades, including the 8th, drove them back out of range. While Buller continued his pursuit of Botha, and Lieutenant-General French moved on Barberton, Reginald Pole-Carew and Ian Hamilton, leading troops from Lord Robert's army, closed upon the 3,000 men under Commandant Pienaar who sought sanctuary at Komati Poort on the Mozambique border.

Cross remained at Lydenburg, however, where the Leicesters were employed on the construction of a fort at the south end of the town and in improving the town's other defences. When not wielding pick and shovel or uncoiling barbed wire, Cross and his companions were on guard or escorting convoys of supplies.

The potency of the Boers, despite frequent news of captures of men, their equipment or livestock, was proved at the end of September when five companies of the Leicesters, with a battery of guns and three squadrons of cavalry left Lydenburg to rendezvous with Buller at Krugersdorp. Not only was the column sniped at for the last eight miles of its march but even when united with Buller's force they could not prevent Boer artillery driving them from their bivouac.

On 6 October Buller left Lydenburg for home, Cross joining the troops lining the road. In the following weeks many volunteer units, including the Leicester's Volunteer Service Company also went home.

On 11 December, having been delayed by family illness and a fall from his horse, even Lord Roberts left South Africa.[82] The war was not over however. It had merely entered a new phase. The defeat of the Transvaal and Orange Free State armies in the field did not signal victory but rather the beginning of a guerilla war, that was to cost yet more in lives, money and reputations.

The Leicesters now found themselves part of Lieutenant-General N.G. Lyttelton's command, based at Middelburg, which had the near-impossible task of securing the lines of communication and supply for the network of columns operating against the Boers. Middelburg itself became a fortress, commanded by Lieutenant-Colonel G.D. Carleton of the Leicesters, with his own battalion, the 1st King's Royal Rifles and 1st Royal Inniskilling Fusiliers as a garrison.

From mid-October until the end of January the Leicesters remained at Middelburg, with companies detached to guard the railway stations at Groot and Little Oliphants River and at Rockdale Farm, four miles from the town. Convoys had to be escorted, reconnaissance patrols sent out and on several occasions, flying columns or troop trains despatched, to relieve posts threatened by raiders.[83]

At the beginning of February 1901, a new series of 'drives' against the Boers began, planned by the new Commander-in-Chief in South Africa, Lord Kitchener, and directed by Lieutenant-General Sir John French.[84] The enemy forces in the territory between the Natal and Delagoa railway lines were to be driven before a moving line of columns, to be surrounded, or forced up against the borders of Swaziland and Zululand, where they would be certain of a hostile reception. Cross's battalion provided the strongest part of Lieutenant-Colonel W.P. Campbell's column, which included detachments of the 18th Hussars, 1st King's Royal Rifles and a variety of long-range and field guns.

Although the columns enjoyed some success in rounding up a few dispirited or wounded Boers, seizing enemy livestock and burning farms, the two or three thousand still with Botha managed to strike viciously at one column, that commanded by Smith-Dorrien, at Lake Chrissie, before withdrawing safely.[85] The British operations then foundered on the usual reef of a collapsing supply system, exacerbated by unusually foul weather. Campbell's column struggled on, the troops living on biscuit and mealies, sweeping the Swazi border and gathering civilians, made destitute by the destruction of their homes and livelihoods, for transfer to concentration camps.

On 28 February 1901 Kitchener and Botha met at Middelburg, in the South African Republic, to discuss peace. The terms offered were eventually rejected (a mere two days after Cross first heard of the talks on 14 March) and the 'drives' continued. Campbell's column had not been idle. While the mounted troops joined the 'chase', Cross and his comrades pushed on into Swaziland to establish a fortified post at Sand or Zand Drift, on the Assegai River. The battalion was still on the Swazi border, finding escorts for supply convoys and parties for outposts and pickets, when Cross's diary ends on 9 April 1901.

The lot of an infantry battalion in the final phase of the war in South Africa was either to remain static as a garrison, or to endure the slow pace of ox-drawn transport as the escort to a supply column. Cross's battalion did both until November 1901 when they helped to build and garrison the Standerton-Ermelo Block House Line, the latest move in Kitchener's attempt to limit the Boers' freedom of movement. The 1st Battalion the Leicestershire Regiment was still defending the line of block houses and barbed wire when the Treaty of Vereeniging at last brought peace and the order that they should dismantle the defences.[86]

Private Cross's diary
July 1900–April 1901

July 1900

Tues 24th Fell in at 8 a.m. and advanced towards Rooi Kopje where the enemy had taken up position. The Gordons formed the firing line Leic and KRR supports the 4.7s came in action shelling the hill incessantly the Cavalry on the left flank. It was getting dusk before we got the order to advance and the Gordons were soon on the hill and the enemy went in all directions. We returned to camp at 9 pm our casualties being 5 killed 17 wounded.[87]

Wed 25th On outpost duty all day.

Thur 26th On reconnaissance again escort to 12 pr. Which shelled the enemy at 1000 yds the M.I. got close up with pom pom we retired in the afternoon with no casualties

Sat 28th had a rest yesterday and went out this morning with 4 Coys Gordons but could find no enemy the Cavalry brought in Cattle and sheep which are being killed.

Mon 30th The remainder of the Batt joined us.[88] My Coy escorted a Batt of Artillery to Zandspruit and stayed there for the night.

Tues 31st Returned from Zandspruit and got the news that Prinsloe and 5,000 boers had surrendered to Gen Hunter.[89] The troops have had a bit of a scrap here and lost 40 through the Cavalry and Artillery retiring and leaving the Infantry behind which is a regular thing here.

August 1900

Wed 1st A flag of truce went out to tell the enemy that Prinsloe had surrendered.

Thurs 2nd Relieved 4 coys Lancashire Fus off outpost at Mooi Macies Fontein

Sat 4th Gen Hilyards[90] guns can be heard in the direction of Volksrust but things are quiet here. The N.C.O.s make us as miserable as possible after taking the lions share of the rations and the captain is as bad as he dare not sleep at night for thinking they are coming it would be a godsend if he was outed.

Sun 5th We have had a visit from Buller[91] and getting ready for another big move the oxen are all being changed for mules as the country is more level. Bank H[oliday] Sunday

Mon 6th Instead of missing the train for Blackpool I was awakened by our Artillery firing and found the boers had started entrenching but soon ran for it. got 1 pint

Tues 7th The whole of the 4th Division arrived here under Gen Littleton[92] and a move is expected we are not sorry as water is

3 miles away and as black as coal. ½ bread and bis[cuit]. We started out early towards Rooi Kop and it was a fine sight to see the thin line of Khaki advance through a grass fire which the boers had lit to retire behind. We drove them back and got to Amersfoort at dusk without much opposition as they had left it to us. The transport did not come in and we got no blankets so started pulling houses down to make fires as it was a bitter cold night. At 8.30 pm I was put in the guards charge for walking 20 yards from my bivouac with Cpl. King of the Volunteers.[93]

Aug 8th A very misty morning a few boers came close up to our outpost and started sniping but were captured by the cavalry. We are having a days rest here as the transport did not get in till 10. This is Christiaan Botha's commando and he managed to get his guns away. We had 40 casualties yesterday 3 of our Regt wounded by a shell Jordan having his arm amputated.[94]

Thurs 9th Our advance guard started at 6 a.m. and it was 2.30 before we got on the move so this gives an idea what it is to move a large convoy. We saw nothing of the enemy today and it is expected they have retired to Ermelo. Halted at Reit Spruit.

Fri 10th Moved off early the 7th Brig[ade] leading it took us 8 hrs to go 6 miles to Vaal River the white flag is flying at all farms.

Sat 11th Advance guard today. Camped at Klipfontein where a grass fire done damage to Maxim and equipment.[95]

Sun 12th Marched into ermelo this is the best little place I have seen out here I was on Garr[ison] Picket so got a good look round. The people tell us the boers have 14 guns.[96]

Mon 13th Buller is looking after the transport which is a big drawback to us. Camped at Klipfontein Farm or Witbank.

Tues 14th Rear guard today marched to Kranspan it is roumoured that Baden Powell is beseiged at Rustenberg[97]

Wed 15th Marched to Twyfelaars 15 miles.

Th 16th We are halting here for a further supply of rations.

Sat 18th It is a treat to get a bath and do a bit of washing. A force visited Carolina but found all quiet.[98] We are ready for another move now as the convoy gets in tomorrow 19th. It is reported that the boers are in force at Belfast and that Hunter has captured some guns from De Wet.[99]

Tues 21st Got english mail yesterday moved off early this morning but did not get far as we had to go to assist the Cavalry who had engaged the boers and it was early morning when we reached bivouac we had 2 casualties halted at Vanwyk's Vlei.[100]

Wed 22nd The casualties were more than at first reported yesterday and 4 Coys nearly got ambushed. Order out in support 4 Casualties they have taken up position 4 miles away.

Th 23rd We drove them away this morning but bullets were more plentiful than biscuits as we are on half rations. Camped at Geluks Farm. 1 killed 6 wounded.[101]

Fri 24th Slept where we drove the enemy from yesterday their position is about 15 miles long the bearer Coy were out all night collecting wounded. Our Regt has 5 wounded.[102] We felt an Earthquake shock this afternoon.

Sat 25th Firing between the outposts all day. We can hear Lord Bobs[103] guns in the distance we have had 100 casualties in the brigade here two of our Regt killed in action today.[104]

Sun 26th The column moved off 5 miles north and attacked N E our regt and Strathconas were on rear guard and had to hold the position till dark and then retire. We had 4 wounded[105] and Strathconas had several. halted at Vogelstruispoort.

Mon 27th I had a fine birthday yesterday I did not know till this morning and it looks like keeping it up. We found the enemy at noon and our Artillery opened fire we had 48 field guns[106] besides long range guns all firing at 2 sec[ond] interval and I have never heard such a bombardment before there was a rain of shells dropping continually on their position and Johnny boer started to run but they got shelled everywhere. Our Regt was in support so we had a splendid view being just by the guns. Th [*sic*] Cavalry and R Bde advanced to the hill and captured 1 pom pom 1 12 p[ounde]r and 1 40 pr but they lost a good many men. I saw Lord Roberts[107] dismount and lay one out and salute him and prop a wounded man against an ant heap. The boers did not have a chance to take all their dead away and we saw some horrible sights caused by Lyddite[108] this is Bergendal.

Tues 28th Rear guard again we saw 16 boers on one small kopje and 4 and 5 in a group lying all over with arms and legs off and a party have been burying them all night it is an horrible sight but we cannot pity them they are turned yellow by lyddite. We saw nothing of the enemy untill nearing machadodorp and our advance guard caught them up capturing 4 wagons. They retired along the Lydenburg road and two train loads of wounded left this morning. I have been in the taking of one of Krugers capitals[109] but it is a hole.

Wed 29th Left machadodorp this morning the country is very mountainous now and difficult for transport. They are getting away as best they can going in all directions and we are close behind them burning all farms. Camp at Helvetia.

Sat 30th [*sic*; 30 August 1900 was a Thursday] There is a halt made here we have destroyed a nice farm today Pole Carews[110] division passed us for Koomati Poort

Sun 31st Gen Buller and Roberts are in camp so we expect another move. Gen French passed through here today he has been to Waterval Boven and released all our prisoners[111] most of them have gone down by train but some came here they look as if a new rig out would do them good, the boers told them we should all be friends in a few days.

Sept

Sept 1st marched to Rietfontein

Sun 2nd Marched out at 9 a.m. they have taken up on some hills and opened fire on us with 5 big guns. Our cavalry and M.I.[112] got on their left flank and lost a lot of horses and 1 man M.I. killed the losses altogether not known. Camped 5 p.m. Crocodile R[iver].

Sept 3rd On outpost duty last night no sign of enemy Maddison killed[113]

Sept 4th We have sent for supplies and are waiting for the flank columns to get up before making another move. Watkinson died of wounds[114] Inlying picket tonight.

Sept 5th the boers opened fire with long toms and shelled us out of camp at 8.30 a.m. we retired about 2 miles and then got the order to take the hill the guns were on. Our Regt formed the firing line and at 5.30 p.m. were letting them have it at 700 yards but they did not stop long we had to remain on the hill till morning without blankets and were nearly frozen to death 5 of Strathconas killed.

Sept 6th We advanced about two miles and then retired to our old camp and found the column had moved so had to do rear guard arriving at Whitclip at 10 pm got blankets at 12.30

Fri 7th Advanced guard started at 8 a.m. arriving at Lydenberg at 1 p.m. We had just got settled down when the boers started firing at 3.30 they burst shrapnell over our Regt wounding 4 and we had to move behind a hill out of sight.[115]

Sat 8th The long toms started at 8 a.m. as the troops started moving out we went through Lydenburg the 8th brigade taking the left flank. Ian Hamilton who joined us yesterday right flank and the 7th Brigade the centre and advanced toward the mountains. We got well up on the left and as soon as our Artillery got in action the boers stopped and started retiring fighting rear guard action 4 Coys of Ours escorted a battery up the hill and had to retire to escort the heavy guns up it was 3 p m when we got on top and all our guns and pompoms were firing at them retiring everyone thought they would make a stand here but I think they are about done. I don't know the casualties but saw 16 of the gay Gordons knocked over with a shell through advancing in close order.[116] It was 8 p m when we arrived in camp fairly done up but we expect a rest here.

Sun 9th Marched into Lydenberg at 12 noon Leicesters Corner[117]

Tues 11th Put on half rations again as the supplies went up with Buller and we have to wait for a convoy.

Wed 12th On Examining guard we have to see everyones pass and are having a bit of fun with the Kaffirs.

Thu 13th On guard over boer prisoners at Lydenberg Prison[118] some of them have been fined £10 for refusing to fight one was at the battle of Talana and had 7 of our bullets through him. they are allowed passes and visitors

Fri 14th Duty is rather hard here I am on inlying picket tonight

Sat 15th We hear that Lord Roberts has issued another proclamation that he will not send surrendered boers out of the country[119] and that Gen Buller has captured 72 wagons and 2 guns. They are taking men on Baden-Powells police[120] but it is only for time-expired men.

Sun 16th The troops went on church parade. Got the news from Buller that Kruger has gone to Europe[121] and handed over to botha. Gen French took Barberton capturing 27 Engines 1000 rolling stock and released 27 officers and 59 men.[122]

Mon 17th Our Regt started building huts but handed over to R B[123]

Tues 18th A deserted boer patrol came in they tell us there is a good many would come if they had the chance. They thought all the women and children had been sent away

Thurs 20th Found a cart full of ammunition in the Crocodile and went diving for it.

Fri 21st Sent 32 prisoners away with 2 Coys of ours escort

Sat 22nd Came off picket at 5 a.m. and went out at 6.30 with 2 Coys of ours 1 Battery Artillery and 2 squadrons hussars as 400 boers are reported they did not stop to fight but we captured their laager arriving in camp at 5 p m

Mon 24th 12 months without a bed or roof and alls well

Tues 25th On prison guard there were plenty of visitors and a good deal of weeping as twenty were being sent away and they think they will be shot. Got the news that Pienaar and 2,000 boers fled into the Portugese territory and handed their arms over.[124]

Wed 26th done a force march of 26 miles and captured a boer laager 2,500 cattle 6,000 sheep 50 horses 19 prisoners and 50 rifles and yesterday 624 cattle 3000 sheep 29 horses.

Thur 27th Reported capture of 250 cattle 1600 sheep 16 prisoners

Fri 28th took two kaffirs in for breaking through picket lines after being warned. News at 24th Guards Brigade entered Koomati Poort only a few rifle shots fired the bridge was found intact but prepared for destruction a very large quantity of rolling stock has been captured also some trucks of Long tom ammunition Pole

Carew reports finding 1 Long tom and 1 Cruesot gun destroyed and 300 rifles 30 Boxes SAA[125] 40 long tom shells 1 log engine. Kitchener reports Selati railway blocked with rolling stock the bridge over the Crocodile is intact so there will be little difficulty in removing this. He reports engines found at barberton to be worth £500,000. Barton[126] made a short march to Krugersdorp captured 9 prisoners 720 Trek Oxen 750 cattle 1200 sheep 24 ponies and 14 good wagons there were 1600 boer prisoners up to 16th September

Sun 30th Fell in at 4.30 this morning 5 Coys Leic 1 Battery R A and 3 Squad[rons] Lancers and Hussars with Pompom and marched to Krugers post a distance of 16 miles to meet Gen Buller. We got half way without opposition and had to fight the remainder the only gun the boers used was a pom-pom. We got in at 5 pm casualties 1 killed 5 wounded cavalry[127]

Oct 1900

Mon 1st Krugers Post is a very small place consisting of a few farms we are bivouacked on top of a hill overlooking a pass. Gen Bullers advance guard came in at 11 am and the convoy is not in at 5.30 he brought 10 prisoners in. The boers opened fire with 2 guns at 4 pm and shelled till 5.30 then started again at dusk and kept it up for 2 hrs in the dark killing 3 and wounding several of Strathconas

2nd The division moved early as the boers had gone during the night we were rear guard started at 10 am. A few followed us up but kept out of range got in Lydenberg 7 pm and it rained all night but luckily we have a house to sleep in.

3rd A wet day on picket Buller is staying here.

4th We hear that Smith Dorrien[128] is relieving us to go on 10 days trek but no orders up to now.

Fri 5th Gen Buller is taking over supreme command as Lord Roberts is going home[129] SALH and Strathconas[130] are handing equipment in.

Sat 6th Gen Buller left Lydenberg the troops lined the road he did not make any speech

Sun 7th Making preparations for a move

Mon 8th A reconnaissance in all directions our Regt left on duty firing heard in direction of Crocodile Valley

Tues 9th Left Leicesters corner at 6 am and joined the Batt[alion] leaving Lydenberg at 7.30 and marched Quagga's Hoek meeting a few snipers in Crocodile Valley but they were soon shifted, Volunteer Coy left us[131]

Wed 10th Marched off at 8 am in escort to guns fighting small rearguard action arrived at Elands Spruit at 5.30 pm

Thur 11th Marched off at 6 am support to advance guard – troubled by snipers all the way but took little notice of them arrived at Dullstroom at 12.30 pm went straight on outpost.

Fri 12th Moved off in advance at 6 am leaving Belfast on the left, got in touch with the enemy who are reported strong with a pom-pom. We had one killed of the Inniskillings 5 of Gordons wounded and 1 Hussar.[132] got in Witpoort at 5 pm

Sat 13th Started at 9 am getting in at 4.30 pm Blinkwater

Sun 14th Started 6.30 am got in at 2 pm bringing in 7 prisoners camped at Hoek Spruit.

Mon 15th Marched off at 6 am and got in communication with Middelburg at 10 am halted at 12.30 pm at Bankfontein

Tues 16th Marched into Middleburg at 12.30 pm it is a large town but very quiet. We have been getting 6 ozs of biscuits for two days and got 2 ozs of rice yesterday so they gave us some bread at 8 pm and we had a good feed. First bread for 3 m[on]ths

Wed 17th Relieved the Cornwalls[133] off duty at the railway bridge the Batt is bivouacked by the line it is a treat to see a train

Fri 19th Relieved by the Inniskilling Fusiliers

Sat 20th A party of boers sniped at F Coy on outpost duty but no one was hurt we had bathing parade.

Sun 21st Church parade. Got tents but wet through first.

Mon 22nd heavy thunder storm swam out of camp

Tues 23rd it took us all day to get dry

Wed 24th Went on outpost duty for 4 days

Fri 26th A Farmer reported a party of boers to our front at 12 noon one of the Liverpools M I[134] galloped in with the news that a patrol was surrounded the Cavalry were soon out but the boers got away again after killing 1 man and wounding seven.[135]

Sat 27th A party went to reconnoitre bringing in 7 prisoners

Sun 28th returned to headquarters

Mon 29th A canteen opened in town and we have managed to get a few things to eat and a bottle of enos.[136]

Tues 30th We are doing running drill every morning before breakfast got paid today £2.

Wed 31st another month gone and there is no more sign of the war being over than there was 12 month ago.

Nov 1900

Thurs 1ˢᵗ Every man got a new suit and we are looking well

Fri 2ⁿᵈ Are allowed to walk out in town from 2 to 6 pm but there is not much to see.

Sat 3ʳᵈ All the women and children sent out to their husbands

Sun 4ᵗʰ Church parade the Batt[alion] looked quite smart in their new clothes we only want a band now the KRR have theirs

Wed 14ᵗʰ A reconnaissance went out composed of 6 Coys Leic 5 Coys Rifles 4 Coys Cornwalls with Artillery and Cavalry we are left on outpost duty and could hear firing this afternoon

Fri 16ᵗʰ A flying column went out

Sat 17ᵗʰ The Battn returned having no casualties[137]

Sun 18ᵗʰ Returned to headquarters off outpost duty.

Mon 19ᵗʰ Artillery fire heard in the direction of Balmoral

Tues 20ᵗʰ 40 of my Coy escorted G Battery R H A[138] by train to Balmoral and found the boers had attacked the outposts there killing 6 and taking 40 prisoners of the Buffs but we arrived too late as they had cleared off after damaging the line which we soon repaired[139]

Wed 21ˢᵗ Returned to Middleburg arriving at 5.30 pm there is a concert in town but we are too tired to attend.

Thu 22ⁿᵈ O[rderly?] Serg[ean]ts are taking entries for sports held tomorrow

Fri 23 The sports were held but very dry

Wed 28[th] Started another reconnaissance at 1 pm and marched to Groat Olifants Rivier

Thu 29[th] Moved out at 4 am and marched to Witbank after leaving here we came across the boers laager they had dinner laid for 45 everything hot ready to serve up but had to do a quick move out of it and our advance guard ate it for them this is Roodepoort.[140]

Fri 30th Started at 4.15 after coming off outpost we drove the enemy in front the 83rd Battery done a lot of firing but we don't know what they done Capt. Scott[141] got captured but shot a boer and escaped we had 3 casualties Kranspoort.

Dec 1900

Sat 1st Marched off at 4.15 a good many farms burned today and the troops have got plenty of loot but the Cavalry get the big share and we are lucky if we get anything. Col Carleton is in charge and never thinks of giving us a rest we have marched 16 miles today and only halted for a quarter of an hour halted at Brugspruitpoort.

Sun 2[nd] Started at 4.15 saw nothing of the enemy burnt a few farms and marched to Olifants Rivier where B & G Co[mpan]y are left to relieve the Cornwalls off outpost duty.

Mon 3[rd] The Battalion marched to Middelburg ant [and?] the DCLI[142] left here for Elands river.

Tues 4[th] 25 men went out with 2 guns to escort a convoy from Middelberg got back at 9 am.

Wed 5[th] 4.30 am Escorted convoy half way to Witbank

Thur 6th On guard duty is hard here out every night

Fri 9th A boer patrol sniped at our outpost but were drove off

Sat 8th A column went out from Middelberg 3 Coys Leic 2 KRR & Innskgs¹⁴³ and 5 guns

Sun 9th Firing heard but no news

Mon 10th Roumour [*sic*] that Paget has surrounded a party of boers¹⁴⁴

Wed 12th The column passed through here on their way back to Middelberg 3 Coys by train the remainder on wagons they had 1 Officer and 6 men wounded Innniskillings

Sat 15th Expecting attack tomorrow as it is the anniversary of Dingaans day¹⁴⁵ every man in the trenches tonight

Sun 16th Dingaans day but no boers about

Mon 24th Went out on escort to guns returning at 11 am we found that an hogshead of beer had come up and the CS¹⁴⁶ was drunk so we all paraded up for some beer and he let us have as much as we wanted it soon began to tell on the men and at 2 oclock nearly everyone was drunk but I was for duty and kept straight The CS and Cpl Cave were put on the peg¹⁴⁷ and 13 ['eight' is here struck through and '13' superscribed] men in the clink so it was a good Xmas Eve.

Tues 25th Xmas day I managed to get a couple of fowls for dinner but was short of vegetables and dough. I was invited out to a farm but the Officer would not sign a pass so Mr. Lansberg brought me some cake and tarts and a few apricots and figs so I did not fare as bad as last year.

Wed 26th On guard at 12.30 turned out but nothing came off.

Th 27th Got 1 pint beer the prisoners [see 24 December] got 10 & 7 days

Fri 28th On patroll in the village for 2 days and nights

Sun 30th Changed posts with B Company as they are getting nights off duty and we are not.

Jan 1901

Sun 6th We are doing duty on the railway 1 night in bed.

Sat 19th On duty on the railway bridge we have made a fine bathing place and do a bit of fishing in the river

Wed 23rd We were told that Lord Kitchener[148] would come by by train the first train that went up was a goods train followed at a short distance by another with Lord Kitchener on half an hour after he passed the train came back at full speed and they reported 200 boers the advance train followed and they both remained in Station while a pilot Engine went up which got through all right and returned the trains started again and when the first engine got to the same spot again up it went with 2 carriages and the second train returned again bringing the remaining carriages back. No one hurt.

Th 24th line blown up again

Mon 28th Marched to Middelberg

Tues 29th Escorted convoy in from Pann[149]

Wed 30th On duty at Uitkijk[150] with guns

Th 31st Sent Registered letters home

Feb 1st *1901*

1st Leic Regt 1 section 21st Batt RA 2 Sq 18th Hussars with pom-pom KRR M I 1 long range 12 pr and 2 maxims with a large convoy left Middelberg under Col Campbell KRRs and marched to Halkfontein we do not know our destination[151]

Sat 2nd Marched off at 6 am and soon got in action the R A fired well we saw a shell knock 2 over. The Cavalry got in an ambush and H Coy had to get them out getting 1 man wounded[152] and the Cavalry 7. We marched to Roodepoort and went to get potatoes and found boxes of everything buried the woman told us where £81 was buried and we had to get it up. The boers are using explosive bullets and the wounded are in an awful mess we had 20 casualties altogether 7 killed and out of the remainder 8 limbs had to be taken off 1 man had 7 in him one every time he tried to load.

Sun 3rd Were on inlying picket last night stood to at 3 am and fell out at daylight. At 9 am the enemy were seen south but the artillery drove them off. At 11 am they attacked C Coy on outpost and my Coy were sent to reinforce the bullets were flying rather close but we got on the hill and let them have it with maxim and rifle and made them retire one of C Coy was hit in the leg.[153] We are collecting all women and children and taking all wagons and eatables that are good and destroying everything else. H Coy fired on a farm where there had been sniping and killed the boer and his cat & dog but the children were unhurt alhough [*sic*] bullets had gone close.

Mon 4th Marched of[f] at 4.30 at 6.30 we met Bothas force[154] with 2 guns and were fighting till dark having 4 wounded 1 being C S Jones.[155] We are in communication with Smith Dorriens column Boshmans Pan

Tues 5th Moved at 5 I was in firing line but they had gone in the night leaving a few snipers which we drove before us. Groblers farm is here with a lot more and we are taking 30 women and several wagons[156] Old Grobbler sent in to say he was coming to surrender. Groblers Spruit.

Wed 6th Marched out at 6 am being in rear we burned several farms where boers had been last night and found a lot of cattle and horses which we are taking with us to Klipfontein.

Thurs 7th Marched at 5.30 we found 11 wounded boers in a farm and one of them was old Grobler who was so bad he could not be moved but was left behind with the boer doctor. We took the other 10 to Chrissie Lake where we met Smith Dorien and Col Henry[157] and learned that Grobler had intended to attack us but made a mistake and attacked Smith Dorrien who has 7000 troops so old Grobler got a good reception and a pill but our force had 70 casualties the wounded boers tell us they had 64 casualties on Sunday 3rd.

Fri 8th Got wet through last night and are not moving today the women children and wounded are sent to Ermelo. Groblers son is a prisoner Baxters 4 sons came in and report 200 boers with 2 guns want to surrender. On outpost

Sat 9th Came off outpost and marched to Hamilton.

Sun 10th Marched to Blauwater without opposition

Mon 11th We have captured thousands of cattle and sheep and at every camp they make us kill a sheep each so that the boers will not get them. halted at Lothaire.

Tues 12th Short march of 8 miles to Bonnybrook.

Weds 13th Short march to Westoe camped by the side of the Asutu River Smith Dorrien is 4 miles away he has been fighting today and captured 40 wagons and 20 prisoners.

Thur 14th Marched into Amsterdam our Column had no opposition but Smith Dorrien was engaged with boer rearguard I went on guard at Post Office the boers have taken nearly everything of value but we got a few Curios. We are resting here for a few days.[158]

[Blank]th Left Amsterdam and marched to Woolvenkop we had a job with the transport and had to leave 1 waggon of Tommy rations but they could stop 5 hrs to bring the Officers loot on we have got to stop here on account of the swolen river and the convoy cannot get to us with rations we have been on short ½ rations for 4 days.

Sat 23ʳᵈ We are collecting mealies ready to issue as rations if we do not get some soon.[159]

Mon 25ᵗʰ Marched off at 6 am to the river which was too high to cross so we had to make another halt Shela river

Tues 26ᵗʰ The ox wagons crossed the river and we made a foot bridge over it. On outpost duty.

Wed 27ᵗʰ Started to cross the river at 5 am and all got over by 8.30 am. We got ½ lb of Mealie and two green colis for our days ration. We passed Aldersons[160] column and got to Piet Retief at 2.30 pm where all the columns meet: ½ lb Mealie.

Thurs 28ᵗʰ Rested. Part of the convoy came in but we are still on mealie.

Mar 1901

Fri 1ˢᵗ Left Piet Retief at 6 am and marched to Zandbank on the Assegai River about 12 miles

Sat 2ⁿᵈ Got 1 biscuit and 6 ozs of mealie went on outpost duty

Sun 3ʳᵈ ¼ Biscuits ¼ lb mealie

Tues 5ᵗʰ Left Zandbank at 7 am and crossed the Swaziland border in a drizzling rain we had a bad drift to cross and had to pull the wagons over with drag ropes. We halted at 2 pm at Mahamba drift ['Kroghs concession' interlined] near Mahamba Mountains

Wed 6th Marched at 6 am we are well in Swaziland the Swazis are a big race and all carry assegais and Kerrys. It has been raining 2 days and we got in wet through and have got to wait till it clears up to get dry. Umptsshenjas[161]

Thur 7th Halted for the day went on outpost duty rained all night.

Fri 8th Marched at 8 am to Kroghs Concession arr[ived] 2 pm

Sat 9th Marched back to Zandbank.

Tues 12th Were put on ¾ rations, put hauser over Assegai.[162]

Wed 13th On outpost duty 14 boers came in there was 28 went into Swaziland and the Swazis killed 14 two of these are wounded

Thurs 14th Peace conferrence being held at Middelberg[163] news later on Sangar building all morning.

Fri 15[th] Six and two in[164] full rations of everything but biscuits, bacon for breakfast. Moved camp a short distance as this is the first fine day for a week and the ground is 6 inches thick of mud.

Sat 16[th] G Co[mpan]y fell in at 8 am and marched to Potgeiters farm where we joined E Coy who took 8 prisoners yesterday this is a nice farm there was plenty of Mealies Pumpkins and Oranges and Lemons but we soon made a mess of them[165]

Sun 17[th] St. Patricks day came off outpost. The Swazis brought two boers in they said they could go nowhere without seeing English so they were hiding in the grass when the Swazies tapped them on the back and said English man want you.

Mon 18th Heavy thunder storm we got swom out and everything wet through. M I relieved by 18th Hussars

Tues 19th Still raining and no sign of a move.

Wed 20th Rain not stopped yet. Two wagons went in to Zandbank to fetch rations. Outpost duty.

Thurs 21st The wagons returned but no mail.

Fri 22nd We are getting a bit of fine weather now but there is thunder about.

Sun 24th Were put on half rations and served out with ¼ lb of tobacco the first for two months no soap yet.

Mon 25th The guide went out to find the boer position and came across one boer at a farm he fired all his revolver cartridges and had his horse killed but the boer got away and he brought in his boots horse 31 sheep 2 cows and calves. We have had several men go to hospital with fever.

Wed 27th Went on duty on an advance post 1 mile from camp

Th 28th Saw boers at 5 pm killing a bullock the cavalry went out but did not capture them

Fri 29th Got relieved by A & D Coys and marched to headquarters at Zandbank.

Sat 30th On guard at Col[onel] Campbells quarters. ¾ Rations

Sun 31st The natives brought news at 1 am that a party of boers were crossing Cralings drift[166] about 5 miles away so he sent 40 M I and 1 Coy of ours to try and cut their wagons off. The M I got back at 9 am having captured 20 boers 7 wagons 420 cattle and some rifles and ammunition. 'B' Coy went to Piet retief [*sic*]. On outpost duty.

April 1901

Mon 1st A convoy went in to Piet retief for supplies put on ½ rations again.

Tues 2nd News received that Allenbys column captured 1 Field gun and two Pompoms.[167] 13 boers drowned in a wagon which they were trying to float over the river. The convoy returned. Outpost again

Wed 3rd We got a ration of bread the first for 2 months and a bit of boer tobacco also a drop of lime-juice. Had to sleep ready to turn out in the night but did not go.

Thurs 4th ¾ rations biscuits. A Pontoon Sec[tion, Royal Engineers] came here and put a bridge over the river and my Section went out to do duty over it.

Fri 5th duty is easy here and I would like to stop until the Regt moves but we are out every other night. A Convoy went out to Allenbys force. Mush L/C[168]

Sat 6th A calf got in the river and was washed down and drowned but we soon had his throat cut and a bit of steak for breakfast.

Sun 7th Passed Easter quietly bathing and sweet spud digging were all we had to do Allnbys [sic] guns could be heard about 5 pm Campbell read news out to Batt[alion] church parade and told them we march NE in a weeks time. 22 guns captured in march.

Mon 8th Commandeered another calf and killed him and made an Irish stew of sweet spuds and veal nothing is too big now if it is eatable. Pontoon moved

Tues 9th Marched to headquarters in the afternoon. Fell in at 5 pm and went on outpost again – nearly at the same place 3 miles

Notes

1 Cross's particulars are recorded in the enlistment register of the 17th, or Leicester Military District, based at Glen Parva, Leicester. The register is deposited at the Record Office for Leicestershire, Leicester and Rutland (henceforth ROLLR): 22D63/85.

2 For the infantry-of-the-line, the Army required a recruit of at least 5 foot 3½ inches, with a 34-inch chest and a weight of 115 pounds (Lieutenant-Colonel J.M. Grierson *Scarlet into Khaki*, ed. Col. P.S. Walton (London, 1988) p. 21).

3 The police discharge certificate (ROLLR: DE 3831/324 no.167) reveals that Cross's addition of two years to his age remained with him and that in the twenty-five years since his army enlistment, he had grown two inches in height.

4 From family information, supported by trade directories and the registers of the Welford Road Cemetery (ROLLR: DE 3100/8/10 and DE 3100/38/3).

5 L.S. Amery *The Times History of the War in South Africa*, Vol. II (London, 1902) p. 103; T. Pakenham (quoting Sir H. Rawlinson) *The Boer War* (London, 1982), p. 107; A.C. Doyle *The Great Boer War* (London, 1902) p. 64.

6 Amery, *The Times History*, pp. 128–9. The question of railway rolling-stock is raised in F. Maurice, *History of the War in South Africa*, Vol. I (London, 1906) p. 126.

7 Maurice, op. cit., p. 128.

8 Letter of 'a private in "A" Company' (1st Leicestershire Regiment) in *Leicester Daily Mercury*, 29 November 1899.

9 Letter of Private A.T. Hill, 1st Leicestershire Regiment, *Leicester Daily Mercury*, 28 November 1899.

10 Amery, *The Times History*, p. 218.

11 Maurice, *History of the War*, p. 545.

12 Private J. Chamberlain, 1st Bn, Leicestershire Regiment, letter, in *Leicester Daily Mercury*, 26 March 1900.

13 The Boer view of the Observation Hill attack is given in Denys Reitz, *Commando* (Harmondsworth, 1948) pp. 72–8.

14 H.W. Wilson *With the Flag to Pretoria*, Vol. II (London, 1901) p. 524.

15 Maurice, *History of the War*, p. 545.

16 B. Kaighin, *A Diary of the Siege of Ladysmith* (Pietermaritzburg,1999) p. 48.

17 H.W. Nevinson, *Ladysmith: The Diary of a Siege* (London, 1900) pp. 274–6.

18 'DF': 2nd Battalion, Royal Dublin Fusiliers. The troops were conveyed by rail, in coal trucks. Transport waggons and men's kits were to follow by road.

19 'Cavalry joined': 18th Hussars.

20 The Dutch Reformed Church adjacent to the Leicestershire Regiment bivouac, five miles from the railway station at Glencoe and three from Dundee.

21 '4 a m': the hour at which the Dundee force paraded is the subject of great disagreement. Amery, *The Times History* (II, p. 154) and Maurice's *History of the War* (I, p. 129) cite 5 a.m. 'as usual'. The Leicestershire Regiment's own account (ROLLR: 22D63/32) states that the brigade 'stood to Arms daily at 4.30 a.m.' and is supported by a number of eye-witnesses; including Lieutenant Reginald Stirling (KRRC), *Melton Mowbray Times*, 8 December 1899, Private W. Wilkinson (Leicestershire Regiment), *Leicester Daily Mercury*, 28 November 1899 and Lance-Corporal Alfred Bishop (Leicestershire Regiment), *Leicester Chronicle and Leicestershire Mercury*, 14 April 1900. Private C. England (KRRC) wrote that 'we had to parade at 4 o'clock, and at five a.m.', *Leicester Daily Mercury*, 28 November 1899.

22 'RIF': Royal Irish Fusiliers; 'RDF': Royal Dublin Fusiliers; 'KRRs':King's Royal Rifle Corps; 'M.I.': mounted infantry.

23 Cross's estimate of British casualties approximates to both that of *The Times History* (226 killed and wounded) and of Maurice's *History of the War* (254). Amongst the casualties were Major-General Sir William Penn Symons, commander of the Dundee force, Colonel John Sherston DSO, his brigade major, and Lieutenant-Colonel R.H. Gunning, commanding officer of the 1st Bn KRRC. The circumstances of Lieutenant-Colonel B.D. Möller's capture by the Boers are fully discussed in the Marquess of Anglesey's *A History of the British Cavalry*, Vol. IV (London, 1986) pp. 38–46.

24 General Petrus (Piet) Jacobus Joubert (1831–1900) Vice-President and Commandant-General of the Transvaal (South African Republic).

25 Lieutenant William M.P.J. Hannah was apparently struck by the base of a shell. Those wounded were Farrier Sergeant Sheppard, 18th Hussars, attached to the Leicestershire Regiment mounted infantry and No. 3604 Private John H. Wood.

26 Elandslaagte, 21 October 1899. A Boer force under J.H.M. Kok occupied a position near the station at Elandslaagte, cutting the railway north of Ladysmith towards Dundee. The Boers were driven off by a strong column from Ladysmith under Major-General J.D.P. French, reinforced by troops under Colonel Ian Hamilton.

27 The medal roll records two Privates Kelly, neither of whose medals had clasps for Talana or Defence of Ladysmith.

28 Cross's memory is presumably at fault. Amery and Maurice both record thirty-three waggons, escorted by two companies of the Leicesters. Lance-Corporal W. Neal, who served with the regimental transport, wrote that '27

mule and bullock wagons went & loaded up': 'A Diary of the South Africa War', in *The Green Tiger* (Leicestershire Regiment magazine), Vol. 27, 1953, p. 61.

29 Cross's description of the withdrawal from Dundee to Ladysmith agrees, generally, with other published accounts. Cross's 'Dasfontein Pass' is presumably the Van Tonder's Nek of *The Times History* (II, p. 201) and Van Tonder's Pass of R.W.F. Droogleever's 'General Yule's Retreat from Dundee', in *Soldiers of the Queen*, No. 78 (Sept. 1994), pp. 18–21. Mention of 'Sundys River' on 24 October is an error for the Waschbank. Indeed, the probably later addition of 'Waschbank 9 a.m.', recording the halt beside the river to allow the rearguard to catch-up, seems proof of Cross's slip.

   The reference to the 'Tintainyona Fight', when Sir George White's force sallying from Ladysmith ran into their enemy first at Tintwa Inyoni and then nearby at Rietfontein, seems also to have been an afterthought by Cross, whose location of the distant gunfire heard by Yule's column must have relied on hindsight.

30 The breakfast received from the 1st Battalion, Gloucestershire Regiment was of 'hot coffee and new bread' (J. Nicholls (ed.) 'No News of the Relief Column', the diary of Private Arthur Nicholls, transcribed 1992, p. 4, in private hands).

31 A cable was received from Queen Victoria.

32 Major-General Sir Archibald Hunter, KCB (1856–1936); Chief-of-Staff to Sir George White.

33 Cross's estimate of the casualties suffered by his own battalion tallies reasonably closely with the Leicesters' own records. The regiment's casualty roll (ROLLR: 22D63/90/2) lists three dead, Privates Booth, Fitzpatrick and Robinson, twenty wounded and six missing – later released. The regiment's 'Historical Notes', a roughly contemporary record, gives the casualties as three killed and eighteen wounded (ROLLR: 22D63/32). Cross's estimate of 'about 100' for the entire force, even without the detachment captured at Nicholson's Nek, is less credible. Sir George White reported losses of sixty-six killed, 249 wounded and 954 missing (*The Boer War: Ladysmith and Mafeking, 1900* (London, 1999) p. 11).

34 The column captured at Nicholson's Nek included five and a half companies of the 1st Gloucestershire Regiment, in addition to the Royal Irish Fusiliers and No. 10 Mountain Battery, Royal Garrison Artillery.

35 Major-General John Denton Pinkstone French (1852–1925) was summoned, with his staff, to command the cavalry in the Cape. The last train also carried the invalid, Major-General Yule.

36 On 2 November White had assigned defensive positions. Five companies of Cross's battalion occupied Cove Redoubt, two companies Gordon Post and another, 'H', was assigned to the armoured train at the railway station. The mounted infantry company was deployed as a cattle guard.

37 'and expecting 14 days seige' [*sic*] seems to have been added later.

38 The convent in Ladysmith had been converted to a hospital.

39 A 'live' royal salute of twenty-one guns was fired in honour of the Prince of Wales's birthday.

40 Attacks were made by the Boers upon Observation Hill and Wagon Hill, both of which had been piquetted but not entrenched.

41 Cross here reports satire as fact. Chlorodyne was provided at Joubert's request, to combat dysentery in the besiegers' camps and gave rise to the invention, reported by H.W. Nevinson (*Ladysmith*, p. 96) 'that Joubert asked for some forage . . . and Sir George White replied: "I would very gladly accede to your request, but have only enough forage myself to last three years"'.

42 Although apparently opposed by Louis Botha and other, more active Boer leaders (Amery, *The Times History*, III, p. 158), Joubert agreed to the construction of a 'neutral' camp for sick and civilians at Intombi Spruit.

43 The Boer siege guns all received nicknames from their intended victims. The 155mm Creusot on Umbulwana was usually named 'Puffing Billy' but, as 'Long Tom' also became a general term for the heavier guns deployed by the Boers, 'Long Tom' or 'Long Tom on Umbulwana' is common.

44 'I.L.H.': Imperial Light Horse.

45 Bester's Farm lay some three miles to the south of Ladysmith, Bester's Valley forming a no-man's-land beyond Caesar's Camp or the Platrand. Bester seems to have been generally distrusted by the garrison and in November 1899 was arrested as a traitor (Nevinson, *Ladysmith*, p. 114).

46 The rumour was incorrect. Joubert was raiding deep into Natal. If Cross's diary was written up some days in arrears, however, the rumour may have been a reflection of the riding accident, on 23 November, which inflicted severe internal injuries on Joubert.

47 Lieutenant F.G. Egerton RN was mortally wounded by a Boer shell on 2 November 1899. Although Egerton took the amputation of his legs calmly, drinking champagne, smoking and joking that his cricketing days were over, he died that night. The Egerton district of Ladysmith is named in his honour. (Nevinson, *Ladysmith*, p. 61; Lewis Childs, *Ladysmith: The Siege* (Barnsley, 1999) p. 89).

48 The inconclusive engagement at Willow Grange, 23 November 1899. A night attack on Boer forces at Brynbella, on the Mooi River, was followed by the withdrawal of the Boers and the occupation of Frere by the British.

49 Natal Carbineers' sports.

50 Cross refers to the raid by the Natal Carbineers and Imperial Light Horse, with detachments of guides, engineers and artillery, under Sir Archibald Hunter, on the Boer emplacement at Gun Hill. Two Boer guns, a 94-pounder and a 4.7-inch howitzer, were destroyed and a machine-gun captured. Cross refers again to the raid in his entry for 8 December 1899. Clearly the diarist was not with the four companies of his battalion which made a diversionary raid to the north of Ladysmith the same night (ROLLR: 22D63/32).

51 News had presumably reached Ladysmith of Lord Methuen's continued advance towards Kimberley after the victories of Belmont (23 November 1899) and Graspan (25 November 1899) and despite the set back at the Modder River (28 November 1899).

52 Cross seems confused. He presumably refers to the raid on 'Surprise Hill' by four companies of the 2nd Rifle Brigade, which led to the putting out of action of another 4.7-inch howitzer.

53 The anniversary of the defeat by the Boers of Dingaan's Zulus at Blood River, on 16 December 1838, was celebrated each year throughout the Transvaal and Orange Free State.

54 Major-General Andrew Gilbert Wauchope (1846–99) was killed at the head of his Highland Brigade at Magersfontein, 11 December 1899.

55 Presumably Cross anticipates the Boer habit of refraining, generally, from bombarding Ladysmith on Sundays.

56 Private Herbert Britland was reported dead from dysentery on 25 December 1899. The other death is presumably that of Private Charles Darlow, two days later (ROLLR: 22D63/90/1).

57 Lieutenant C.P. Russell, 1st Leicestershire Regiment, died of enteric fever at the Intombi Field Hospital on 5 January 1900 (S.A. Watt, 'Intombi Military Hospital and Cemetery' in *South Africa Military History Journal*, Vol. 5, No. 6).

58 Lord Roberts, having been appointed 'Field Marshal Commanding in Chief the Forces in South Africa' in December 1899, actually arrived in Cape Town on 10 January 1900 (A. Wessels, *Lord Roberts and the War in South Africa* (Stroud, 2000) pp. 19 and 26).

59 Lieutenant-Colonel William Henry Dick-Cunyngham VC was mortally wounded by a near-spent bullet whilst bringing up the remainder of his battalion, 2nd Gordon Highlanders. He had been wounded in the arm at Elandslaagte and returned to duty on 13 December 1899 (Childs, *Ladysmith*, p. 102).

60 Archibald James Leofric Temple, Earl of Ava, Lieutenant, 17th Lancers, attached to Sir George White's staff.

61 The Leicestershire Regiment's casualty roll lists only two: Privates J.H. Hunt, slightly wounded, and J. Richardson, severely wounded.

62 The narrow escape of Sergeant-Major F. Arculus and Quartermaster-Sergeant A. Johnson was widely noted – but on 20 November 1899.

63 'Chevril', and other horse-products, were manufactured in the long engine-shed at Ladysmith's railway station. The horse-halves were boiled in iron trolleys, sunk into the engine-pits.

64 'Kranz Kloof'; a ravine at the centre of the Boer Tugela line, immediately north of Vaal Krantz. Presumably Cross could see the bombardment preliminary to Sir Charles Warren's crossing of the Tugela, on 18 January 1900.

65 No. 3835 Private John Arthur Arnold, reported dead of disease on 17 January 1900 (ROLLR: 22D63/90/1).

66 The Leicestershire Regiment's casualty roll records Private Thomas Whitehead killed in action on 21 February and Private E. Evans wounded (ROLLR: 22D63/90). The 'historical notes' on the 1st Battalion (ROLLR: 22D63/32) has a marginal note of '3 casualties in H. Coy. 2 killed 1 wounded 21.2.00'.

67 The defenders of Ladysmith were listening to the fighting at Spion Kop, which had been seized by Brigadier-General Woodgate's brigade of the relief column on 23 January and held at great cost until the early hours of the following morning.

68 'On the 18th January the Enemy brought into position an old mortar that threw a round shot with a wooden fuze. it often tried to reach our outposts but failed' (ROLLR: 22D63/32).

69 Cronje, still at Magersfontein, was under increasing pressure from the army corps massing under Lords Roberts and Kitchener.

70 Cingolo and Monte Cristo, heights occupied by the Boers on the southern bank of the Tugela River, were stormed by the relief column on 17 and 18 February respectively.

71 Colonel Francis William Rhodes (1851–1905), the elder brother of Cecil Rhodes. Implicated in the plotting that led to the Jameson Raid, Rhodes was imprisoned by the Boers and placed on the British Army retired list. He served with the Imperial Light Horse.

72 Douglas Mackinnon Baillie Hamilton Cochrane, twelfth Earl of Dundonald (1852–1935), Colonel commanding 2nd Mounted Brigade.

73 Cross is clearly confused as to the correct date, a sign perhaps of his increasing fatigue or illness. 1 March 1990 was actually a Tuesday. Cross's dating remains at fault until 2 April which he correctly gives as Monday.

74 The relief column marched into Ladysmith, along streets lined by the garrison, on 3 March 1900.

75 A service company, drawn from the 1st Volunteer Battalion, Leicestershire Regiment.

76 Letter of No. 584 Sergeant T. Wain, Mounted Infantry Company, Leicestershire Regiment, in *Leicester Daily Mercury*, 4 May 1900.

77 The letters of 3180 Private J. Dexter and 3142 Private L. Warsop, recording their experiences as stretcher-bearers at Spion Kop were printed in the *Leicester Daily Mercury* (and elsewhere) on 26 February 1900 and 19 March 1900 respectively.

78 ROLLR: 22D63/32.

79 Ibid.; the battalion's diary records 'the men working 10 hours a day for some weeks'.

80 *The Times History* is generally critical of Buller and has influenced many subsequent writers. D. Judd and K. Surridge, in *The Boer War* (London, 2002), for example, portray a prevaricating Buller left to his own devices by an exasperated Roberts. G. Powell in *Buller: A Scapegoat?* (London, 1994) pp. 180–6 has Buller pestered by Roberts, given contradictory and changing

instructions, yet facing the worse terrain and more active enemy. Thomas Packenham, *The Boer War* (London, 1982) p. 379, has evidence that Buller was ordered by Roberts to remain on the defensive, despite his protests.

81 B. Williams (ed.), *The Times History of the War in South Africa*, Vol. IV (London, 1906) pp. 339–42.

82 Wessels, *Lord Roberts*, p. 94.

83 ROLLR: 22D63/32.

84 E. Childers (ed.), *The Times History of the War in South Africa*, Vol. V (London, 1907) pp. 159–60.

85 Ibid., pp. 166–8.

86 Lieutenant-Colonel E.A.H. Webb, *A History of the Services of the 17th (The Leicestershire) Regiment* (London, 1912) p. 224.

87 Cross's total is confirmed by the casualty roll which records one Gordon Highlander killed, two died of wounds and fifteen wounded, one KRRC killed, one Manchester wounded and one Connaught Ranger killed and one wounded.

88 Four companies had been detached under Captain W.S. Melvill on 21 July, to assist in the capture of Rooikoppies. The battalion was reunited at Meerzicht (ROLLR: 22D63/32).

89 Although some 1,500 escaped through 'Golden gate', Marthinus Prinsloo, with 4,314 men, three guns, 2,800 cattle, 4,000 sheep, 5–6,000 horses and two million rounds of ammunition were captured by forces under Sir Archibald Hunter. Williams, *The Times History*, IV, pp. 339–42.

90 Major-General Henry John Thoroton Hildyard (1846–1916) commanding 5th Division.

91 General Sir Redvers Henry Buller (1839–1908) VC, Commander-in-Chief in South Africa, from 1899 until superseded by Lord Roberts.

92 Major-General Hon. (later Sir) Neville Gerald Lyttelton (1845–1931) commanding 4th Division.

93 No. 6759 Corporal A. King, Service Company, 1st (Volunteer) Battalion, Leicestershire Regiment.

94 The regimental history records three casualties 'wounded with the Maxim gun which was slightly damaged by a splinter of a Boer shell' (ROLLR: 22D63/32) but the casualty rolls record only 3577 Private C. Wesley and 4248 Private H. Jordan wounded at Amersfoort. Jordan, a left-handed man, apparently lost his left hand to shellfire (Diary of Private W. Cox – private possession).

95 An incident blamed by Private Frank Rippon, of the Leicesters' Volunteer Service Company, on the cooks of the King's Royal Rifle Corps (ROLLR: DE5172).

96 Williams, *The Times History*, IV, p. 438, suggests 'Buller had to reckon with 3,000 to 4,000 Boers with fourteen guns and some pom-poms'.

97 Major-General Robert Stephenson Smyth Baden-Powell (1857–1941). Williams, *The Times History*, IV, p. 361 records that Baden-Powell's and Ian Hamilton's forces joined outside Rustenburg on 6 August but the next day

were ordered to retire to Commando Nek, which they reached on 9 August, having evacuated not only Rustenburg but also Olifant's Nek.

98 Three squadrons of Strathcona's Horse captured Carolina on 14 August, driving off a small force of Boers and destroying enemy supplies. Williams, *The Times History*, IV, p. 439.

99 Christiaan De Wet (1854–1922) commander of the Heilbron Commando, then General and Chief Commandant of Orange Free State forces.

100 18th Hussars, with a detachment of 5th Lancers and a company of Mounted Infantry, were caught in a fire-fight with the Bethal Commando, entrenched on the Frischgewaagd Ridge. Half battalions of the Leicesters and Gordon Highlanders were sent to their aid, with a battery of guns. They remained in action until 11 p.m. The Leicesters casualties, both severely wounded, were 5066 Private A.W. Underwood and 3907 Private B. Pick. See Williams, *The Times History*, IV, p. 444 and ROLLR: 22D63/90.

101 Casualties reported at Geluk's Farm, 23 August 1900 (ROLLR: 22D63/90): 3709 Private John Thomas Wilford, died of wounds; 4623 Private J.W. Chesney, missing – since died; 5069 Private H.C. Corbett, severely wounded; 5818 Private C. Hall, severely wounded; 1499 Private A.H. Morris, severely wounded – invalided home 31 January 1901; 4094 Private G. Phipps, slightly wounded; 4238 Private H. Snow, slightly wounded and 6508 Private J. Webb, slightly wounded.

102 3514 Corporal A. Coote, severely wounded; 1424 Private J. Litton slightly wounded – invalided 30 November 1900; 854 Private F. Preston, dangerously wounded – invalided 13 November 1900; 6696 Corporal W. Norton (Volunteer Service Company), severely wounded and 6724 Private R. Tomlinson (VSC), severely wounded.

103 Frederick Sleigh, Baron (later Earl) Roberts (1832–1914), Field Marshal and Commander-in-Chief in South Africa.

104 5069 Private H.C. Corbett died of wounds received on 23 August and 4590 Private Arthur Horsfield killed in action.

105 The casualty roll (ROLLR: 22D63/90) records only two: Sergeant E.J. Horner, 3rd Battalion Leicestershire Regiment (Militia) slightly wounded and 3848 Private J.H. Trigg severely wounded.

106 Williams, *The Times History*, IV, p. 452, states 'Buller's thirty-eight guns'.

107 Cross, with his battalion in support, would have been well placed to see Lord Roberts, who rode over from Belfast to observe the bombardment with Buller and Lyttelton. Williams, *The Times History*, IV, p. 453.

108 Lyddite: high explosive developed at Lydd in Kent in 1888. Composed largely of picric acid, the explosive tended to stain its victims and the area around them yellow.

109 Machadodorp served as the seat of the Transvaal government from 5 June until 27 August 1900.

110 Lieutenant-General Reginald Pole-Carew (1849–1924) commanding 11th Division.

111 The prisoners were presumably those at Nooitgedacht, released on the orders of General B.J. Viljoen, who was appalled at the conditions in which they were held (Williams, *The Times History*, IV, p. 457). The prisoners were asked by their captors not to loot the farms on their way back to their friends.

112 Two squadrons of South African light horse, Strathconas, and 4th Division Mounted Infantry.

113 3365 Private George Maddison, killed in action, 2 September 1900, at Badfontein.

114 2268 Private Joseph Watkinson, died of wounds, Badfontein.

115 The regimental history (ROLLR: 22D63/32) records the incident and the wounding of five men by shrapnel and shell splinters but the casualty roll names only three: Private J. Parker, severely wounded; 2555 Private G. Robinson, severely wounded and 5141 Private G. Matthews, slightly wounded.

116 Williams, *The Times History*, IV, p. 466, records one man killed and twenty wounded of the Volunteer Service Company, 2nd Gordon Highlanders, as they were 'moving to a flank in column . . . the Volunteers nevertheless, continued their advance with perfect steadiness'.

117 'Leicester corner' was presumably the section of the town's defences, with its fort (Fort Howard) entrusted to Cross's battalion.

118 Cross seems to refer to prisoners held by the Boers at Lydenberg. These included citizens of the South African Republic fined for refusing to join their commando; see Fransjohan Pretorius, *Life on Commando during the Anglo-Boer War 1899–1902* (Cape Town, 1999) p. 188.

119 Lord Roberts issued a proclamation for the Transvaal on 14 August, repeated for the Orange River Colony (as the Orange Free State had been renamed) on 1 September that Boers who had not yet taken the oath of loyalty would be liable to transportation on capture.

120 The South African Constabulary, raised by Baden-Powell, 1900–3.

121 Stephanus Johannes Paulus Kruger (1825–1904), the Transvaal's State President, sailed for Europe aboard the Dutch cruiser *Gelderland* from Lorenço Marques on 19 October 1900.

122 Williams, *The Times History*, IV, p. 472 lists forty-four locomotives, with two entire trains, eighty British prisoners, 2,500 Boer refugees and 'vast stores of supplies' amongst the haul at Barberton.

123 2nd Battalion Rifle Brigade.

124 The majority of the Boers trapped against the Portuguese border at Komatipoort were led across into internment by Commandant J.J. Pienaar of the Johannesburg Commando on 24 September 1900.

125 Small arms ammunition.

126 Major-General Geoffry Barton (1844–1922), commanding 6th (Fusiliers) Brigade.

127 The small force of Leicesters, with cavalry and guns, commanded by Lieutenant-Colonel Wolseley Jenkins, 19th Hussars, rendezvoused with

Buller at Kruger's Post. The camp was shelled by a Boer long-tom, killing Second-Lieutenant H.W. Cuming, 1st Devonshire Regiment, and another of the South African Light Horse, and wounding eight others. Williams, *The Times History*, IV, p. 480; L. Creswicke, *South Africa and the Transvaal War*, Vol. VI (Edinburgh, 1901) p. 111 and ROLLR: 22D63/32.

128 Major-General Horace Smith-Dorrien (1858–1930) commanding 19th Brigade.

129 Presumably a slip of the pen, in view of the following entry.

130 South African Light Horse and Strathcona's Horse: a Canadian mounted unit, raised and equipped at the expense of Lord Strathcona and Mount Royal, the Canadian High Commissioner in the UK, and commanded by Colonel S.B. Steele, of the North-West Mounted Police.

131 The Volunteer Service Company departed for home at 5 p.m., with the Gordon Highlanders' Volunteers, as escort to a convoy and guard for fifteen Boer prisoners being taken to Pretoria.

132 The Natal Field Force casualty roll records no. 2226 Private P. Devinney, 1st Royal Inniskilling Fusiliers, killed at Witpoort, 12 October 1900. Only two Gordon Highlanders are recorded as wounded and no Hussars.

133 2nd Battalion Duke of Cornwall's Light Infantry.

134 1st King's (Liverpool) Regiment, mounted infantry company.

135 The casualty roll records the death of no. 5322 Private G.W. Clayton, 1st Liverpools, at Middelburg on 26 October 1900.

136 Presumably the fruit salts tonic.

137 The column, commanded by Lieutenant-Colonel G.D Carleton (Leicestershire Regiment), consisted of 18th Hussars, 21 Battery Royal Field Artillery, one 5-inch gun, six companies Leicesters, and four companies KRRC. The force marched to Elandslaagte and back to Middelburg, via Schietpad and Sterkstroom (Diary of Lieutenant W.H.W. Young – ROLLR: 22D63/92/1).

138 Royal Horse Artillery.

139 General B.J. Viljoen's Boers made simultaneous attacks on British posts at Balmoral and Wilge River, on 19 November 1900. Though beaten off, an outlying post of the 2nd East Kent Regiment (The Buffs) suffered six men killed and thirty-one captured. Childers, *The Times History*, V, p. 61 and H.M. and M.G.M. Jones, *Gazetteer of the Second Anglo-Boer War* (Milton Keynes, 1999).

140 A strong force, consisting of six companies Leicesters, 18th Hussars, 21st Battery RFA, a pom-pom and a 12-pounder quick-firing gun commanded by Lieutenant-Colonel Carleton (Diary of Lieutenant W.H.W. Young – ROLLR: 22D63/92/1) narrowly missed Viljoen; see Childers, *The Times History* V, p. 61.

141 Presumably Major E.R. Scott, second in command of the battalion.

142 2nd Battalion Duke of Cornwall's Light Infantry.

143 1st Battalion Royal Inniskilling Fusiliers.

144 This presumably refers to the action at Rhenoster Kop, 29 November 1900. Major-General Arthur Henry Fitzroy Paget (1851–1928) with the 1ˢᵗ West Ridings and 1ˢᵗ Royal Munsters, nine guns and 1,200 Yeomanry and Australian and New Zealand mounted troops, attempted to encircle Viljoen. The attack ended in failure but after a day's fierce fighting (and eighty-five British casualties) the Boers withdrew, leaving a few men behind who had not received word to withdraw. Childers, *The Times History* V, pp. 62–3 and Marquess of Anglesey, *History of the British Cavalry* IV, p. 211.

145 'Dingaan's Day': see note 53 above.

146 Colour Sergeant.

147 'on the peg', i.e. under arrest. The corporal was probably no.3876 Corporal H.S. Cave, who appears in the medal rolls as a private once again!

148 Major-General Horatio Herbert Kitchener, Baron Kitchener of Khartoum (1850–1916). Kitchener accompanied Lord Roberts to South Africa, where he served as Chief-of-Staff. On Roberts's return home, Kitchener succeeded him as Commander-in-Chief. He remained in South Africa until the conclusion of the war in May 1902.

149 Pan was a settlement with a station on the railway from Pretoria to the Portuguese border at Komatipoort, some 12½ miles east of Middelburg. It was defended by a small British garrison. See Jones and Jones *Gazetteer*.

150 Uitkyk; another defended station on the Pretoria–Komatipoort line, five miles from Middelburg.

151 The column commanded by Lieutenant–Colonel W. Pitcairn Campbell, 2ⁿᵈ KRRC, was one of three despatched into the Ermelo district in the hope either of destroying the enemy there or of driving them against the Swaziland frontier. Childers, *The Times History* V, pp. 159–60 gave Campbell 250 men of the 18ᵗʰ Hussars, 120 of the 1ˢᵗ King's Royal Rifles mounted infantry company, the 1ˢᵗ Leicesters' 850 men, a 5-inch howitzer, one 12-pounder naval gun, and a section (two guns) each of the 21ˢᵗ Battery Royal Field Artillery and pom-poms.

152 No. 3591 Private J. Shelton, reported slightly wounded, 2 February 1901.

153 No. 5049 Private A. Hill.

154 Christiaan Botha's attention was, in fact, not upon Colonel Campbell's column but on that commanded by Smith-Dorrien, which was approaching Lake Chrissie.

155 No. 2350 Colour Sergeant G. Jones and 3075 Corporal T. Barnett were reported severely wounded and 5396 Private W.C. Heggs, slightly wounded. Jones, known as 'Cruet' was sent by the commanding officer with twelve men to push fifty yards forward. Though sheltered behind an ant-hill, Jones was severely wounded in the right arm (letter of Colour Sergeant A. Wood, quoted in ROLLR: DE5935/1 'The Boer War Letters').

156 Private W. Cox in his diary recalled a cool reception from 'Mrs. Grobelear' [Grobelaar]. She was brought in by the column, in her own wagon.

157 Colonel St G.C. Henry, commanding the cavalry attached to Smith-Dorrien's column: 5th Lancers, 2nd Imperial Light Horse and 3rd Mounted Infantry.

158 The inscription 'Amsterdam Cricket Club' on Cross's diary suggests a possible occupation during the period of rest or, if the diary was copied up at a later date, that the book itself was one of the 'curios', perhaps from the post office.

159 For the break-down in the supply system due to flooded rivers, see Childers, *The Times History* V, pp. 175–6.

160 Brigadier-General E.A.H. Alderson, commanding a column consisting of 13 and 14 Battalions, Mounted Infantry, King's Own Yorkshire Light Infantry, Canadian Scouts, Volunteer Company, Mounted Infantry and two batteries.

161 Mshungu's Drift.

162 Childers, *The Times History* V, p. 176, records the use of 'wire ropes, pontoons, or rafts' to cross swollen rivers impassible to wagons.

163 Lord Kitchener and Louis Botha met to discuss peace terms at Middelburg on 28 February 1901.

164 Cross enlisted on 15 January 1895 and so, on 15 March 1901, had completed six years and two months' service.

165 Private Cox recalled that the farmhouse was itself wrecked; its doors and window frames being burnt as fuel.

166 De Kraalen Drift. Campbell's haul of prisoners, wagons and livestock is confirmed by Childers, *The Times History* V, p. 180 and Jones and Jones, *Gazetteer*, p. 54.

167 Colonel Edmund Henry Hynman Allenby (1861–1936), commanding a column, succeeded in capturing a gun and two pom-poms at Langdraai Drift, on 31 March 1901. Childers, *The Times History* V, p. 180.

168 Presumably a friend of Cross's promoted to lance-corporal.

Index to John Wilson's Journal

Abercrombie, Sir James, 54, 93

Aire, Siege of, 81

Anne, Queen, 8, 13, 29, 48, 58, 94, 97, 115

d'Arco, Comte, 41, 45, 117–18

Arleux, 9, 81–2

Ath, 28, 105

Athlone, Earl of, 22, 29–31, 33, 36, 38, 100

Atkinson, C.T., 6

Asch, 35, 106

Augsburg, 45, 47

Baden, Prince Louis of, 43–6, 48, 90, 98, 118–19

Bavaria, Elector of, 19–26, 41, 46–8, 50–6, 103–4, 118

Bavay, 79

Berwick, Duke of, 37, 66, 99–100

Bethune, siege of, 81

Bishop, Cpl, 84

Blackadder, Col J., 6

Blenheim,
village, 49–55, 120–1
battle of, 49–58, 98, 114–15, 119–21

Blood, Brig H., 42

Bonn, 39

Bouchaine, 91, 105

Brabant, Lines of, 36, 58

Bruges, 69, 92–3, 105

Brussels, 21, 28

Cadogan, W., Earl of, 34, 36–7, 98–9

Casualties, 17–18, 26, 44–5, 56–7, 63–4, 66–7, 80, 83, 91–2, 121, 125

Catinat, Marshal N. de, 28, 114

Cave, Maj Gen, 23, 26

Charles, Archduke, Charles III of Spain and VI of Austria, 39

Chelsea, Royal Hospital, 64, 93

Churchill, Gen C., 40, 48, 53, 99, 120

Coblenz, 40, 105, 117

Coehorn, Baron M. van, 18, 33, 37, 99, 113

Courtrai, 60–1

Cranenburghs, 29, 32–3

Cranstoun, Col, 6

Cutts, Lord J., 22–5, 30, 36–7, 40, 45, 50–55, 99, 113, 120

Danube, river, 41, 48–50, 53, 118

Deane, Pte, 6, 118, 122

Donauwörth, 41, 43, 45, 48–50, 98, 105, 117–18

Douai,
siege of, 81
town, 65, 74, 82, 105

dragoons, 17, 22, 25, 31, 35, 43, 54, 79, 89, 92–3

Duikenburgh, 32, 43

Dunkirk, 84, 92–4

Eckeren, battle of, 39

Eugene, Prince, of Savoy, 41, 48–52, 55, 57–8, 62, 64, 66–7, 72, 75–6, 78, 80, 90, 119–20, 123

Evans, Brig, 24, 65, 68

Fagel, Gen F.N., 32–3, 100

Ferguson, Gen 40, 59

foot guards, 17
Fort Kehl, 47, 119
Fort Knocke, 84–90
fusiliers, 22

Genappe, 34, 76
George I, King of England, 8, 13, 94, 98, 101
Ghent, 64, 67, 92–3
Goor, Lt Gen van, 42–3, 45, 68
Grave, 30, 32–4
grenadiers, 19, 22, 24–5, 42–4, 59–60, 62, 70, 83
Guiscard, Comte, 20–1

Haliday, Ens. W., 15–16
Hanover,
    Elector of, 34
    Ernest Augustus, Prince of, 34
    Maximilian, Prince of, 47
Hare, Dr, 6
Harrison, Brig, 8, 13, 112
Hertford, Earl of, see Seymour, A.
Hesse-Cassel, Landgrave of, 21–2, 38, 43, 45, 76, 116
Höchstadt, 52–3, 55, 120–1
Holstein-Beck, Prince of, 57, 61, 121
Holstein-Ploen, Duke of, 20, 22
Hompesch, Lt Gen Comte, 42–4, 48, 50, 118
Hornes, Comte, 43, 45
hospital, 56, 63
hussars, 43, 47, 55, 75, 79, 119
Huy, 39

Ingoldsby, Lt Gen R., 40, 45, 48
Ingolstadt, 47–8

Kaiserswerth, 29–30, 33–4, 106
Kane, Brig R., 6, 84

Lech, river, 46, 48
Lediard, T., 5, 67, 111–12, 118, 121
Lesley, Sir J., 15–16, 112

Lille,
    city, 106
    siege of, 62–9
Lottum, Comte, 71–3
Lumley, Gen H., 40, 42, 44, 93

Maas (Meuse) river, 17, 19–21, 26, 34–5, 40, 106, 115
Mackay, Gen H., 114
Mackay, Hon. R.H., 114
Main, river, 50, 106
Malplaquet, battle of, 75–9, 91, 98, 103, 124–5
Marlborough, Duke of, 8, 13, 34–8, 41–2, 44, 46–52, 55, 58, 68, 72–6, 80–1, 84, 90, 97, 101, 111, 116, 119, 122
Marsin, Marshal F. Comte de, 51, 55
Menin, 63, 66, 85, 89–90
Mérode-Westerloo, Fd Marshal, Comte de, 6, 114
Mesgrigny, M. de, 71–2, 123
Millner, Sgt J., 6, 125
Mons, 75, 80, 98, 125
Mook, 30, 34
Moselle, river, 40, 58
Motte, Comte de la, 37, 69
Munich, 47

Namur, 17–28
Nebel, river, 49, 120
Neuburg, 46, 48
Nieuport, 92–4, 106
Nijmegan, 30–4, 106, 115
Nordlingen, 56, 118, 120
Northumberland, Duke of, 8
Non Plus Ultra, lines of, 81

Orchies, 74, 124
Orkney, Gen G.H., Earl of, 39, 42, 45, 51–5, 66, 69, 100, 121, 123–4
Ormonde, Duke of, 8, 13, 84, 101
Ostend, 61, 93–4

Oudenarde, battle of, 62, 98, 105
Overkirk, Fd Marshal H., 64

Pallandt, Maj Gen, 43, 45, 118
Parker, Capt R., 6, 84
pioneers, 74

Quesnoy, siege of, 91

Ramillies, battle of, 60–1, 98, 101, 117
Ramsey, Maj Gen, 17, 20, 101
regiments,
    1st Foot Guards, 42, 118
    1st Royal Regt, 42, 65, 107, 117
    2nd Royal Regt, 43, 94, 107, 117
    Bavarian Guards, 52
    Blood's, 108
    Blue Guards, 33
    Brewer's, 29, 108
    Bridges, 108
    Buchan's, 24–5, 113
    Carbineers, 93
    Churchill's, 59
    Collingwood's, 29, 109
    Collum's, 93
    Corthorp's, 24, 113
    Disney's, 94, 109
    Duke of Argylle's, 69, 109
    Earl of Hertford's, 94, 108
    Evans's, 93, 109
    Ferguson's, 35, 59
    Godfrey's, 59, 74, 108
    Hamilton's, 24–5, 94, 108–9, 113
    Hanover Guards, 67–8
    Horse Guards, 2nd Troop, *see* Lifeguards
    Howe's, 29, 36, 43, 59, 63–5, 67–8, 74, 80–1, 108
    Imperial Dragoons, 52
    Ingoldsby's, 42, 59, 74, 108
    Kane's, 92–3
    Lee's, 93
    Lifeguards, 7, 10–11, 13, 15–16, 102

    Lord John Hay's, 35
    Makay's, 24–6, 108, 113
    Marquis of Harwich's, 93
    Meredith's, 42, 109
    Mordaunt's, 59, 108–9
    Newton's, 93, 109
    North and Grey's, 67–8, 74, 94, 108
    Preston's, 94
    Primrose's, 43, 94, 108
    Ross's, 35
    Rowe's, 35, 43, 108
    Stern's, 94
    Stuart's 29, 108
    Temple's, 63–4, 109
    Tiffany's, 29, 109
    Webb's, 74, 83–4, 107
    Wynne's, 93, 109
Rhine, river, 22, 29–30, 33, 40, 48, 50, 98, 106
Rivara, Comte, 23, 25
Roermond, 35, 39–40
Ross, Gen, 40, 42–4, 48
Rowe, Maj Gen, Lord, 30, 32–3, 40, 48, 50, 98, 106
Royal Dragoons, 6
Rutlingen, 50

St Ghislain, 76
St Pierre, Col, 6
St Venant, 81
Salish, Lt Gen E. van, 18, 102
Salsine Abbey, 19, 24
Sambre, river, 19–21, 106
Scheldt, river, 29, 66, 75, 106
Schellenberg, 41, 106, 117
Schwerin, Maj Gen, 23, 26
Seymour, A., Earl of Hertford, 7–8, 11, 80, 102, 112
Stenheim, 56
Sterne, Col, 6
surgeons, 45, 93
Surville-Hautfois, Gen Marquis de, 71–4

Tallard, Marshal C., Comte de, 37,
    47–8, 50–3, 56, 58, 101,
    115–22
Tilly, C., Graf von, 30–4
Tongres, 39
Tournai, siege of, 74–7
Treves (Trier), 58

Ulm, 58, 118
Utrecht, Treaty of, 90

Valenciennes, 74, 82
Vaudemont, Prince de, 21–3, 29, 102
Vehlen, Comte, 47, 119
Vendome, Marshal L.-J., Duc de, 66

Venlo, 35–6, 39–40
Villars, Marshal C.-H., Duc de, 30,
    80–2, 90–1, 98, 102–3, 124–5
Villeroi, Marshal F., Duc de, 21–3, 28,
    47, 49–50, 101, 119

Waal, river, 32–3, 106, 115
Waterloo, 28, 106
William III, King of England, 8, 13,
    17, 29, 97, 100
Withers, Gen, 30, 35, 40, 103
Wood, Lt Gen C., 44, 50
Würtemberg, C., Duke of, 30, 33, 79,
    104
Wynendael, battle of, 67

Index to William Leslie's Letters

Agew, Brig J., 151, 186
Alexander, Col W. (alias Lord
    Stirling), 153, 186–7
Amhurst, Gen, 158
Armstrong, Lt W., 140, 170, 193
Aughton, Gen Sir J.A.D., 167,
    192–3
Aughton, Lady M., 168, 193

Balcarres, A.L., 6th Earl of, 147, 184
Balfour, N., 158, 188
Balgonie, Lord (Bal), *see* Leslie, A., 7th
    Earl of Leven and 6th of
    Melville
Bedford, Long Island, 151, 153
Belches, A., 143, 182
Belsches, J., 171–2, 181, 188, 193
Beresford, Lord, 147, 184
Blacquiere, Col J. de, 146, 184
Boston, Mass., 149, 185
brigades,
    2nd, 159, 163
    4th, 149, 151, 153, 156
    6th, 152–3, 156
    Hessian, 150–1, 159–61, 163, 165
Bronx, 159, 160
Brookland, battle of, 153
Browne, Capt A., 153, 186
Browne, Lt T., 153, 186
Burlington, 163

Campbell, Lt C., 142, 182
Carnegie, W., 154, 187
Carrickfergus, 143
casualties, 152–3, 157, 160–1, 172
Cornwallis, Lord C., 163, 165, 190

Delaware, river, 163, 165
Drogheda, 143

Erskine, A., 168, 193
Evelyn, Capt W.G., 159, 189

Finch, Hon. Capt J., 167, 192
Fort Constitution, 159
Fort Independence, 161
Fort Lee, 159, 162
Fort Washington, 150, 158–9, 161–3,
    190

Gardiner, L., Viscount Mountjoy, 147,
    184
Goodenough, Major E., 149, 185
Graham, Capt J., 145, 184
Grant, Gen., 149, 151, 185
Grant, Lt Col J., 153, 186
grenadiers, 157, 161

Halifax, Nova Scotia, 149
Hall, Lt E., 175–6
Harcourt, Col W., 164, 191
Harlem, 160
'Hearts of Steel', 140, 142
Hepburn-Murray, Sir A. Bart, 140,
    150, 152–3, 170, 186, 193
Hillsborough, 153, 165
Howe, Gen W., 149, 157–61, 164, 181,
    191
Howe, Adm. R., 164, 191

Instone, S., 154, 187

Kings Bridge, 158–9, 161

Knyphausen, Baron W. von, 160, 162, 189

Lee, Gen C., 164, 191
Leslie, A., 7th Earl of Leven and 6th of Melville (Balgonie), 139, 141, 143–4, 149–50, 171, 181, 193
Leslie, A.L., Earl of Leven and Melville, 139
Leslie, D., 6th Earl of Leven and 5th of Melville, 137, 139, 146, 149, 151, 157, 159, 165, 167, 171, 173, 176, 179
Leslie, Brig D., 168, 193
Leslie, Gen A., 149, 157–9, 162, 165, 167, 169, 175, 185, 191
Leslie, Hon. W.,
    birth, 137
    death and burial, 137, 165–72
    commemoration, 173–9
Leslie, Lady A. (Lady Northesk), 166, 174, 191
Leslie, Lady. J. (Jenny), 139, 143, 150, 171, 178, 181, 194
Leslie, Lady M.E., 147, 184
Leven, Lady, 163, 181
Leslie-Melville, W.H., 179, 194
Lindsay, C., 168, 193
Long Island, battle of, 149, 151–4, 157–8, 190

Mackay, Capt A., 144, 183
McDonald, P., 166, 169
McLaggan, Mr, 142, 182
McPherson, Capt J., 165–7, 169, 172, 192
Martin, S., 174–5
Mawhood, Lt Col, C., 167, 171–2, 192
Melville House, 139, 150
Mifflin, Brig T., 166, 169, 192
Moneypenny, Col A., 142, 181
Montgomery, Miss B., 147, 184
Montgomery, W., 147, 184
Morgan, M.A., 140, 152, 186

Mountjoy, Visc., see Gardiner, L.
Murray, Capt W., 142–3, 181, 184
Musgrave, Major T., 159, 189

New Jersey, 162–4, 168, 179, 190
New York, 149–50, 153–5, 157–8, 162, 166, 175, 190–2
Nicholson Square, 139, 144, 150
North, river, 159
Northumberland, 2nd Duke of, see Percy, H.

Percy, Brig H., 2nd Duke of Northumberland, 159–61, 188
Philadelphia, 63, 175, 178, 190
Pluckemin, 167–8
Prescott, Gen R., 162, 189
Princeton,
    battle of, 137, 165, 176, 178
    college, 164–5
    town, 171–2

Rall, Col J.G., 165
regiments,
    16th Light Dragoons, 165, 167, 191
    1st Foot Guards, 161, 167, 192
    7th Foot, 140, 146, 149, 153, 156, 165–6, 170–3, 178, 185–7, 192–3
    23rd Foot, 153
    33rd Foot, 161, 190
    35th Foot, 160, 189
    40th Foot, 149, 153, 172
    42nd Foot, 140, 157, 161, 181–4, 193
    44th Foot, 153, 182, 184, 186
    46th Foot, 149, 193
    49th Foot, 160, 189
    55th Foot, 149, 165, 172, 193
    56th, 181
    64th Foot, 149, 185
    Handasyde's, 139
Rhode Island, 162
Robertson, Lt J., 145, 183

Rosebery, Lord, *see* Beresford
Rush, Dr B., 137, 150, 165–6, 169,
    175–6, 178–9, 181, 190–2,
    194

Ships,
    Eagle, 154, 187
Staten Island, 149, 151, 194
Sullivan, Gen J., 153, 187

Trenton, 163, 165, 171
Trew, Capt F., 166, 169, 192

Wardrop, A., 171, 193
Washington, Gen G., 165, 167–8, 172,
    175–6, 179
Webster, Dr A., 165–6, 190–2
Webster, Capt John, 162, 165, 167–8,
    173, 190
Webster, James, 162, 190
White Plains, battle of, 150, 159–61,
    189
Witherspoon, Gen G., 164, 190

York Island, 157–61, 189

Index to Private Cross's Diary

Alderson, Brig E.A.H., 244, 260
Allenby, Col E.H.H., 247, 260
Amersfoort, 224, 229
Amsterdam, 243–4
Artillery,
    G Battery, RHA, 238
    21st battery, RFA, 241, 258–9
    83rd battery RFA, 239
Assegai, river, 227, 244–5
Ava, Earl of, 216, 253

Baden-Powell, Maj Gen R.S.S., 229,
        233, 255
Badfontein, 225, 257
Balmoral, 238, 258
Barberton, 225, 234, 257
Barton, Maj Gen G., 235, 257
Beith, 208
Belfast, 199, 224, 230, 236, 256
Bergendal, 225, 231
Bester's Farm, 211, 252
Botha, C., 229, 242, 259
Botha, L., 220, 224–5, 227, 252,
        260
Brocklehurst, Maj Gen, 224
brigades,
    2nd Mounted, 224, 254
    3rd Mounted, 224
    7th, 224–5, 229, 233
    8th, 202, 223–5, 233
    11th, 223
    19th, 257
    67th (Fusiliers), 257
    Guards, 234
    Grimwood's, 204
    Natal Field Force, 203–4

Naval, 209
Buller, Gen Sir R., 205–6, 212–15,
        217–20, 223–5, 228–9, 231,
        233, 235–6, 254–6

Caesar's Camp, 205, 210, 252
Campbell, Lt Col W.P., 226–7, 242,
        246–7, 259–60
Cape Town, 215, 253
Carleton, Lt Col, 226, 239, 258
casualties, 207–11, 213, 215–17, 227,
        229–32, 235, 239–40, 242–3,
        250–1, 254–6, 258
Chrissie Lake, 226, 243, 259
Cingolo, 218, 256
Colenso, 219, 223
concentration camps, 226
Cove Redoubt, 214–15
Crocodile, river, 232, 234–6
Cronje, P., 218, 254

De Wet, C., 224, 230, 256
divisions
    4th, 225, 228, 255, 257
    8th, 231, 256
Dick-Cunyngham, Lt Col W.H., VC,
        215, 253
Dundee, 201–3, 206–8, 223, 250
Dundonald, Earl of, 218, 224, 254

Egerton, Lt Hon. F.G., RN, 211,
        252
Elandslaagte, 203, 207, 216, 220, 250,
        253, 258
Eland Spruit, 236
Ermelo, 243, 259

Flag Hill, 204
French, Maj Gen Sir J., 203–4, 210, 225–6, 231, 234, 250–1
Frere, 212, 252

Geluk's Farm, 230, 256
Glencoe Junction, 201–2, 206–7, 220, 250
Gordon's Post, 211, 251
Grobelaar, 'Old', 242–3
Gun Hill, 205, 213, 220, 252
Gunning, Col, 207, 250

Hamilton, Col I., 204, 225, 233, 250, 255
Hannah, Lt W.M.P.J., 207, 250
Helpmakaar, 203, 208
Henry, Col St G.C., 243, 260
Hildyard, Maj Gen, H.J.T., 228, 255
hospital, 207, 210–11, 213, 217, 252–3
Howard, Maj Gen, 223–4
Hunter, Maj Gen Sir A., 209, 220, 224, 228, 230, 251–2

Impati, 206–7
Intombi Spruit, 210, 252–3

Joubert, Gen P.J., 207, 210–11, 224, 250, 252

Kitchener, Lord F.W., 224, 226–7, 235, 241, 254, 259–60
Klip River, 213
Klipfontein, 229, 243
Komati Poort, 225, 234, 257, 259
Kranz Kloof, 216, 253
Krugersdorp, 225, 235
Kruger, S.J.P., 233, 257
Kruger's Post, 235, 258

Ladysmith, 199, 201–4, 206, 208–11, 218, 220, 223, 250–4
Laing's Nek, 199, 201, 224

Leicester's Corner, 233, 236, 257
Lombard's Kop, 209, 211, 221, 223
Long Hill, 204
Lyndenburg, 225, 232–3, 235–6, 257
Lyttleton, Lt Gen Sir N.G., 226, 228, 255–6

Machadodorp, 225, 231, 256
Meerzicht, 224, 255
Methuen, Gen Lord, 212–13, 253
Meyer, L., 202, 207
Middelburg, 226–7, 236, 242, 245
Modder Spruit, 204, 208
Möller, Col B.D., 202, 207, 250
Monte Cristo, 218, 254
Mooi Maciesfontein, 228
Mooi River, 212, 252

Nicholson's Nek, 203, 209, 251

Observation Hill, 205, 212, 249, 252
Oliphant's River (Groot and Little), 226, 239
Onderbrook, 219, 220, 223

Paget, Maj Gen A.H.F., 240, 259
Pan, 241, 259
Pienaar, Comdt J., 225, 234, 257
Piet Retief, 244, 246
Pole-Carew, R., 225, 231, 234–5, 256
Pretoria, 221, 224, 246
Prinsloo, M., 224, 228, 255

regiments
    5th Dragoon Guards, 217
    5th Lancers, 256, 260
    18th Hussars, 202, 207, 223, 226, 241, 245, 250, 256, 258–9
    Imperial Light Horse, 211, 213, 252, 254, 260
    Mounted Infantry, 207, 227, 232, 241, 245–6, 250, 256–7, 260
    Natal Carbineers, 202, 252

South African Light Horse, 236, 257–8
Strathcona's Horse, 230, 232, 235–6, 256–8
Connaught Rangers, 255
Devonshire Regt, 215, 258
2nd Duke of Cornwall's Light Infantry, 237, 238–9, 258
2nd East Kent (Buffs), 238, 258
1st Gloucestershire, 208, 251
2nd Gordon Hldrs, 215, 224, 227–8, 233, 236, 253, 255–7
1st King's (Liverpool), 237, 258
1st King's Royal Rifle Corps, 207, 209, 226–7, 238, 240, 242, 250, 255, 258–9
Lancashire Fusiliers, 228
1st Leicestershire, 199, 201–2, 207, 209, 216, 220, 223–7, 230, 233, 235, 238–41, 249–59
2nd Leicestershire, 199
Manchester Regt., 210, 216, 255
2nd Royal Dublin Fusiliers, 202, 206–7, 250
1st Royal Irish Fusiliers, 226, 236–7, 240, 251, 258
2nd Royal Irish Fusiliers, 207, 209, 226
2nd Rifle Bde, 231, 234, 238, 253, 257
Royal Irish, 207
Royal Engineers,
    Balloon Section, 216
    Pontoon Section, 247
1st West Riding, 259
1st Vol. Bn Leicester Regt, 219, 223, 225, 229, 255, 257–8
Johannesburg Police, 225
Natal Police, 202, 203
Rhodes, Col F.W., 218, 254
Riefontein, 203, 232, 251

Roberts, Lord, 215, 223, 226, 230–1, 233, 236, 253–7, 259
Rockdale farm, 226
Roodeport, 239, 242
Rooi Kopje Ridge, 224, 227, 229, 255
Russell, Lt C.P., 215, 253

Sand Drift (Zandspruit) (Sand Bank), 227–8, 244–6
Scott, Major E.R., 239, 258
Shela, river, 244
Shirston, Col, 207, 250
Signpost Ridge, 220, 223
Smith-Dorrien, Gen H., 226, 235, 242–3, 258–9, 260
Standerton-Ermelo Blockhouse Line, 227
Surprise Hill, 217, 219–20, 253
Symons, Maj Gen Sir W.P., 201–2, 207, 250

Talana Hill, 199, 201–2, 206–7, 233, 250
Tintwa Inyony, 208, 251
Tugela River, 205, 213, 223–4, 253–4

Umbulwana, 211, 252

Vaal, river, 229
Van Wyk's Vlei, 224, 230

Vereeniging, treaty of, 227
Vogelstruispoort, 230

Waggon Hill, 205, 215, 220, 252
Wakkerstroom, 224
Wauchope, Maj Gen A.G., 213, 253
White, Sir G., 201–6, 210, 212, 217, 251–3

Yule, Brig, J.H., 201–3, 251